Theme Attica
For the latest updates and more, go to
www.facebook.com/ThemeAttica

Athens with Kids
(and not only)

1st Edition, May 2013

Tania J. Kollias

ISBN 13: 978-1480145481

Cover, content, editing, lay-out, photos unless otherwise credited, and mistakes by the writer. Page decorations: Clio's art. Contact/feedback: *www.facebook.com/ThemeAttica*

Front cover photo: Κλειω on the Hill of the Muses.
Back cover photo: Stroll in the Ancient Agora.

Bio Blurb
Tania Kollias is an accredited journalist and editor currently living in Athens, Greece. She has worked in newspapers, magazines and related fields for more than two decades, contributing to publications such as the *New York Daily News*, *Daily Mail* and *Globe & Mail* among others, and has written travel guides for the likes of Frommer's, Fodor's, DK and Expedia. Originally from Vancouver, Canada, after finishing a Communications degree (SFU), she travelled to some 30 countries in North America, Europe, Asia and Africa, and has worked in Vancouver, Melbourne, Tokyo and Athens. This is her (my) first self-published travel guide. Hopefully what is lacking in presentation is made up for in content. Much gratitude goes to my family and friends for their invaluable support, especially my dear daughter, who I couldn't do this without and who (proudly!) features throughout.

How to Use this Book
While not "Athens for dopes", *Athens with Kids (and not only)* is fairly detailed on the practicals, especially the hows and wheres, since having children with short legs, attention spans and appetites, when time is also short, means that every moment counts. It's also a foreign country, plus things go out of date very rapidly here. I write guides with myself in mind, and will also be using this book for my own outings, with updates on *www.facebook.com/ThemeAttica* until the next edition is published.

Chapters are organized by what a visitor needs to know upon arrival, so travel info is first, then accommodation, which is set out according to area or neighbourhood in relation to the orienting Acropolis Hill, as are most of the chapters.

Once you've chosen a place to stay, you can then see where the nearest supermarket or taverna is, do your souvenir shopping, and check out what sites and activities there are in your neighbourhood, including dedicated chapters on special events, playgrounds, pools, beaches, and, for most listings, how stroller accessible they are.

See the maps at the back of the book for quick orientation—and then get a free, detailed map on arrival at the airport or download one.

If parents want a kid-free break, there's a "Parent Time Out" chapter (include the kids too, if they also need a hair cut, want to soak at a spa or watch a sports match).

Included are English-language worship services for those wanting to keep up with (or sample) the family's spiritual journey.

In listings organized by category (eg shopping), its location (area) is also highlighted.

Each chapter has its own logic, so read the chapter's intro for clarification. For example, accommodation is rated according to price, while the most important places to go are rated according to "must-sees" and organized by geography and "order of appearance" in a vicinity, not alphabetically. Playgrounds lose ratings for various reasons (noted). *TJK.*

Contents

Chapter 1: Intro to Athens   5
Orientation Briefs   6

Chapter 2: Travel   8
Arrival by Air   8
Car Rental   11
Arrival by Cruise Ship   12
Public Transport & On Foot   12
Ferry Travel   15
Intercity, Long-distance Buses   16
Intercity Railway   16

Chapter 3: Accommodation   19
Choosing a Base   19
Self-catering   20
Hotels & Hostels (by area)   21

Chapter 4: Food & Restaurants   31
Babies & Toddlers   32
Feed & Change Spots   33
Street Food   33
Farmer's Markets (*Laiki*)   34
Bread & Cheese   34
Middle Eastern Pastries   35
Groceries & Supermarkets   36
Dining Out (by category, area)   38
Ice Cream & Frozen Yogurt   46

Chapter 5: Shopping   50
What to Buy   50
Where to Buy   51
Shops (by category)   51

Chapter 6: Places to Go, Things to See   65
Athens Landmarks & Attractions   66

Chapter 7: City Tours   95
Bicycle Tours   95
Coach Tours   96
Mini-trains   97
Walking Tours   97

Chapter 8: Field Trips—Indoor   99
Places to Go (by proximity to central Athens)   99

Chapter 9: Field Trips—Outdoor   105
Places to Go (by proximity to central Athens)   105
DIVING EXCURSION, LESSONS   112

Chapter 10: Leisure & Entertainment   114

Live Shows, Events, Exhibitions   115
Bowling   117
Cinema   118
Golf   119
Ice Skating   119

Chapter 11: Events & Holidays   121

National Holidays   121
Other Annual Events in Greece   124

Chapter 12: Parks, Playgrounds & Indoor Play Areas   127

Playgrounds (by area)   128
Amusement Parks, Indoor & Supervised Play Areas   145
Playgrounds & Supervised Play Areas, Greater Athens   148

Chapter 13: Drop-in Hotel & Destination Pools   154

Heads Up   154
Swimming with Babies   155
Hotel Pools (by area)   155
'Destination' Pools   161

Chapter 14: Athens Area Beaches   164

Heads Up   164
Attica Beaches (by proximity to Athens)   165
Beach & Island Day Trip: Aegina & Angistri   169

Chapter 15: Parent Time Out   171

On the Town   171
Special Events & Concerts   176
Spectator Sports   176
Sports Cafes   177
At a Day Spa   177
At a Salon   179

Chapter 16: Biblical Athens & Worship   180

Attend a Greek Orthodox Church Service   180
English-language Church Services   181
Non-Christian, Buddhist & Meditation Services   183
Excursions to Monasteries   184

Chapter 17: Special Interest—Jewish Athens   186

Chapter 18: Planning & Reference (emergencies, tourist info, etc)   189

Index   202
Maps   209

Panoramic view of Athens from Lycabettus Hill

Chapter 1: Intro to Athens

Greece is a country where all your senses "wake up". Great for families with lots to do, the many festivals and events that take place will also be memorable.

Kids will (hopefully) like seeing places they've heard about at school, read in books (Percy Jackson series, etc) or seen on TV, such as Hercules (Irakles) or Ulysses (Odysseus), while younger ones will enjoy the atmosphere and attention.

There are many free things to see and do that are easy to get to, and eating and drinking can be cheap too if you DIY rather than go to restaurants or tavernas for every meal.

The weather is usually fair but take care in the heat, most people speak English, and children are adored and accepted almost everywhere.

The youngest children are welcome well into the night (10pm is the dinner hour) at tavernas or neighbourhood restaurants, where you can always find bread and a plate of chips/fries or spaghetti.

For the Athens Olympics in 2004, an urban renewal and archaeological site unification project was completed which links the main sites, parks and city squares of Athens by turning main thoroughfares into pedestrian cobblestone walkways. This change to pedestrian-only has been great for businesses, residents and of course, visitors. Many parts of the pathways have been used since antiquity, the city being continuously inhabited (a rarity) for at least 3,000 years.

The main sites located in Athens are easy to navigate along the mainly pedestrian streets, one of which is the walkway around the Acropolis. Most of it is cobblestone which is rattling with a stroller, but there are places along the sides that are either flat or pebble. The walkway has many places to stop.

Important sites and landmarks are fairly close together, so getting around on foot is doable, however the sidewalks and pavements are often blocked or in disrepair, which makes strollering a challenge but not impossible. You need to watch out for trees and poles on sidewalks as well. Most people use the roads. Take extra care while crossing busy streets, as drivers do not heed the "little green man" walk signal. Cars usually go first.

Orientation Briefs

GEOGRAPHY & MAIN ROUTES

Athens is a big city (pop. 4m+) in a basin, surrounded by low mountains and the sea. At street-level it may not look particularly appealing when arriving from the airport, train station or sea port, the plethora of low-rise apartment blocks built in the 1960s and 1970s stretching in all directions. But the setting is beautiful, and if you're staying in the right place, mainly **near the Acropolis**, you'll find even the street-level view pretty spectacular too.

The **port of Piraeus** and the expanse of Aegean Sea abruptly stops the development spread in the south, the north side creeps up **mounts Penteli** (Pendeli) (1,109m/3,638ft) and **Parnitha** (Parnes) (1,413m/4,636ft), and **Mount Hymettus** (Ymettos, Ymittos) (1,026m/3,366ft) to the east with its aerials. The hills of **Aegaleo** (Egaleo, Aigaleo) (469m/1,539ft) face the city's west.

The central urban sprawl is relieved further by eight hills: **Acropolis, Aeropagus, Pnyx** (Pnika), **Hill of the Nymphs** (*Nymphaion*), **Hill of the Muses** (*Mouseion*), **Lycabettus** (*Lykavittos*), **Strefi**, and **Ardittou**.

GET YOUR BEARINGS

Athens International Airport (*www.aia.gr*) is about an hour's drive (30km/19mi) east of the city, behind Mt Hymettus, on the Messogeia or Attica Plain.

Attiki Odos (*www.aodos.gr*) is a toll highway that rings the city and reaches the airport.

The **main arterial routes** from the centre are **Vasillisis Sofias/Kifissias Avenue** to the Northern (north-eastern) suburbs, **Messogeion Avenue** towards Messogeia in the east and the airport, **Piraeos (aka Pireos) Avenue** west and south towards the port of Piraeus, **Syngrou** and **Vouliagmenis avenues** heading south towards **Poseidonos Avenue**, which goes along the coast where the nearest beaches are located, **Patission Avenue** heading northwest, and **Athinon (Kavalas) Avenue**, which is the **National Road/Highway No. 1** heading west or north out of the city.

From in front of **Parliament** at **Syntagma Square**, eight-lane **Amalias Avenue** (*pictured*) feeds the main arterial routes to the north (Vas. Sofias/Kifissias Ave) and south (Syngrou, **Kallirois** and Vouliagmenis aves).

The **main central square** in town is **Syntagma**, where Parliament is located, and **Ermou Street** is the main pedestrianized shopping street which runs west from Syntagma through the **Monastiraki** district (a bit scruffier), then alongside **Thissio**, an upscale residential and café/bar area, where the walkway around the Acropolis (**Apostolou Pavlou Street**) is lined with street sellers.

Gazi, the main nightlife area, is just beyond Thissio at the end of Ermou St, around Kerameikos Metro station.

Historic and touristy **Plaka** is south of Ermou St and goes up the north slope of Acropolis Hill, where the orienting Parthenon is located.

Four main streets—**Athinas**, **Stadiou** (southbound) or **Panepistimiou** (signed as **Elef. Venizelou**, northbound) and **Ermou**—link **Syntagma Square, Omonia Square** and **Monastiraki Square** in what's called the **commercial or historic triangle**. It's a busy area with small shops and businesses, contains the **Central Market** (**Agorà**), and gets seedy at night and the closer to Omonia and vicinity you get. It takes about 10 minutes to walk to each square of the triangle.

Museo, where the **National Archaeological Museum** is located, is just beyond Omonia, and backs onto **Exarchia**, the trendy/edgy student district.

UNIFICATION OF ARCHAEOLOGICAL SITES

The pedestrian **Acropolis walkway**, ready by the Athens Olympics in 2004, links up the ancient sites and extends from Gazi up **Ermou St** all the way to Parliament at Syntagma Square. At Thissio Metro station on Ermou St, it veers south along **Apostolou Pavlou St** towards the Acropolis and veers around the south slope past the **Herodes Atticus Odeon** (*pictured*), **Theatre of Dionysus** and **Acropolis Museum** as **Dionysiou Areopagitou St**.

Opposite the entrance to the Acropolis, a walkway extends into **Filopappou Hill** (**Filopappou Monument, Ancient Assembly**, picnic spots, nature trails). Carrying on along the path to the Acropolis entrance brings you to Plaka, and another path (**Adrianou St**) that goes alongside the train tracks from Thissio Metro station brings you to an entrance of the **Ancient Agora** and onwards to Monastiraki Metro station.

Latinized spelling

Note that streets can change names after even a block (labels are on buildings at intersections), while Greek rendered in Latin characters also varies, such as Aiolou/Aeolou St, Irodion/Herodion (theatre), Irakleidon/Iraklidon St etc, and names that have a recognized English variant (Lycabettus, Corfu) may be rendered in the Greek (Lykavittos, Kerkyra) or English translation (Constitution/Syntagma Square—"square" is *plateìa*). Keep an open mind when reading signs and labels.

You won't have to travel on a three-wheeler, still a common sight around the flea market. Sites in a compact area make walking a viable option

Chapter 2: Travel

Arrival by Air

Greece is about the size of Nicaragua or Alabama, but has 32 airports, some operating seasonally, around the mainland and islands serving an 11 million population that more than doubles with tourist arrivals in summer.

Athens International (Eleftherios Venizelos) Airport (*210-353-0000, www.aia.gr*), is a south-east European hub handling up to 15m passengers a year. The busiest regional airports are on the islands of Crete, Corfu and Rhodes, and the northern port city of Thessaloniki (*2310-473212, www.thessalonikiairport.com*), 16km/10mi from town.

Domestic airlines are **Olympic** (*210-355-0500, www.olympicair.com*) and **Aegean** (*210-626-1000, www.aegeanair.com*).

Flying with babies and toddlers

Flying with babies is not too difficult, you normally get a seat near young families with the bassinet hook-up in front for babies up to six months, milk and water is available and they can heat bottles, and the bathrooms have change tables. The water and liquids restriction at security is waived for parents with babies and toddlers. If you think you need help, try the service *www.nannyintheclouds.com*.
  Make sure babies are sucking on something for take-off and landing.
  A terrycloth, plastic-backed change mat is handy if youngsters want to sleep stretched out on the floor. Strollers are usually brought right to the door of the plane, and delivered there again on arrival.
  I've let my tired bigger kid ride on the luggage cart, but it's "not allowed".

Luggage

If children are carrying some of their luggage for long periods, it's recommended they don't carry more than 15 percent of their body weight to avoid stress on growing spines. Lightweight backpacks with evenly set straps and not wider than their body are best, with the weight in the centre and close to the body, near their lower back.

Keeping children occupied on the journey

Attendants give crayons, colouring books and puzzles for older kids, and have cartoon channels, and/or bring a portable DVD player (charge it at airport plug-in stations, bring a multi-plug adapter) with a supply of favourite shows. This is also useful at the hotel for when you want to rest but the kids don't. Bring favourite toys for babies, paper if the children like to draw, as well as books, electronic gadgets or mobile devices with suitable apps, and adaptor plugs and batteries. Batteries are widely available in grocery stores and corner shops.
  Suitable from three years, **Leap Frog** (*www.leapfrog.com*) has small, educational toys such as Text and Learn (*pictured*), with a keyboard and simple games that is handy for keeping children's attention on and off the plane, during waits, quiet time in the hotel, etc. The Hong Kong-based **Vtech** (*www.vtechkids.com*) has a Vreader (*pictured*) with interactive stories and learning games, as well as a kids' camera, which also has simple games.
  Other items that are useful for keeping children occupied during waiting, travelling or resting times are play and educational apps for mobile devices, such as games, comics, drawing, piano… that are little or no cost to download.

Athens International Airport

Since Greece is an EU frontier country, most flights to Athens are from European and Middle Eastern destinations, with **direct flights** year-round to New York,

Toronto and Montreal, plus Newark, Atlanta and Philadelphia in summer.
The Athens International Airport (AIA) website (_www.aia.gr_) lists regular and charter airlines, including discount operators from Europe.

While lacking the character of the beloved old airport on the south coast, AIA has won awards since opening in 2001, as it's not too big and easy to navigate. Facilities include a post office, ATMs, currency exchange, free internet, pharmacy, restaurants and snack bars, newsagents and duty-free shopping, an electronics shop (**Germanos**, _210-353-4956, www.germanos.gr_) located in the Departures hall (you need to ask to get in if arriving; cell phones start at around €40), and a **child's play area** (_9am-9pm, 210-353-2414 or 210-353-2445_) as well as a **free museum of antiquities**.

There are also **baby rooms** for changing and feeding, and manned **airport information desks**.

Note that **luggage carts** at arrival need a €1 coin in a machine, so if you need one, get change.

Private tour company desks (_**Amphitrion** 210-353-0568_ and _**Pacific** 210-353-0160_) to **book a hotel on arrival** are open 24 hours and located in the Arrivals hall.

You can get the **Athens Spotlighted discount card** only at the airport, at one of two booths _in the Baggage Claim area or in the Arrivals hall level Business Centre 6am–10pm, and from info booth nos. 5 & 6 in the Arrivals hall from 10pm to 6am._

For Athens info and **free maps**, head to a City of Athens info point, _next to information counter no. 5 (extra-Schengen) or no. 6 (intra-Schengen) at Arrivals level_, or get assistance at airport information kiosks. Most hotels have free maps as well.

Getting to town, ports, railway

Located 27km/17mi east of Athens at Spata, the trip into town takes about 40 minutes, and the airport is served by stroller/luggage accessible regular **public bus** (_www.oasa.gr_ has route maps) that runs 24 hours.

A **ticket**, bought from a booth outside the Arrivals hall adjacent to the bus-stop, costs €5 for 90 minutes, and is valid on all public transport.

The **X95** city bus runs to **central Syntagma Square (town centre)**, **X96** goes along the south coastal road (Poseidonos Ave) from the seaside resort of Varkiza and past Vouliagmeni, Voula, Glyfada, Elliniko, Alimos and Faliro to **Piraeus port** and Piraeus Metro station, and **X97** runs to **Dafni Metro station on Line 2** in southern Athens.

Long-distance KTEL buses take passengers to the **port of Lavrion** (north Aegean island destinations) via the town of Markopoulo, and the **port of Rafina** via the town of Artemis (Loutsa), from a bus-stop near Sofitel (past the escalator).

Also you can take the **Metro subway** (_www.stasy.gr for "Tube" maps and times_) into Athens centre and the **suburban rail** (_dial 14511 toll charges apply, www.trainose.gr, in Greek_), if you want to bypass the centre or go to **Athens main railway station (Larissa)** and onwards to Corinth or Patras for Italy-bound ferries, but the suburban also goes to the port of Piraeus for ferries to most Aegean Sea islands.

The Metro and suburban rail (**Proastiakos**) (_pictured_) both cost €8, €14 for two or €20 for three persons, good for 90 minutes and are transferable to all modes of transit in the city. The trains operate ~5.30am–11.30pm.

Buy the tickets at the counter or booth and cancel them in the machine before entering the platform.

The Metro and suburban trains are across an overpass towards the luxury-class **Sofitel Athens Airport hotel** (*210-354-4000, www.sofitelathens.gr*), which incidentally has a **spa**...

Taxis are metered with extra charges for luggage and tolls, and these are posted on the dashboard, along with the driver's ID. Drivers are notorious for ripping off tourists unfortunately, so a flat rate of €35 direct to central Athens hotels from 5am–midnight and €50 midnight – 5am (*see www.aia.gr for info and map*) has been implemented from the airport. Taxis are located outside the Arrivals hall.

Child **car seats** are not required in taxis or other temporary transport.

Car Rental

You can **rent a car** (**Avis, Budget, Hertz, National/Alamo, Sixt** have desks at the airport) and head out, or break up the journey with **airport parking** offers, ie €25 (Fri–Sun) and €50 (3–7 days).

Athens streets are confusing and traffic is heavy, so driving in the centre is not recommended, but there are some good car rental deals that make sightseeing around the mainland—from Ancient Mycenae to Ancient Olympia, or Meteora and Mt Olympus, for example—easier.

The major international car rental agencies are also represented in town: a few are **at the beginning of Syngrou Ave**, opposite the Temple of Olympian Zeus.

Ask the agent about including child **car seats**, specifying your child's age, height and weight. Children up to 135cm/53in/4ft5in should be in the back seat with car seats or booster cushions so the regular seatbelt fits across their body correctly.

Check the fine print, eg that the Collision Damage Waiver is included, and double-check when you pick up your car.

Go over the **condition of the car** with the agent before taking it. Also be aware that maintenance may be lacking if it was a great deal. Check the tires aren't bald...

Drive with care, as drivers are generally unpredictable and aggressive, with many accidents each year. If drivers behind you are flashing their headlights, move to a slower lane.

You'll notice you're not meant to stop for pedestrians either!

Finding **street parking** is difficult and day parking can cost €20 a day, so find a hotel with free parking, or ask beforehand if it's easy to find parking on the street in the vicinity.

Speed limits are 120kmh/75mph, 50kmh/30mph in built-up areas, and 80kmh/50mph on country roads. **Road signs** are in Greek and English but may be hard to spot (obscured or last-minute)—including traffic lights, which are usually at the side of the road.

Fuel (gasoline/petrol) is quite expensive, nearing €2 a litre. It's uncommon to use washrooms at gas/petrol stations. There are frequent rest stops and restaurants along the highways.

EU nationals don't need an **international driver's permit** but other nationals do. The permits are issued to Greek nationals by **ELPA** (Greek Automobile Association, 210-606-8800, _www.elpa.gr_), ie issued by the country of residence (driver's licence). ELPA also has **road assistance** (_10400_).

Arrival by Cruise Ship

If you're arriving on a cruise ship in the port of Piraeus (Athens), time is usually very limited, so walk around the port to the Piraeus Metro station terminus which will take about 20 minutes, and then another 20 minutes into the centre of Athens (**Thissio** or **Monastiraki** Metro stations on Line 1), or catch a bus (_tickets from a booth_) from the bus-stops (terminus) on **Akti Miaouli Ave** _near the international passenger terminal_, or get a taxi, which takes about 15 minutes and costs around €10.

To get your bearings, a **Port of Piraeus map** is at _www.olp.gr/en/coastal-shipping/posts-ships-gates_, also reproduced at the end of this book. The _Piraeus Metro station is in front of_ **Gate E6**, _cruise ships are at_ **Gates E11 and E12**.

Public Transport & On Foot

The centre of Athens and the main sites within it are compact enough to navigate on foot (_pictured, Vas. Sofias Ave_), with many areas pedestrianized. The only irritants are the many obstacles along the sidewalks/pavement, cars getting priority, and having to be extra careful when crossing the street. Look both ways, including on one-way streets, and even when the pedestrian light is green. Unsynchronized pedestrian crossing lights, meaning you may have to zigzag up a street or be stuck in the central meridian/island, also irks. Otherwise you can take the very convenient, clean and safe **Metro** (_www.stasy.gr_) which runs from around 5.30am–midnight and till ~2.30am on Fri–Sat. All stations have an elevator, but they may be inconveniently located, such as opposite the Larissa (Athens) railway station. The **tram** (_www.stasy.gr, runs from Syntagma Sun–Thurs ~5.30am–midnight, Fri–Sat till ~2am. Last tram from SEF (Piraeus) leaves at ~1.15am Fri–Sat_), which goes from central Syntagma Square and down the coast to either Voula or Faliro, is slow but great for strollers and a trip to the seaside for young children. Or use the **local buses and trolleys** (*www.oasa.gr*), which *run from ~5am to 10pm and sometimes till midnight*. Bus-stops are handily named. *All buses have a stroller-accessible area* (look for the wheelchair label), and someone will usually help you take a stroller off the bus. A **single journey ticket** on one mode of transport costs €1.20, while a **90-minute integrated ticket** good for any direction on all transit modes is €1.40. Children 7–12 yrs, 13–18 yrs and 65+ yrs with ID pay half-price. There is also a daily ticket (all modes) for €4, and a weekly ticket for €14. **Public transport maps:** *www.aia.gr* (*see Access and Parking*), or *www.ametro.gr*.

METRO (subway, tube)

Line 1 (Green) Piraeus—Kifissia
• Piraeus (*port*) (*pictured*) •
Neo Faliro (*Peace &
Friendship Stadium—SEF,
Marina Zea*) • Moschato •
Kallithea • El Venizelos-
Tavros • Petralona • Thissio
• Monastiraki (*Plaka,
Ancient Agora, Central
Market*) • Omonia • Victoria
(*Natl Archaeological
Museum*) • Attiki • Agios
Nikolaos • Kato Patissia •
Agios Eleftherios • Ano
Patissia • Perissos •
Pefkakia • Nea Ionia • Neo
Iraklio • Irini (*Olympic
Stadium*) • Nerantziotissa (*Suburban rail transfer, The Mall Athens*) • Maroussi •
KAT • Kifissia.

Line 2 (Red) Anthoupoli—Agios Dimitrios
• Anthoupoli • Peristeri • Agios Antonios • Sepolia • Attiki • Larissa (Athens) Station (*railway*) • Metaxourgio • Omonia • Panepistimiou • Syntagma (*Parliament, National Gardens*) • Akropoli (*Acropolis, Plaka*) • Syngrou-Fix • Neos Kosmos • Agios Ioannis • Dafni • Agios Dimitrios (*Metro Mall*). *Summer 2013 extension to:* Ilioupoli • Alimos • Argyroupoli • Elliniko.

Line 3 (Blue) Airport or Douk. Plakentias—Egaleo
• Airport • Koropi • Kantza • Pallini • Doukissis Plankentias • Halandri • Nomismatokopio • Holargos • Ethniki Amyna • Katehaki • Panormou • Ambelokipi • Meg. Mousikis (*Concert Hall*) • Evangelismos • Syntagma • Monastiraki (*Ancient Agora*) • Kerameikos (*Thissio, Gazi*) • Eleonas, • Egaleo.

TAXIS

Athens has a vast number of taxis (*pictured, Syntagma Sq*) that are crying for business these days. Most take multiple fares going in the same direction, but each pays the same fare separately—it's just car sharing. If you are a passenger you have the right to refuse taking on more passengers but this is rarely done—you don't want to antagonize your driver, especially when you don't know where you're going. You can put strollers in the boot/trunk and have your baby or child in the back seat with you, no special seats are required for taxi rides, and few use seatbelts.

Fares are reasonable, with a minimum fare of €3.16 (give €3.50 or €4), but you can get quite far with this.

When hailing a cab, note that the rate nearly doubles between midnight and 5am, so it's tariff 2 on the meter.

A taxi is generally difficult to get around 3pm (shift change) and 11.30pm (waiting for midnight's double-tariff to kick in), as well as during heavy rain.

You can **order a taxi** or make an appointment for an additional €3–€5 from one

of many taxi companies, such as **Attika** (*210-341-0553*), **Proodos** (*210-345-1200*) or **Cosmos** (*1300*). Or if you have a smartphone you can order a taxi from **Taxibeat** (extra 50 cents per fare) from wherever you are, and tailormake your specs. Download the app at *www.taxibeat.com*.

Scams

Drivers know they have a bad reputation and some are making efforts to smarten up, however if you feel you're being ripped off, which is common and especially with foreigners, don't pay or get out of the car until you are at your hotel, where you then ask the clerk for assistance, or else ask to be driven to a police station, which will hopefully get the driver back in line. Make a note of the license plate, and the driver's name if you can see it—they have photo ID posted in the taxi.

A common ruse is turning on the meter as double tariff (the "2" is lit rather than the single tariff "1") and saying that it means two fares or two passengers—it doesn't. Another is when you hand over a high denomination note and they give back change for a lower denomination, swearing that's what you gave them.

Another is not dropping you off right at your hotel

Surcharges
- Meter begins/flat rate: €1.19
- Minimum charge: €3.16
- Rate per kilometre inside city limits: €0.68
- Rate per kilometre outside city limits: €1.19
- Rate per kilometre midnight to 5am: €1.19
- Waiting (per hour): €10.85
- Radio call—simple: €1.92
- Radio call—appointment: €3.39 to €5.65
- Airport—to & from: €3.84
- Port, railway, bus stations: €1.07
- Baggage over 10kg: €0.40 each bag

(and thus risking a confrontation with a local), saying they can't reach it (pedestrian street, etc), and then getting aggressive, saying they'll drive off with your luggage if you don't pay. All the hotels are accessible by car, so ask to be taken to your hotel door and let the hotel staff deal with it, while also asking to see the driver's ID to take note of it. Take a picture of it if you can't read the Greek—and of the driver!

Ferry Travel

Greece has super-fast ferries, regular ferries, catamarans and Flying Dolphins (hydrofoils). All serve snacks and drinks, from beer to fruit juice, and sandwiches, savoury pies/pitas (most babies love feta cheese—a common pie filling), cookies and chips. It's more pleasant out on deck for children so the slower ferries might be the better option for shorter domestic routes than taking a flying dolphin, such as to nearby islands.

For toddlers, consider buying a harness or reins though (*pictured*), as the railings are too wide and they will want to enjoy the experience and run around.

Derek Gatopoulos

For international travel, given the length of time and costs involved, it may be cheaper to **fly from Italy.** Try *www.skyscanner.net*, *www.flyairone.it*, and *www.airtickets.gr* for online deals.

Ferries do ply routes from **Ancona**, **Bari**, **Brindisi** and **Venice** to the island of **Corfu (Kerkyra)**, the town of **Igoumenitsa** on the west coast mainland, and the town of **Patras**, where most travellers head to reach Athens. The sailing lasts from 10 to 17 hours and is usually overnight; deck prices start at around €30.

Tickets can be bought in advance, online, at travel agencies around the port, at booths inside the port, and on the boat if necessary. The **X96 bus** goes from the airport to the port of Piraeus.

Check *www.greekferries.gr* for prices and *www.openseas.gr* and *www.gtp.gr* for boat **schedules.**

• **Agios Konstantinos Port Authority** (*to Evia island and the Sporades islands: Skopelos, Skiathos, Skyros, Alonissos*), 22350-31759.
• **Corfu (Kerkyra) Port Authority** (*Patras or Italy-bound*), 22610-45551, 39824, *www.corfuport.gr*
• **Igoumenitsa Port Authority** (*for Ioannina and northern Greece*), 26650-99300, *www.olig.gr*

- **Lavrion Port Authority** (*north Aegean islands*), 22920-27711, 22920-22089, *www.oll.gr*
- **Patras Port Authority** (*Corfu or Italy-bound*), 2610-365113, *www.patrasport.gr*
- **Piraeus (Athens) Port Authority** (*Saronic, Aegean islands, Rhodes, Crete*), ferry info on *14541*, €0.89 per call from a landline and from €1.50 for mobile/cell phone calls. You can call them to see if a boat is going if it's windy, for example, as well as for schedules and islands served, *www.olp.gr*
- **Rafina Port Authority** (*Aegean islands*), 22940-23605, 22940-22840, *www.rafinaport.gr*

Intercity, Long-distance Buses

KTEL Terminal A
The **X93 bus** from the airport ends at KTEL Terminal A intercity bus station for **Patras** and destinations in the **Peloponnese and western Greece.**
- *100 Kifissou St, Kolonos, 14505 wait for English, www.ktel.org, apps available.*
Get there: *From central Athens you take bus no. 051 from Menandrou St near Omonia Square.*

KTEL Terminal B
For other destinations in central Greece such as **Meteora** and **Delphi**, head to KTEL Terminal B intercity bus station.
- *260 Liossion St, 14505 or 210-831-7186.*
Get there: *From Kato Patissia Metro station on Line 1 and then a 5-minute walk west, or bus no. 024 from central Syntagma Square on Amalias Ave.*

KTEL Aigyptou Square & Mavromateion St Terminals, Museo
The KTEL Aigyptou Square and Mavromateion St terminals serve the south and east Attica coast, such as **Sounion** and **Marathon.**
- *Aigyptou Sq, Patission St, Museo, 210-880-8080*
- *Mavromateion St, Museo, 210-880-8000, www.ktelattikis.gr*
Get there: *Victoria Metro station on Line 1 and walk ~10 min, past the National Archaeological Museum, or take trolley nos. 2, 3, 4, 5, 6, 7, 8, 9, 11, 13 or 15 north-bound.*

An **intercity bus** from **Patras** (*KTEL 2610-623887*) **to Athens** leaves every 30–45 minutes and takes ~2.5 hrs.
Buses leave **Igoumenitsa** (*KTEL 26650-22309*) western Greece, every couple of hours for the town of **Ioannina** in mountainous Epirus, journey ~2 hrs.

Note: Toilets are not in use on regional buses, which may make a rest stop.

Intercity Railway

Trains to Greece from the Balkans, Eastern Europe, Russia and Turkey normally terminate in the northern port city of Thessaloniki, but the routes have been suspended due to Greece's current economic crisis, which includes the Hellenic Railways Organization, **OSE** (*1110 schedule, in Greek, 14511 customer service, charges apply, www.ose.gr, www.trainose.gr*). You could buy the **Thomas Cook European Rail Timetable** online for schedules, or check *www.seat61.com* for current info on international route availability.

Sleepers or couchettes are available for international journeys, but the trips are long (2–3 days) and hard going, and extra safety precautions (as well as food and water in some cases) are needed.

Entering **via ferry to/from Italy** to Patras and then by train (or bus if the train's not running) to domestic destinations is the usual route.

DOMESTIC JOURNEYS

There are many trains a day between **Athens and Thessaloniki** taking from 4.5 hrs to eight hours overnight. **Athens (Larissa) Station** (*pictured*) is quite small (snack-bar/**cafe**, luggage storage).

Domestic tickets are quite cheap and you can buy them online through *www.tickets.trainose.gr*. Or buy at the station, or at OSE ticket offices.

Athens Larissa (Stathmos Larissis) Station (OSE)
• *31–33 Deliyianni St, 210-821-3882, internally 1110, www.ose.gr*
Get there: *Larissa Metro station on Line 2.*

OSE ticket offices
• *Mon–Fri 8am–3.30pm* • ***1 Karolou St, Omonia**, 210-529-8829.*
• *Mon–Fri 8am–3pm* • ***6 Sina St, Panepistimio**, 210-362-7947 (intl), 210-362-1039 (domestic).*

The **Patras train station** (*2610-639102 or 2610-639108*) is opposite the ferries, but if coming from Corfu or Italy and there isn't a train to Athens (*3.5hr journey*), you could opportunistically go to nearby **Ancient Olympia** instead where there's also a village to stay.

TOURISTIC RAIL JOURNEYS

If railways are your thing, there are **two rack-and-pinion touristic railways**.

Kalavryta, Peloponnese

One is the .75-gauge cog-rail train along a gorge and up the mountainside from **Diakopto/Diakofto** (*OSE 26910-43206*) on the **Corinth-Patras** line near Patras that branches off to the historic (WWII atrocities) and pretty ski resort village of **Kalavryta** (*OSE 26920-22245*). Originally constructed in the 19th century with French and Italian know-how, the track has since undergone an upgrade. Diakopto (161km/100mi) is ~2 hours' journey from Athens. The cog rail journey (22.3km/13.8mi) takes about an hour.

From Patras you can also get to Kalavryta by **KTEL bus** (*26920-22224, tickets €7.80*).

• *Cog rail (Odontotos) leaves Diakopto daily at 8.45am, 11.15am, 2.30pm. Tickets €9.50.*

Pelion peninsula 'Moutzouris' (Smudgy)

The other is a .60-guage train to villages in the scenic **Pelion peninsula**, over stone and iron bridges and with views to the Pagasitic Gulf, near the main town of **Volos** (320km/200mi, ~3.5 hours from Athens) on the eastern mainland, which operates in summer.

The Pelion train was built by Evaristo de Chirico, father of surrealist painter Giorgos Chirico, and ran for 80 years before being retired in 1971. It was revived in 1996 as a tourist attraction. It leaves **Ano Lehonia**, 13km/8 miles southeast of Volos (*local bus no. 5 leaves from the KTEL bus station*), and goes to the village of **Milies**, with a 15-minute stop at **Ano Gatzea**.

It's a 16km/10-mile trip going about 20km/12mi per hour. Info and **tickets** from the **Volos railway station** (*24210-24056*).

• *Leaves daily during summer months at 10am; returns at 3pm. Journey takes 1 hour, 30 mins. Adults round-trip tickets €18, one-way €10, children 4–12 yrs €6 one-way, €10 return.*

On a sailboat (card for Nana), Feb 2013 ☺ 5.5 yrs

Grande Bretagne, King George Palace and NJV Athens Plaza, Syntagma Sq

Chapter 3: Accommodation

Choosing a Base

Athens is a tourist city full of hotels, but as with the rest of Europe, rooms are small and may feel cramped. Especially with the current conditions, however, you can find very good deals. **Room rates** are regulated and posted on the room door, but these are maximum prices and the rate you get is usually lower. When booking, request their best current rate, and get a written record of the price agreed and the room if possible, ie if you're paying more for a room with a view. **The Hellenic Chamber of Hotels** (*www.grhotels.gr*) posts the rights and obligations of hotel owners and guests, which include things like the hotelier may ask for up to 25 percent of the total cost as down payment, charge 20 percent of the room rate to add a bed, and half the day rate to stay till 6pm (check-out is normally by noon). You also usually have to leave your passport or ID at the hotel.

A double room (*dìklino*) may have two single beds (*dìo mòna krevàtia*), so check if you want a double bed (*diplò krevàti*). Ask about special requirements such as cots (usually a pack-and-play), bottle-warming ability (a large, Greek-style coffee pot known as a *brìki* or an ice bucket do nicely as a bain-marie), if there's a fridge, extra beds or connecting rooms if needed, stroller-accessibility, if babies are allowed in the hotel pool, how much babysitting costs, etc.

Location

My first consideration when choosing places to stay is the vicinity, and the best places are located in a wide area around the Acropolis, which is conveniently in central Athens. These include the neighbourhoods of **Thissio**, **Plaka**, **Syntagma**, **Kolonaki**, **Makriyanni** and **Koukaki**, and towards the Metro station of **Monastiraki** area.

Where's the nearest playground?

Travelling with children 0-3 years old will be much different than with older children, as their attention span (or lack thereof) takes precedence. The playground location (*see Chapter 12*) will probably be a higher priority for where you decide to stay.

These are either residential, or areas frequented by tourists, and are easy to hit the main sites. These are districts I personally feel at ease walking in, day or night.

Other residential areas to consider are along Metro Line 3 from Syntagma heading towards the airport, so anywhere around **Evangelismos**, **Megaron Mousikis**, or **Ambelokipi** stations.

The accommodation options listed are suggestions, but if you stick to these areas, hotels not listed should also generally be fine. Bear in mind I have not stayed in them since I live here, but I have been in to check most of them.

Apart from three major hotels right on Syntagma Square and the other luxury options, the hotels were also selected for their **quiet location**—what I personally seek when on a holiday—and are **easy to access** or are short walks from a Metro station.

There are many good deals outside of these areas, but the neighbourhoods may be and feel quite rough, and as mentioned, I only recommend staying in areas I myself feel comfortable walking around in, day or night. If you don't plan on being out in the evening or doing much around the vicinity of your hotel, such areas include **Omonia**, **Karaiskaki**, **Metaxourgio** and **Vathis squares**, which are a bit further from the main sites of the centre on Lines 2 and 3, also have many hotels, and are closer to the National Archaeological Museum.

Check a map, such as the **Greek National Tourism Organization's** excellent **free map**, which you can download from *www.visitgreece.gr*. Check a trusted review site and hotel photos, but note that many hotels say they are centrally located when they aren't, and area experts may have incentives.

Self-catering

There are no all-inclusive hotels in central Athens, but there are a couple of self-catering options that are listed below. Eating at tavernas is a great experience and most are child-friendly, but if you can't do it every day (meals are around €15+ per person at tavernas, although fast-food and street food are available—a souvlaki/gyros is ~€2), an alternative is to stay at a **studio or one-bedroom apartment**. They typically have a sofa-bed in the kitchenette, enabling you to make your own food (and the children's) on your schedule (and theirs).

You could online search for **vacation rental properties** and **places to stay**, getting some very good deals through sites such as _www.airbnb.com_, _wimdu.com_,

A large Greek coffee pot (briki) makes a fine bain-marie for bottle-warming

www.vacationhomerentals.com, _www.ownersdirect.co.uk_, and _athens.craigslist.gr_.

Or pay nothing or next to nothing if you are willing to open your home to visitors and book through **home-swapping sites** such as _www.homelink.org_ or _www.intervac-homeexchange.com_.

Note: One asterisk denotes the most common price for a standard hotel, which is ~€50 to ~€90 a night, including taxes and often including breakfast. Check prices online or directly with the hotels, which usually offer deals.

Hotels & Hostels (by area)

PLAKA, SYNTAGMA

Syntagma is the central square of Athens and anchors the main shopping district, which extends into the surrounding areas and west down Ermou St. Plaka is the oldest neighbourhood in Athens, with its picturesque, village-like streets—the two main ones lined with tourist shops—and top-end neoclassical houses, especially around the south-east slope of Acropolis hill.

* Achilleas

A well-situated three-star option for families (and emphasized on their website), is this popular hotel that also caters to business people. Located in the shopping area near Syntagma Square and close to Plaka and Monastiraki as well, it's on a quiet street near pedestrian Ermou St, the central shopping "mall", thus easy to navigate and find. It's also next to a pharmacy (handy for baby food). 34 rooms. Doubles from ~€80.

• 21 Lekka St, Syntagma, 210-323-3197, www.achilleashotel.gr
Get there: Syntagma Metro station on Lines 2 and 3, then 10 minutes' walk.

* Acropolis House

Stay in a restored 19th century house among others near Syntagma on the edge of Plaka, close to the Children's Museum and within striking

Adonis Hotel and Acropolis House are across from each other on a flagstone lane, Plaka

distance of the National Gardens and Zappeion playgrounds. A popular budget choice; no air-con rooms are cheaper. 19 rooms. Doubles from €65 high season, discounts available.

• *6–8 Kodrou St, Plaka/Syntagma, 210-322-2344, www.acropolishouse.gr*
Get there*: Syntagma Metro station on Lines 2 and 3, then 10 minutes' walk to the south end of Voulis St.*

* Adonis Hotel

At Syntagma and straddling Plaka, this is another convenient choice (*pictured, at left*), especially for easy bolting access to the airport. Close to Plaka and the Children's Museum, playgrounds at the National Gardens, and walking distance to the Acropolis and other important sites. Some rooms have big balconies, and the roof garden breakfast area overlooks the Acropolis. 26 rooms. Doubles from €65 in high season.

• *3 Kodrou St, Plaka/Syntagma, 210-324-9737, www.hotel-adonis.gr*
Get there*: Syntagma Metro station on Lines 2 and 3, then 10 minutes' walk to the south end of Voulis St.*

* Adrian Hotel

Convenient to reach Metro lines to the airport and port of Piraeus, this refurbished hotel is on the lower edge of Plaka and a short walk to the Acropolis, Ancient Agora, shopping, and family-oriented dining at Monastiraki Square. On Plaka's main pedestrian street (but reachable by car), there's a small café-lined square opposite. Acropolis-view from the roof garden. 22 rooms. Doubles from €85 low season with breakfast, children up to 6 yrs free sharing with 2 adults.

• *74 Adrianou St, Plaka/Monastiraki, 210-322-1553, www.douros-hotels.com*
Get there*: Monastiraki Metro station on Lines 1 and 3, then 10 minutes' walk into Plaka.*

** Athens Cypria Hotel

This is a well-situated hotel with restful rooms just off pedestrian Ermou St in the shopping area near Syntagma Square. Easy access to the main Metro lines at Syntagma or Monastiraki for flights or port-bound trips. It's a popular business hotel so July and August are ideal times to book. **Snack bar**. 115 rooms. Doubles start ~€100 but look for special offers. An American buffet breakfast is included.

• *5 Diomias St, Syntagma, 210-323-8034 or 210-323-0470, www.athenscypria.com*
Get there*: Syntagma Metro station on Lines 2 and 3, then 10 minutes' walk.*

** Ava Hotel

The Ava (*pictured*) is lux-class accommodation with spacious studios suitable for long-term guests and families. On a narrow street off busy Amalias Ave with Hadrian's Arch, Temple of Zeus and Zappeion Gardens (playground) across the street, and Plaka and the Acropolis also nearby, it's a convenient and comfortable place to stay. Special offers available. 15 suites. Rates from €130 to €390.

• 9–11 Lyssikratous St, Plaka/Zappeion, 210-325-9000, www.avahotel.gr
Get there: Akropoli Metro station on lines 2 and 3, then 5 minutes' walk north.

* Central

True to its name, this modern hotel is in an easy-access area straddling Plaka and the central shopping district on a fairly quiet street. Acropolis views from the back rooms, and larger rooms with balconies face the front. Rooftop **snack bar** is open year-round; rare **parking**. 84 rooms. Doubles from ~€90 with breakfast.

• 21 Apollonos St, Syntagma, 210-323-4357, www.centralhotel.gr
Get there: Syntagma Metro station on Lines 2 and 3, then 10 minutes' walk.

*** Electra Palace

Not to be confused with the **Electra Hotel** on central pedestrian Ermou St (run by the same company and also very well located), this is a lux-class hotel and the largest in Plaka that's also near central Syntagma Square and the National Gardens (playground). **Spa** with **indoor pool**, **restaurants** and **parking** are on site, as well as a rooftop **pool**. Some of the richly-decorated rooms have an Acropolis view. 122 units. Doubles from ~€160.

• 18 Nikodimou St, Plaka/Syntagma, 210-337-0000, www.electrahotels.gr
Get there: Syntagma Metro station on Lines 2 and 3, then 10 minutes' walk.

**** Grande Bretagne

Athens' most historic hotel (part of the Starwood Luxury Collection) is in a class by itself as the most luxurious option in the city's "mile zero". Royalty and heads of state are frequent guests. Rooms are luxurious, service is top-notch, restaurants, bars, award-winning **spa** with **indoor pool**, and an outdoor **pool** and roof garden, Acropolis-view **restaurant** are draws in their own right. 321 rooms. Doubles start ~€300.

• Syntagma Sq, Syntagma, 210-333-0000, www.grandebretagne.gr
Get there: At Syntagma Metro station on Lines 2 and 3.

** Hermes

One of the three better class hotels on centrally located Apollonos St, the Hermes straddles the shopping area, Plaka and Monastiraki districts. Modern décor throughout, and family and connecting rooms on request. Child's **playroom** off the breakfast room on the mezzanine floor. 45 rooms. Doubles from ~€95.

• 19 Apollonos St, Syntagma/Plaka, 210-323-5514 or 210-322-2706, www.hermeshotel.gr
Get there: Syntagma Metro station on Lines 2 and 3, then 10 minutes' walk.

**** King George Palace

The luxury hotel next-door to the Grande Bretagne is newly part of the Starwood group of hotels, as is the GB, opening under the new management in summer 2013. Right on Syntagma Square, it is very easy access to the Metro, has a **spa** with **indoor pool**, restaurants, bar, and a **rooftop pool** that may be reserved for the best suite in the house. Special meals can be arranged, while you can have a

gorgeous Acropolis view from the **restaurant** on the 7th floor. 78 rooms. Doubles from ~€270.
• *3 Vas. Georgiou St, Syntagma 210-322-2210, www.classicalhotels.com*
Get there: Opposite Syntagma Metro station on Lines 2 and 3.

*** New Hotel
Indeed one of Athens' newest hotels, opened in 2011, this one is run by the same group as the Periscope in Kolonaki. It's very centrally located at the top of Plaka in central Athens, and near the main sites, on a busy street but across from the National Gardens and Zappeion (playgrounds), and close to the Children's Museum where toddlers and up will be engaged for an hour-plus, free of charge. Local and Brazilian décor and luxury-standard features such as turn-down, pillow menu, free newspaper and a steam room massage, it has a **bar/restaurant** that uses organic products, connecting rooms, and offers services from laundry, babysitting and guided tours, to 24-hour room service and a butler. 79 rooms. Starting ~€160 for a double.
• *16 Filellinon St, Syntagma/Plaka, 210-327-3000, www.yeshotels.gr*
Get there: Syntagma Metro station on Lines 2 and 3, then 5 minutes' walk.

* Niki Hotel
This hotel is another really good option where location is concerned, being on a quiet street near Syntagma (Metro, shopping), the National Gardens and Zappeion (playgrounds), Plaka, and an **organic restaurant** and grocery shop across the street. The rooms are smallish, higher floors have balconies, and there's a café/bar downstairs. 23 units. Doubles from ~€80.
• *27 Nikis St, Syntagma/Plaka, 210-322-0913, www.nikihotel.gr*
Get there: Syntagma Metro station on Lines 2 and 3, then 5 minutes' walk.

*** NJV Athens Plaza
The third hotel in a row right on Syntagma Square is in the most central part of town, in the commercial and shopping area. Get a bird's eye view of all events from here, including (normally peaceful) protest marches, plus of the Acropolis and surrounding greenery in the National Gardens. The room décor is restful whites and creams. **Restaurant** and bar on site. 182 rooms. Doubles from ~€160.
• *Syntagma Sq, Syntagma, 210-335-2400, www.njvathensplaza.gr*
Get there: Opposite Syntagma Metro station on Lines 2 and 3.

OTHERS TO TRY AROUND SYNTAGMA

Astor
Conveniently located in a busy pedestrian area, with some traffic. Official rates ~€80–€100 for a double but check for special offers.
• *7 Voulis St, Syntagma, 210-335-1000, www.astorhotel.gr*

Athos
This one has 18 rooms (~€55–€90), and is on a very quiet side-street, well located between Plaka and the shopping district off Apollonos St.
• *3 Patroo St, Syntagma/Plaka, 210-322-1977, www.athoshotel.gr*

Diamond Homtel
This recently-established (2011), discreet and plushy, blink-or-miss boutique
hotel is in a very quiet location at the Plaka (south) end of Voulis St.
~€100 a night.
• *24 Voulis and Mitropoleos sts, 210-323-2443, www.athensdiamondplus.com*

Myrto
Also quiet and very well-located is the Myrto with 12 rooms (doubles €55–70),
extra bed €10, family apt for 5–6 people €100-125 including breakfast.
• *40 Nikis St, Syntagma, 210-322-7237, www.hotelmyrto.gr*

MAKRIYANNI (ACROPOLIS), KOUKAKI
This mixed-income, residential-and-tourist-blend area gives a taste of living like
the locals. Now dominated by the **Acropolis Museum**, it's very close to town and
Plaka, and is walking distance to the entrance of the Acropolis and Filopappou
Hill park, as well as Zappeion Gardens (playground) and the Temple of Olympian
Zeus. It's also well-located for easy access to south coast beaches.

* Art Gallery Hotel
Stay in a residential neighbourhood at this circa 1950s house that was once the
home of an impressionist artist. This family hotel has a charming, old-fashioned
feel and is located near a Metro station, the main route to the seaside, and close to
the Acropolis. 21 rooms. Doubles from ~€60 winter, €90 summer.
• *5 Erechthiou St, Koukaki, 210-923-8376, www.artgalleryhotel.gr*
Get there: *Syngrou-Fix Metro station on Line 2, or trolley nos. 1, 5, 15, bus-stop: Gargaretta; bus no.
230, bus-stop: Akropoli Museo or Erechthiou. Also many buses (trolley no. 10, bus nos. A2, B2, E22,
E90, 040, 550) on arterial Syngrou Ave. to Syngrou-Fix Metro station (bus-stop: Syngrou-Fix stn) and
5 minutes' walk.*

* Athens Backpackers
For tight budgets you can stay in dorm-style hostel rooms in this friendly place
that's popular with young people and well-located near the Acropolis Museum,
Plaka, Zappeion Gardens (playground), and the main route to coastal beaches.
There's a launderette and sports bar nearby, the rooftop bar has an Acropolis
view, and low-cost excursions and tours are arranged here too. 60 rooms. Price
per bed from €17 winter and €26–28 summer. Double rooms €75–€85 winter,
summer €85–€95.
• *12 Makri St, Makriyanni, 210-922-4044, www.backpackers.gr*
Get there: *Akropoli Metro station on Line 2, then 2 minutes' walk.*

* Athens Studios
Self-catering apartments with Ikea furnishings have proven very popular with
travellers at this central location near the Acropolis Museum, Plaka and Zappeion
Gardens (playground), and is on the main route to south coast beaches. This hotel
is easy to find, at the point where Veikou and Dimitrakopoulou sts meet, and is
just around the corner from and run by Athens Backpackers. Laundry, info,
restaurant and bar are downstairs; lots of restaurants nearby. 35 rooms. Apt for
2–3 people €75–€85 winter, €85–€95 summer.
• *3A Veikou St, 210-923-5811, Makriyanni, www.athensstudios.gr*
Get there: *Akropoli Metro station on Line 2, then 2 minutes' walk.*

*** Divani Palace Acropolis

Part of a local chain, this large hotel is near the Acropolis Museum, Temple of Olympian Zeus and Filopappou Hill as well as the Acropolis. It has somewhat larger rooms with balconies, and a supermarket conveniently located across the street. Many tour groups go through its doors. Also an outdoor **pool** and rooftop **restaurant**. 253 rooms. Doubles from ~€140.

• *19–25 Parthenonos St, Makriyanni, 210-928-0100, www.divanis.gr*
Get there: *Syngrou-Fix Metro station on Line 2, many buses (trolley no. 10, bus nos. A2, B2, E22, E90, 040, 550) along Syngrou Ave. (bus-stop: Syngrou-Fix Stn) then 5 minutes' walk from the station.*

** Herodion

For a comfortable stay in a popular, mid-sized hotel with larger rooms in a central residential location close to the Acropolis, Acropolis Museum and other sites, you can also relax in the **Jacuzzi** on the roof and enjoy the view. **Restaurant** on site. 90 rooms. Doubles from ~€130.

• *4 Rovertou Galli St, Makriyanni, 210-923-6832, www.herodion.gr*
Get there: *Akropoli Metro station on Line 2, then 5 minutes' walk.*

* Hotel Tony

Stay within walking distance of the Acropolis entrance near Filopappou Hill in this easily-found pink building located on a residential street (of apartment blocks, but this is Athens). Also near the main route to the seaside (Syngrou Ave). It has self-catering studios well-suited for families or longer stays. 21 rooms. Double studios ~€85 and apartments ~€120.

• *26 Zacharitsa St, Koukaki, 210-923-0561 or 210-923-5761, www.hoteltony.gr*
Get there: *Syngrou-Fix Metro station on Line 2 and a 10 minutes' walk, or trolley bus nos. 1, 5, 15 bus-stop: Zinni, and 5 minutes' walk.*

* Marble House

A budget option on a quiet cul-de-sac beside the **Evangelical church** (Sunday services with English translation), the homey hotel (*pictured*) is in the residential Koukaki area, with many shops, from bakeries and dairy stores to herbs and children's clothes, including a small organic shop. Close to the Acropolis Museum and walking distance to playgrounds—there's a big one at the end of the road (Dimitrakopoulou St). Doubles from €40 without bathroom, €45 with bathroom. 16 rooms.

• *35 Anastasiou Zinni St, Koukaki, 210-922-8294, www.marblehouse.gr*
Get there: *Syngrou-Fix Metro station on Line 2, then 3 minutes' walk. Trolley nos. 1, 5, 15, bus-stop: Zinni. Trolley no. 10, bus nos. A2, B2, E22, E90, 040, 550, bus-stop: Syngrou-Fix stn on nearby Syngrou Ave, the main road to coastal beaches.*

* Philippos Hotel

A small, family-run hotel in a quiet residential neighbourhood near the Acropolis and Acropolis Museum as well as the large park area of Filopappou Hill. Run by the same owners as the nearby Herodion, it has a **coffee shop** with drinks served throughout the day, or go to the **restaurant** at the Herodion. There are steps at the entrance which is mid-landing. 50 rooms. Doubles from ~€85.

• *3 Mitseon St, Makriyanni, 210-922-3611, www.philipposhotel.gr*
Get there: *Akropoli Metro station on Line 2, then 5 minutes' walk.*

NEOS KOSMOS

This busy, built-up, working class area is just outside the town centre by a couple of Metro stops, on the far side of Syngrou Ave—the main route to the seaside—and arterial Kallirois Ave nearer to town. Not really a noteworthy place to stay but not bad either. Bonus for baklava lovers: **Kostis bakery** *(70 Ilia Iliou St, 210-901-5882, at the Metro/tram station exit)* is located here.

**** Athenaeum Intercontinental

While not quite in the town centre (there's a shuttle or a 15 minutes' walk to town), this large, deluxe hotel caters to those wanting no-nonsense, well-run, roomy-sized luxury. There's a **pool** on site as well as a **spa**, **24-hour restaurant**, and a cinema complex with a bowling alley and arcade games nearby to entertain older kids. There's a large playground with a café behind the hotel, while wooded Nea Smyrni Alsos (park) is also nearby. 543 rooms. Doubles from ~€200.

• *89–93 Syngrou Ave, Neos Kosmos, 210-920-6000, www.intercontinental.com*
Get there: *Neos Kosmos Metro station on Line 2; or trolley no. 10, bus nos. A2, B2, E22, E90, 040, 550, bus-stop: Panteios or tram-stop: Kasomouli, then 5 minutes' walk.*

* JK Apartments

The hotel with the fresh white façade is located on the other side of busy Syngrou and Kallirois aves that lead to the south coast, but it is easy to access, across the street from the tram line and Neos Kosmos Metro station. The hotel has a plush feel with

baroque furniture, but seems a little neglected.

Nice plunge **pool** (*pictured*) on the roof with steps (rare) in a shallow end, and arguably the best bakery in town (Kostis) across the street. 21 rooms. Doubles €70 year-round.

• *71 Ilia Iliou St, Neos Kosmos, 210-901-0933, www.jkhotel.gr*
Get there: *Opposite Neos Kosmos Metro station on Metro Line 2, tram-stop: Neos Kosmos.*

* Luxurious Furnished Apartments

Staying in apartments is the newest trend, and especially appealing for families who may also prefer to self-cater. These two are spacious and clean, designed by an architect and mother of three, and conveniently located near Akropolis Metro station on Line 2. 70m2 each, €90–€130 for two or four people.

• *25 Hatzichristou St, Makriyanni or 8-10 Vouliagmenis Ave, Neos Kosmos, 693-700-0787, www.athensdesignapartments.com*
Get there: *Akropoli Metro station on Line 2, then 5 minutes' walk (both properties).*

THISSIO, PSYRRI (WEST)

This lively area on pedestrian streets near the Acropolis and main archaeological sites is a magnet for Athenians as well as tourists, and really gives you a taste of the best of Athenian life. Suitable for older and younger children, there's a much-used **playground** nearby (due to an absence in town). The neighbourhood is a mix of apartment blocks and 19th century mansions, and full of outdoor cafes up Irakleidon St towards and around Thissio square, with its remarkable views of both the Acropolis and Lycabettus hills. Street sellers line pedestrian Apostolou Pavlou St beginning from Thissio Metro station.

* Jason Inn

This hotel, part of a small chain, is well-located near Thissio Metro station and the pedestrian walkway to the main sites, as well as the nightlife areas of Thissio, Psyrri and Gazi if you can squeeze in a night out. Take in gorgeous views over breakfast or dinner in the roof garden **restaurant** (*eves only May–October*). 57 rooms. Doubles ~€80. Children up to 6 yrs free sharing with two adults.

• *12 Agion Asomaton St, Psyrri, 210-325-1106, reservations 210-520-2491, www.douros-hotels.com*
Get there: *Thissio Metro station on Line 1, then 2 minutes' walk.*

* Phidias Hotel

The location is the draw at this otherwise drab hotel (see travel site reviews) located on the pedestrian walkway around the Acropolis (*pictured, 3rd bldg on the left*) in the trendy and convenient Thissio district. There's a **playground** across the street that abuts the Ancient Agora, a park, many **cafes**, and an open-air cinema up the road. Near the Thissio Metro and within walking distance of the main sites. 15 rooms. Rate is ~€80 in July.

• *39 Apostolou Pavlou St, Thissio, 210-345-9511, www.phidias.gr*
Get there: *Thissio Metro station on Line 1, then 2 minutes' walk.*

MONASTIRAKI, PSYRRI (EAST)

Monastiraki is a busy, central area that gets scruffier further down (north on) Athinas St towards Omonia Square, and nicer towards Plaka and Thissio and west towards Gazi. It also forms part of the central shopping district and Ermou St "mall". It has lots of flea market and souvenir shops, plus sidewalk cafes lining the tracks between Monastiraki and Thissio Metro stations. Family-oriented souvlaki restaurants are nearby at Monastiraki Square and Mitropoleos St.

* Athenstyle

This is a hostel with dorms as well as spacious private rooms and suites with kitchenettes and big balconies (*pictured, with Acropolis view*), very conveniently located close to the Monastiraki Metro station on Lines 1 (Piraeus port) and 3 (airport) and for hitting any of the sites. Trivia: Lord Byron boarded on this steet at no. 11, writing the poem, "Maid of Athens" for the young daughter of the owner back in 1809. Breakfast, **restaurant** (*opens 7pm*) and bar (*opens 6.30pm*) on the rooftop, there is an elevator, but steps from the last floor to the roof. Ground floor lounge and **free internet** and game-room in the basement. Families with children under 10 yrs are asked to take a private room. 21 rooms. Doubles and studios €70 and €75. Dorm beds from €20.

• *10 Agias Theklas St, Psyrri, 210-322-5010, www.athenstyle.com or www.athenstyle.gr*
Get there*: Monastiraki Metro station on Line 3, Athinas exit, then 2 minutes' walk.*

* Tempi Hotel

Tempi is a popular and friendly budget hotel centrally located in the shopping district on a pedestrian street that ends at the Tower of the Winds in the Roman Agora. Facing a square with a flower market that has become lively with cafes, it has a **communal kitchen** but no elevator, however the owners will assist with luggage and strollers. 24 rooms, 12 with common bathroom. Triple with shower €70 high season, €53 low season.

• *29 Aiolou St, Monastiraki, 210-321-3175, www.tempihotel.gr*
Get there*: Monastiraki Metro station on Line 3, then 5 minutes' walk.*

KOLONAKI, EVANGELISMOS

Kolonaki is the centre's most upscale residential and shopping area, full of boutiques, galleries, a lively café/bar scene, and the best fashionista-watching opportunities. Lycabettus (Lykavittos) Hill juts up from the north, and central Athens is within walking distance. It's near main traffic routes for destinations north of the city, where many embassies are located, as well as the airport.

**** Hilton Athens

This landmark, luxury hotel (*pictured*) (the area is known as "Hilton") is convenient for the American Embassy (adjacent area known as "Embassy"), Concert Hall (Megaron Mousikis), and getting to points north of the city. It is one Metro stop from central Syntagma Square and then across busy streets—a downside, but there's a large outdoor **pool** and **children's pool**, **restaurants**, rooftop bar, and a **spa** with **indoor pool** on site. It's a comfortable, spacious and secure place to stay with modern rooms. 508 rooms. Doubles go from ~€200.

• *46 Vas. Sofias Ave, 210-728-1000, www.athens.hilton.com*
Get there: *Evangelismos Metro station on Line 3, then 5 minutes' walk.*

** Periscope

Located in central Athens' most upmarket area, surrounded by designer boutiques and the city's best-dressed people, this hotel offers sophisticated, minimalist rooms. Close to downtown shopping, Lycabettus Hill (café/restaurant, theatre) and nearby museums, also not far from the main sites. Kids will enjoy looking through the rooftop periscope and zooming in on sites in the city. **Restaurant** on the premises. 21 rooms, doubles from €145 to €170 in high season.

• *22 Haritos St, Kolonaki, 210-729-7200, www.periscope.gr*
Get there: *Evangelismos Metro station on Line 3, then 10 minutes' walk uphill, or bus nos. 022, 060 bus-stop: Loukianou.*

Apartment bldg & house, Sept 2012 ☺ 5 yrs

Derek Gatopoulos

Simple, fresh, delicious: Dining Greek-style, al fresco

Chapter 4: Food & Restaurants

Greek food needs little introduction. Natural food's rich flavour, especially fruit and vegetables, still tastes like it should—ripe and juicy rather than cultivated for looks, shelf-life and transport. Plus being served a meal at the shoreline or at a sidewalk café under the stars… Enjoy these simple pleasures while here, remembering what juicy tomatoes and peaches taste like, along with rich yogurt and fragrant honey—another sensory experience for the memory bank.

Babies & Toddlers

*Baby foods are usually at the end
of supermarket aisles*

Greek cuisine is not generally spicy,
and babies with teeth can eat bite-
sized pieces of soft foods such as
cooked vegetables and soft fruit.
But as good as the honey is, the
sweetener is not advised for babies
under a year old due to a risk of
infant botulism.

All kinds of **milk** are readily
available, and for bottles, apart from
access to a microwave, a large,
long-handled Greek or Turkish
coffee-pot (*briki*) partially filled
with hot water is perfect for
immersing glass bottles. Buy one or
ask if your hotel has one.

If using **formula**, check to see if your brand is available in Greece. For
example, formula made by Cow and Gate is called Almiron. The Aptamil
equivalent is also Almiron by Nutricia. If you take the formula label to a
pharmacist in Greece they can tell you the equivalent or nearest substitute.

Stage 1 (up to six months) is only available in **pharmacies** at present.
Pharmacies are plentiful but close 2pm–5pm and don't reopen in the evenings
(5pm–8pm) on Monday and Wednesday. There are pharmacies open in every
neighbourhood outside those hours however, and their locations are posted on a
chart in pharmacy windows. Ask a Greek-speaker (passers-by will be happy to
help) to read it, and tell you where the nearest is located.

Many pharmacies, but limited hours

You can buy **baby cereals** in tins at
supermarkets (*see Groceries and Supermarkets
section*), and find **baby and toddler foods**
such as cottage cheese, feta, which most babies
love, and all kinds of fruit to cut up, such as
pears. At restaurants mashed potatoes are rare
(considered hospital food), but ground
beef/mince patties are available as well as
salads and dips, and bread is always placed on
the table.

Babies from six months old until their teeth
come in at around a year old are at the most
difficult stage to feed while on holidays as you
need to puree the food. For babies in-between
solids and cereals, there are a handful of
supermarkets that sell **prepared baby food**

(*see Groceries & Supermarkets section*). A small jar of mixed organic veg or fruit (under 200g) is about €2 and €1.70 for 250g of regular. Otherwise consider asking your hotel and maybe even the restaurant to blend a vegetable or fruit mix for you, and for over eight months meat as well, eg a mix of your dinner. Check with the hotel beforehand if this is your case, or consider bringing a small hand-held blender (and plug adaptor that can handle 220V).

Feed & Change Spots

Central Syntagma Sq has places to sit and feed babies

Central Athens has a dearth of green spaces, but if you see green or open space, most of these public squares have benches to keep your schedule and feed or change a baby. Apart from the parks and playgrounds (*see Chapter 12*), pleasant and safe places to stop to feed babies and toddlers while in town are at central **Syntagma Square** on benches around the grass area and the fountain, in front of the Metro station exit. If you or your child needs to use the washroom, try the cafés located there, or pop across the street to McDonald's. There are public toilets inside the **National Gardens** at Syntagma as well, which is another nice feeding spot.

The **pedestrian walkway around the Acropolis** has a few discreet places to stop where you can comfortably nurse, especially in the vicinity of the entrance to the archaeological site, on Dionysiou Areopagitou St in **Makriyanni**.

Around **Monastiraki and Thissio**, head to the park area on the south side of **Thissio Metro station**. In **Psyrri,** pop inside the Technopolis gasworks complex.

Street Food

Roasted chestnuts and corn-on-the-cob are available in the winter months

It's perfectly acceptable to eat on the streets in Greece. Morning snacks in particular, such as *kouloùria* (sesame-covered bread rings) are widely available at roadside stalls. Do-it-yourself meals are also easy with the plethora of *tiròpita* (cheese pie) shops found all over town that sell cheese pies and savoury variants with spinach, chicken, potato and ham. The spinach pies may have feta in them, and you can offer the filling to toddlers as a way to sneak in their green vegetable quota. *Bougàtsa* is a semolina-cream-filled pie, usually sprinkled with icing sugar and served warm. Buy a few pieces of fruit from a stand, rinse with a bottle of water and pat yourself on the back for providing a filling and healthy meal.

Other common street stall foods are corn-on-the-cob, roasted chestnuts, various nuts and seeds, and a coconut confection in summer. In winter you might want to heed the call of the *salèpi* (*salep, sahlab*) seller and try the mildly sweet, viscous warm drink traditionally made with orchid tuber flour, which has been used medicinally to soothe coughs, asthma, stomach aches and diarrhoea since antiquity. The Ancient Romans believed it was an aphrodisiac.

Farmer's Markets (*Laikì*)

The 'laiki' has some great deals, like the bag of apples (foreground) for 50 cents

Farmer's markets set up in different neighbourhoods Monday to Saturday. The road is closed to traffic (cars cannot be parked at the curb, which are usually cordoned along the sidewalks the day before to remind car-owners), and stalls sell fresh fruit, vegetables, olives, herbs, flowers, fish, clothing (underwear, socks, etc) and sundry household items. You can also buy small amounts, and if only one or two pieces they may just give them to you for free. *Make sure you wash and peel; pesticides are used.*

To experience this unique part of Athenian life (products are cheaper as the day wears on), there's one in **Koukaki** (for **Makriyanni** area as well) on Fridays, *from early morning until* ~*3pm* on **Matrozou St** May to October, and on **Zacharitsa St** November to April. In **Kolonaki** it's on Fridays on **Xenokratous St**, and organic produce sets up in **Dexameni Square**. There's also one in **Neos Kosmos,** just beside **Syngrou Ave** around **Kasomouli tram** stop on Saturdays. And of course there's the permanent *Agorà* or **Central Market** on **Athinas Street**, between **Monastiraki and Omonia squares**, *open Mon–Thurs 6am–3pm, Fri–Sat 6am–6pm.*

Bread & Cheese

Bakery and cheese shop meals are another option. Buy a loaf of bread, such as the simple white *horiàtiki* (village bread) with or without sesame seeds (*susàmi*), whole-grain (*olòkliri*) or brown (*mavro psomì*), multi-grain (*polìsporo*) or sour dough (*prozìmi*). The "bun flower"—buns stuck together in a daisy shape—is called a Margarita. Croissants, some chocolate-filled, and ready-made sandwiches are also widely available in bakeries.

Bakeries also usually sell milk, juice, yogurt, butter or marg, soft drinks and beer, and sometimes bottle or barrel wine.

Then head to a traditional **dairy shop** that sells cheese by the barrel. Greeks are the biggest consumers of cheese per capita at some 27 kilos a year—even more than France—so it's definitely worth taking the opportunity to try the specialties. You will always find feta, which toddlers especially seem to love and which can be found in a milder soft form at these shops, as well as the wonderfully soft and mild *anthòtyro* sheep cheese, a soft *mizìthra* which when hard is grated on pasta, and the unfortunately named but mild and semi-soft *manoùri*. Hard cheeses include *gravyèra* (gruyere), *kassèri* and *kefalòtyri*, and you can also usually find *haloùmi*, the unique, squeaky-when-chewed, rubbery Cypriot cheese. At **tavernas** you can order cheese fried, as *saganàki* and best eaten when still hot.

Middle Eastern Pastries

Pastries to look for at patisserie-bakeries (*zaharoplasteìa*) are the familiar Middle-Eastern pastries and bite-sized morsels such as baklava and its many variations (***pictured***), including *galactoboùreko*—a syrup-y vanilla cream pie made with filo pastry, and the unique Constantinople-origin pastries and puddings. *Kazandibì* is a pudding usually made with rice and "burnt" on both sides giving a unique, rich taste. *Tauk giouksoù*, *keskoùl* and *malèvi* are also mild cream desserts to try that young children may enjoy.

Greek baklavas cost around €16.50 per kilo. You can buy as little as you like, including a few different morsels in a box.

Hatzi
Around **Syntagma**, there's a branch of cosmopolitan Thessaloniki's (Salonica's) Hatzi bakery/café.
• *5 Mitropoleos St, **Syntagma**, 210-322-2647; 34 Akadimias St, **Panepistimio**, 210-360-0644, www.chatzis.gr*

Karaklou Gulluoglu
Also try Turkish-origin Karaklou Gulluoglu (***pictured***), which has yummy biscuits/cookies as well as what could be described as dainty spinach pies.
• *Behind the post office, 10 Nikis St, **Syntagma**, 210-321-3959, www.karakoygulluoglu.com*

Konstantinidis
If you're staying in **Koukaki/Makriyanni** there's well-known Konstantinidis that also sells **ice cream**.
• *98 Syngrou Ave, **Koukaki**, 210-924-7370, www.konstandinidis.gr*

Kostis
If around **Neos Kosmos** Metro or tram station you're in luck, as one of the best in town is Kostis, opposite JK Apartments (hotel), right at the station, which also sells **ice cream**.
• *70 Ilia Iliou and Kassomouli sts, **Neos Kosmos**, 210-901-5882.*

Groceries & Supermarkets

Supermarkets around town are more like mini-markets due to the lack of space. **Formula** for babies up to six months is available at pharmacies; for older children you can buy formula, cereals, children's yogurt and other items from supermarkets or mini-supermarkets that also sell fresh fruit. Ask at your hotel for the nearest one or check the list below. **Prepared baby food** is not always available, but if they have it, it would be with the baby cereals and shelf (long-life) milk. *Hours are usually Mon-Fri 8am–9pm; Sat 8am–8pm.*
    A list of **kosher foods** and where they can be bought is on *www.chabad.gr*, and **halal restaurants and food** can be found around **Omonia** and towards **Psyrri**, *down Sofokleous and Evripidou sts* from the **Central Market** (**Agorà**), but be careful around there, where many illegal migrants and addicts congregate. A list of outlets is on *www.halalfooddirectory.com*. Supermarkets also have health food sections.

CENTRAL SUPERMARKETS & HEALTH FOOD SHOPS

Artemisia
A health-food shop in **Makriyanni**.
• *3 Parthenonos St, **Makriyanni**, 210-924-8840.*

Bazaar
Bazaar supermarket (*pictured*) is a discount chain which has a small selection of baby food jars at the **Syntagma** branch.
• *28 Petraki St, one street parallel south of Ermou St, near **Syntagma** Sq, 210-321-3590.*

Carrefour Marinopoulos
Carrefour Marinopoulos is in **Kolonaki**, which is near **Syntagma Square**.
• *9 Kanari St, **Kolonaki**, 210-362-4907, www.carrefour.gr*

Fruit shop
There are a few fruit and veg shops around, but one centrally located is at the *corner* of *Xenofontos and Nikis sts*, **Syntagma**.

Green Store
There's a small health-food shop (*pictured*) with some organic produce, further west of Makriyanni in **Koukaki**.
• *57 Dimitrakopoulou/Noti Botsari sts, Koukaki, 210-924-1842.*

Health Ecology
This well-known health-food shop near **Omonia Square** stocks organic produce as well as dried goods and also has a **vegetarian restaurant** to eat there (including upstairs—which is handy if you have young children) or take away.
• *Daily 8am–9pm.* • *57 Panepistimiou St, Omonia, 210-321-0966.*

Marinopoulos
Marinopoulos is a supermarket in **Kolonaki**.
• *43 Xenokratous and 48 Deinokratous sts, Kolonaki, 210-725-3863, www.carrefour.gr*

Market In
This is a small supermarket in **Thissio,** further down heading towards the bridge (Gefyra) and Gazi.
• *33 Nileos St, Thissio, 210-347-7267.*

Organic shop
There's an **organic grocers** opposite the Temple of Zeus, **Makriyanni**.
• *3 Syngrou Ave, Makriyanni.*

Sofos
There's a Sofos mini-market near **Syntagma**, and another in **Monastiraki**.
• *Kolokotroni and 13 Praxitelous sts, Syntagma, 210-321-3533; 78 Mitropoleos and Aiolou St, Monastiraki, 210-322-6677.*

Spar supermarket
There's one in **Makriyanni** across from the Divani Palace Acropolis hotel, and on the pedestrian "tram" street in **Thissio**.
• *4 Parthenonos St, Makriyanni; 11-13 Irakleidon St, Thissio, 210-342-5100, www.veropoulos.gr*

Tesseris Epoches
This organic shop at **Syntagma** has products and fresh fruit, right around the

corner from the fruit shop. They sell prepared baby food in jars. It's beside a vegetarian restaurant, **Avocado** (*see Special-interest dining section*), near Xenofontos St.
• *Mon–Fri 8.20am–8.30pm, Sat 8.20am–6.30pm.* • *30 Nikis St,* **Syntagma**, *210-322-9078.*

Vasilopouloi Delicatessen
A supermarket between Omonia and Syntagma Squares on **Stadiou St,** (Panepistimio Metro station), this is a rather expensive mini-market delicatessen (***pictured, right***) that stocks **imported and specialty** items. Next to the City of Athens Museum.
• *3 Paparigopoulou St,* **Klafthmonos Sq**, *210-322-2405,*
www.ab-delicatessen.gr

Dining Out (by category, area)

Greeks are picky about their food, and quality and freshness are paramount. The caveat here is that food normally found in touristy places may not reach the highest standards, so aim to eat where the locals do. You'll also get the generous portions Athenians are accustomed to.

Families are welcomed and children get special treatment, including at most restaurants, where running around between the tables is tolerated, since Greeks spend a lot of time socializing rather gregariously themselves, and certainly don't expect the children to sit quietly either.

Tavernas & local cuisine
The extended family remains largely intact in Greece, so the idea of getting a neighbourhood babysitter is unusual, and being a hot country where people go to bed late after being inside during the heat of the day, children are taken almost everywhere, including tavernas, restaurants, and café-bars, where alcohol is served. There are usually cafes or restaurants at **museums** so the children can also eat while there.

Barrel wine, also for sale

Tavernas are either *psistarìa* (grill houses) or *mageirìa* (cook houses) (***pictured, opposite***) which are a good bet, especially for an evening meal. Very helpfully, you can go back to the kitchen to view the dishes at *mageirìa*. Children are usually around at all times, although the Greek dinner hour is 10pm. Many tavernas open at 5pm or 6pm in the evening.

At a taverna you'll be able to find something that children will like, even if it's just the chips (fries). It's no fun waiting with antsy, cranky kids and then rushing through the meal. So for really young children that cannot wait for an order to be freshly cooked, ie a steak, ask the waiter for food that is ready, such as *moùssaka*, salad or an appetizer, at least to keep them occupied until the chips arrive.

A basket of bread is always brought to the table together with the utensils and serviettes.

A typical meal for two or four people comprises a salad, dip, appetizer, plate of chips/fries (also ubiquitous), and the main course meal, plus a barrel wine you can often purchase bulk (***pictured, opposite***) or beer, and juice or soft drinks for the kids. Non-carbonated lemonaid of any brand is known as "*Fanta Ble*" (blue).

The menu has **salads** such as Greek salad (cucumber, tomato, onion, feta, olives) drizzled in olive oil, but there may be a choice of other salads as well, such as lettuce or carrot and cabbage.

Starters include dips like *tzatzìki* (yogurt, cucumber and garlic), *fava* (bean), and *taramousalàta* (fish roe), and other *mezè* (appetizers) can be anything from fried eggplant/aubergine, zucchini/courgette or fried long green or red Florentine peppers, to peppers stuffed with feta, patties made of various ingredients and deep fried, mini-cheese pies, and boiled zucchini/courgette served with oil and lemon.

Main courses can run from roast chicken and potatoes to steak (*brizòla*), and the biggest pork chops (steaks) you're likely to ever see, thick and juicy.

There's also plain pasta dishes such as child-favourite spaghetti with meat sauce (*makarònia me kimà*), or *pastìccio*, macaroni-type pasta with mince/ground beef in a béchamel sauce and baked, and tummy-filling *moùssaka*, made with mince and potato and a béchamel sauce. Spicy sausages are another choice, as well as bread-fortified, spicy meat patties (*keftèdes*). *Kalamàri* is deep-fried squid, but grilled octopus (*ch-tapòdi*) is another specialty (and hit or miss taste-wise), as are mussels (*mìdia*).

Dessert is rarely part of the menu at traditional Greek tavernas, but they may have fresh fruit, such as cut-up watermelon that's brought to the table following a meal (or ask), a mild semolina cake, or baklava—the Middle-Eastern sweet made of layers of filo pastry and walnuts drizzled with honey syrup. Tavernas may also have thick Greek yogurt drizzled with honey, both being specialties and together as divine now it was in antiquity. Restaurants will have a dessert menu.

Tipping

As for tipping, a service charge may be included but it's customary to round up the bill or leave about 10 to 15 percent. ***Note: Most restaurants are cash only.***

Fast food

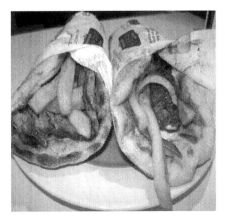

Greece's fast food is *souvlàki*. A *souvlàki* or *gyros* to go is ~€2. Nutritious and filling, they are usually made with chicken or pork sliced off a vertical roaster, or come as kebabs on a skewer, which you can also get as mince (ground beef). "With everything" (*ap'òla*) includes fresh tomatoes, onions, fries/chips and a sauce in the pita. Kids will probably like them plain—with the chips and without the onions. Many places around town have *souvlaki* (look for the *gyros* roaster or grill).

Gyristroula
In Thissio/Monastiraki you can also sit down at this busy place, just opposite Thissio Metro station on the pedestrian walkway. Hot dogs and sandwich fare is next door at **In Between** (*9 Agion Asomaton Sq, 210-331-7576, noon-midnight*) which also delivers.
• *9 Asomaton Sq, **Thissio/Monastiraki**, 215-215-2692.*

O Petros
Just by the Metro bridge between Thissio and Gazi near Pireaos St, opposite the Technopolis cultural centre, you can get souvlakia here; they also deliver.
• *3 Persefonis St, **Gazi/Thissio**, 210-347-2301, 698-945-2060.*

Pita Pan
You can take away or sit down upstairs at this place around the corner from McDonald's.
• *2 Ermou St, **Syntagma Sq**, 210-331-2212, www.pitapan.gr*

Ta Souvlakis tou Hasapi
Get them to go at this hole-in-the-wall near Syntagma and Plaka.
• *1 Apollonos St, **Syntagma/Plaka**, 210-322-0459.*

Restaurant chains

Everest
Everest (*www.everest.com.gr*) is a **sandwich chain** with many outlets.
• *Beside McDonald's, **Syntagma Sq**.*
• *Ath. Diakou and Makriyanni sts, **Makriyanni**.*
• ***Omonia Square**.*
• *Sina and 68 Solonos sts, **Kolonaki**.*
• *Panepistimiou at Ippokratous St, **Panepistimiou**.*
• *59-61 **Akadimias St**, towards **Omonia Sq**.*

Goody's

Goody's (*www.goodysnet.com*) is Greece's **burger-chain** equivalent. Branches at

• *72 Ermou St, **Monastiraki**.*
• *17 Stadiou and Christou Lada sts, **Syntagma**.*
• *Syngrou Ave at Syngrou-Fix Metro station Drakou St exit, **Koukaki**, which also has an indoor play area upstairs.*

Hard Rock Café

This chain is also here, if it's a must-go.

• *Daily 10am till late.* • ***18 Filellinon St**, **Syntagma**, 210-325-2758, www.hardrock.com*

McDonald's

McDonald's is right at **Syntagma Square** alongside a **sandwich shop** and near **bakeries** that sell savoury pies and ready-made sandwiches.

• *Ermou St at **Syntagma Square**, www.mcdonalds.gr*

Pizza

You can find **pizza** parlours all over town; most offer delivery. **Pizza Hut** (*18118, www.pizzahut.gr*) is also available to order out.

• *30 Stadiou and 4 Korai sts, **Korai Square** (between Stadiou and Panepistimiou sts), inside the arcade.*

Starbucks

Ever-popular Starbucks (*gr.starbucks.com*) serves coffee/tea, desserts and sandwiches.

• *Mon–Fri from 7am/7.30am, Sat–Sun from 8am/9am until 10pm/10.30pm.*
• *4 Theofanous St, **Ambelokipi**, corner of Kifissias and Alexandras aves, 210-645-1563.*
• *38 Patriarchou Ioakeim St, **Kolonaki**, 210-725-5797.*
• *80 Mitropoleos and Aiolou sts, **Monastiraki**, 210-322-4962.*

TGIFriday's

Branches of family restaurant TGIF (*www.fridays.gr*), are in town as well

• *Sun–Thurs 1pm–1am, Fri–Sat 1pm–2am.*
• *2 Neofitou Vamva St, **Kolonaki**, 210-722-7721, near Vas. Sofias Ave (near Evangelismos Metro station on Line 3).*
• *Alexandras and Kifissias aves, **Ambelokipi**, 210-647-5417.*
***Get there**: Ambelokipi Metro station, Panormou exit, 5 min walk).*

Tavernas & Greek restaurants

For the nearest (though not necessarily most authentic) "local taverna" recommendations, ask at your hotel, but here are some suggestions.

MONASTIRAKI

Adrianou St

For a refreshment there are many **cafes** on pedestrian Adrianou St between Monastiraki and Thissio Metro stations, along the train line opposite the Ancient Agora, with tables set up on the street. Not to be confused with the other Adrianou St in nearby Plaka, the main pedestrian street with all the tourist shops.

• *Adrianou St, Monastiraki.*

Mitropoleos St

For a meal especially during the day or for an early dinner, head to the end of Mitropoleos St on **Monastiraki Square**, at Monastiraki Metro station. This area is closed to traffic and family-friendly with tables set out in the street, with very reasonably-priced souvlaki meals. The two main restaurants across from each other are **Savvas** and **Thanasis**. You can also eat *lachmajùn* here (at **Savvas**), a spicy kind of Eastern pizza with mince/ground beef as the topping on pita or Arabic bread.

• *Monastiraki Sq and Mitropoleos St, **Monastiraki**.*

SYNTAGMA

Kentrikon

For a lunch break, nearby is an air-conditioned restaurant called Kentrikon. On Kolokotroni St just before Stadiou St and behind the National History Museum is the big "Kentrikon" sign. Go into the pedestrian lane and it's on your left. This long-established diner open only for lunch and early dinner has an extensive menu and reasonable prices, so there should be something there for everyone. You can also just have a refreshment break here.

• *Mon–Sat noon–6pm.* • ***3 Kolokotroni St, Panepistimiou/Syntagma Sq,** 210-323-2482.*

PLAKA

The tavernas in Plaka are very touristy so it's best to find places where Greeks go.

Platanos Taverna

A traditional taverna in Plaka that is frequented by Greeks is Platanos Taverna, on a pedestrian-zone square with tables under a plane tree.

• *Mon–Sat noon–4.30pm/7.30pm–midnight, Mar–Jun also Sun noon–5pm.* • *No credit cards.*
• *4 Diogenous St, Plaka, 210-322-0666.*

Scholarhio (Kouklis)

One taverna that is popular with both tourists and locals, and is also child-friendly (upstairs), is Scholarhio (Kouklis) Ouzerie (*pictured*), where you can choose *meze* (starters) selections off a tray. They offer a set menu for four people with ten small dishes, drinks and dessert for €14 per person.

• *Daily 11am–2am.* • *14 Tripodon St, Plaka, 210-324-7605, www.sholarhio.gr*

Taverna Tou Psara

This place has received good reviews from locals over the years for taverna dining in Plaka.

• *16 Erechthios St, at the end of Flessa St, Plaka, 210-321-8733 to 4.*

THISSIO

Steki tou Ilia

This taverna is really two, ie it has two locations on the same pedestrian path alongside the train tracks from Thissio station (towards Piraeus) that, also to confuse matters, changes names further down the street.

A highlight is a plate of lamb (for one person or more) which is ordered by the kilo and put on a platter with wedges of lemon to share. Then a salad and other *mezè* as taste dictates, usually a Greek salad (*horiàtiki*), *tzatzìki* (yogurt dip) for the bread, and another vegetable, along with wine from the barrel (*hìma*). There is no *souvlàki* here, and crucially for kids, no ketchup for the chips/fries at the Thessalonikis St location. They do offer mustard, and they won't mind if you bring your own ketchup. If one location isn't open, especially during August, go to the other. Expect to pay €15+ per person for an entrée, salad, a couple of meze and a drink (beer or barrel wine). No credit cards.

* At the location opposite **Agios Athanasios church**, in summer customers dine within the **fenced off garden** beside the church yard.

• *Mon–Fri 7.30pm–1am, Sat 1pm–1am, Sun 1pm–7pm.* • *5 Eptahalkou St, Thissio, 210-345-8052.*

* The other location is further along, and dining is inside in winter and on the **pedestrian street** in summer.

• *Tues–Fri 6pm–1am, Sat–Sun 1pm–1am, Mon closed.* • *7 Thessalonikis St, Thissio, 210-342-2407.*

MAKRIYANNI (ACROPOLIS), KOUKAKI

Delinolanis
A restaurant with a discreet mezzanine seating area that's convenient if you have small children, and also just to stop for an ice cream, a branch of the Delinolanis chain is around the corner from Syngrou-Fix Metro station, Drakou St exit. Looking spotless with white baker's hats, they also serve traditional Greek food (including pasta), "fast food" (burgers and chips/fries) and are **open 24 hours.**
• *100 Syngrou Ave, **Koukaki**, 210-898-3000.*

Drakou St
Pedestrian Drakou St outside the **Syngrou-Fix Metro station exit** is also popular and busy with locals, with tavernas, cafes, and a "beer garden" café—**Vini** *(10 Drakou St, Koukaki, 210-922-6225).* Look for the "Guinness" sign *(pictured)*.

Makriyanni St
There are a few restaurants (tavernas) and cafes beside the Acropolis Museum on pedestrian Makriyanni St, as well as around the end of pedestrian **Dionysiou Areopagitou St**, the walkway around the Acropolis, near busy **Amalias Ave** at Hadrian's Arch. All have tables set up in the street and cater to the many tourists in the area, which is not necessarily a good thing in terms of authentic Greek food.

Strofi
This is a white tablecloth (more expensive) taverna following a refurbishment a few years ago. It has good Greek fare and is located fairly close to the Acropolis entrance. Roof garden, Acropolis-view dining is popular.
• *Entrees ~€11–€25* • *Daily noon–1am* • ***25 Rovertou Galli St, Makriyanni**, 210-921-4130, www.strofi.gr*

Special-interest dining

ANCIENT GREEK

Archaion Gefseis
At "Ancient Flavours", you and your older children will remember the experience of dining on the food (tasty—check out the menu on the website) eaten by the

ancients and served by toga-clad waitstaff. Exotic foods include deer, rabbit and quail with pomegranate.

• *Tues–Sat 7pm–1am, Sun noon–5pm, closed two weeks in Aug.* • **22 Kodratou St, Metaxourgio,** *210-523-9661, www.archeon.gr*
Get there: *Metaxourgio Metro Station on Line 2, then 5 minutes' walk towards Lenorman St.*

BRUNCH

Byzantino

Byzantino has a **daily buffet** with a huge selection of starters, seafood, etc, and hot-plate selections of meat, fish and pasta, as well as lots of sweets and fruit for dessert. Sure to find something agreeable and familiar here, especially for picky eaters. But you'll pay for the privilege at €37.50 excluding drinks, free up to 5 yrs, half-price to 12 yrs.

• *Daily 12.30–midnight.* • **Athens Hilton, 46 Vas. Sofias Ave, Hilton, Ilissia,** *210-728-1000, www.hiltonathens.gr*
Get there: *Evangelismos Metro station on Line 3.*

New York Sandwiches

NYS serves French toast, pancakes, eggs Benedict, bagels with cream cheese and other deli fare (*pictured*) for **brunch** *until 6pm on weekends*, but you should book ahead. They also deliver.

• *Daily noon–midnight.* • **3 Sinopis St, Ambelokipi**, *behind Athens Tower (Pirgos Athinon), Vas. Sofias and Alexandras/Mesogion aves, 210-777-8475, www.nys.gr*
Get there: *Trolley nos. 3, 7, 8, 10, 13, bus nos. 408, 419, 550, 601, 603, bus-stop: Athinaion.*

ETHNIC

There are many ethnic restaurants in Athens, but here are three that are convenient to satisfy a craving.

Furin Kazan

Catering also to a large take-out clientele, Furin Kazan is near **Syntagma** and the place to go if you're craving clean-palate **Japanese** cuisine.

• *Dishes €8 to €22.* • *Mon–Sat noon–midnight, Sun 2pm–midnight.* • **2 Apollonos St, Syntagma,** *210-322-7170.*

Gostijo

Jewish restaurant in Chabad House in **Psyrri** specializes in **kosher** meat (*besari*) and Sephardic dishes, also a mini-shop of kosher products. May deliver to visitors at their hotels.

• *Daily from 5pm, Fri Shabbat dinner and Sat Shabbat lunch by reservation, Sat night (Motzari shabbat) open one hour after sundown.* • **10 Aisopou St, Psyrri,** *210-323-3825.*

Indian Kitchen

The latest Indian food entrant and the only one to venture into upmarket **Syntagma** thus far. While a little pricey, it's a handy place to get spicy food. Also vegetarian choices.

• *Entrees €11–€12, vegetarian €6–€8.* • *Daily noon–12.30am.* • **6 Apollonos St, Syntagma,** *210-323-7720.*

VEGETARIAN

Avocado
Avocado (*pictured*) is Athens' newest (opened 2011) vegetarian restaurant which also regularly holds free meditation sessions upstairs. Beside a **health-food store** (**Tesseris Epoches**) that also sells fresh produce. • *Entrees are ~€8, fresh juice from €3.50 to €6.80 for a protein shake.* • *Mon-Sat 11am–10pm, Sun 11am–7pm.* • **30 Nikis St, Syntagma Sq**, *210-323-7878,* www.avocadoathens.com

Health-Ecology
Near Omonia Square, this is more of a breakfast and lunch or take-out diner, with ready-made dishes you order cafeteria-style, and it also has space upstairs to sit down. There's a **health-food store** beside it which also has fresh fruit (organic). • *Mon–Fri 8am–9.30pm, Sat 8am–8pm, Sun 10am–3.30pm.* • **57 Panepistimiou St, Omonia Sq,** *210-321-0966.*

Improv Vegetarian Restaurant/bar
This place in Gazi is a rock bar with vegan food as well as American and Mediterranean styles, recommended for its specialty beers, organic wine and food dishes. • *Tues–Sat 6pm–3am.* • **8 Iakhou and Evmolpidon sts, Gazi**, *one block south of main Iera Odos St, 213-024-0875, www.facebook.com/improvathens.*

Ice Cream & Frozen Yogurt

Packaged **ice cream** is widely available in help-yourself freezers at almost every kiosk and corner store for one or two euros. Bakeries also often sell ice cream in summer, as scoops or as individual mini sticks and cones. One scoop cone is typically €1.50, soft ice cream is €2.

The latest craze to take the capital is **frozen yogurt**, and these shops are popping up all over (*pictured, Lazaridis*). A little pricey but yum!

THISSIO

En Athinais
Nevermind if you can't find the name, this is an ice cream bar (and real bar) at the top of Nileos and Irakleidon sts.
• *12 Irakleidon St, **Thissio**, 210-345-3018.*

Gefsi Peripatou
A little sandwich shop sells scoop and soft ice cream near the Thission open-air cinema, on the walkway around the Acropolis and ancient sites.
• *11 Apostolou Pavlou St, **Thissio**, 210-347-0406.*

In Between
At In Between there's scoop and soft ice cream (plus hot dogs and sandwich fare), just across the pedestrian street from the Thissio Metro station. They also deliver.
• *Noon–midnight.* • *9 Agion Asomaton Sq, **Thissio**, 210-331-7576.*

KOUKAKI, MAKRIYANNI (ACROPOLIS)

Bo
An ice cream café-bar-restaurant near Syngrou-Fix Metro station.
• *Pedestrian Drakou St at 42 Dimitrakopoulou St, **Koukaki**.*

Gelato
Very near Akropoli Metro station, across from the post office on the edge of Plaka, is this top-quality ice-cream shop that also has yogurt with fruit.
• *8 Dion. Areopagitou St, **Makriyanni**, 210-321-7879.*

Makriyanni St
There are a few ice-cream-selling **cafes** on pedestrian Makriyanni St, beside the Acropolis Museum outside the Akropoli Metro station exit (*pictured*).

Mama Psomi
Ice cream is usually sold at bakeries in summer; one is Mama Psomi, a charming, traditional bakery near the **Tony Hotel**.
• *42-44 Zacharitsa St, **Koukaki**, 210-922-7686.*

SYNTAGMA, PLAKA

Everest
This sandwich shop (*www.everest.com.gr*) sells frozen yogurt.
• ***Syntagma Square**, right beside McDonald's.*

Fleiyo

Right behind the main post office, Fleiyo has yogurt and mini pastries and doughnuts that are child-sized and priced around €1. Seats in front; they also deliver.

• *10 Nikis and Ermou Sts, **Syntagma**, 210-323-7736.*

Kydathinaion, Adrianou sts

There are ice cream shops on both Adrianou and Kydathinaion sts, the main pedestrian streets in **Plaka**. One is opposite **Ruby's** jewellers *(105 Adrianou St)*.

Milk Bar

Milk Bar (*pictured*) has both frozen and yummy fresh Greek yogurt.

• *39 Kydathinaion St, **Plaka**, 210-324-5153.*

To Horiatiko

This well-known bakery has ice cream scoops.

• *Aiolou and 67 Ermou sts, towards **Monastiraki** on the edge of Plaka, 210-323-7766, www.horiatiko.gr*

MONASTIRAKI

Athens Best Yogurt (ABY)

• *36 Pandrossou St, **Monastiraki**, 210-321-5791.*

Fro-yo

• *55 Ermou St at Kapnikareas (church in the road) St, **Monastiraki**, 212-100-6147, www.froyo.gr*

Ice Scream!

Lazaridis is on the edge of the flea market, near Monastiraki station. It's got the big cones outside.

• *19 Pandrossou St, **Monastiraki**, 210-322-0709, www.icescream.gr*

Mattonella Gelateria

An ice cream parlour (*pictured, left*) is also across from Monastiraki Sq.

• *82 Ermou St, **Monastiraki**, 210-325-1717.*

Yiaourtaki

Right opposite Monastiraki Square in Psyrri, this place (*pictured, right*) serves fresh (intermittently) and frozen yogurt.

• *82 Ermou St, across from **Monastiraki Sq**, 694-974-1599.*

Yum...me

A frozen yogurt bar just west of Kapnikarea church on

central Ermou St, which has bean-bag chairs outside on the pavement.
• *73 Ermou St, just below Aiolou St, **Monastiraki**, 210-323-7115.*

KOLONAKI

There are two frozen yogurt shops on **Tsakalof St** in the block between Kolonaki Square and Iraklitou St—one is beside the **Everest** sandwich outlet on the corner.

Picnic tip

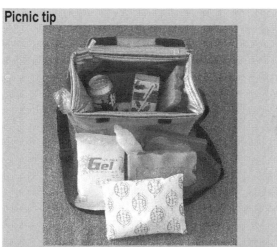

If you're making picnic lunches for yourself and/or your children, consider bringing some **freezer gel packs** to keep cold sandwiches and other food that can spoil, especially when the weather is hot to avoid excessive bacteria and food poisoning. You can also find freezer packs at **Ikea**, while sometimes pharmacies give cold packs to keep refrigerated medicines cold until you get home, which can be reused. Ice cube bags from the supermarket kitchen items section might work but obviously for less time. **Insulated tote bags (*pictured*)** are available where camping/picnic supplies are sold, and online.

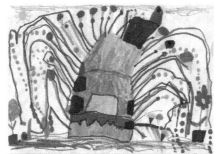

Ice-cream-making machine, Nov 2012 ☺ 5 yrs

Ornate silver buckles from the 19ᵗʰ century and other items can be found in antique shops, including at Avyssinia Square, Monastiraki

Chapter 5: Shopping

What to Buy

Things to buy include beautifully-crafted gold and silver **jewellery, worry beads, karagiozi puppets, icons, statues and pottery**, especially **decorative plates, herbs, toiletry items made with olive oil or other natural products**, and sweets such as **sesame bars** and **Turkish delight**, anything with **masticha**—the prized flavour from the sap of a tree grown on the island of Chios (*Mastiha Shop, 6 Panepistimiou (El. Venizelou) and Kriezotou sts, Panepistimio, 210-363-2750, www.mastihashop.com*), and **honey** from wild flowers, thyme or pine nectar.

Metaxa (the more stars the better) is a smooth **brandy**, and numerous **local wines** include **Nemea** (from indigenous red *agiorgitiko* grapes) and aromatic **Moschato** (Muscat), one of the oldest cultivated grapes. **Cavas** or wine shops and even some tavernas sell decent wine in bulk. Good-quality **leather shoes** and sandals are the most popular purchases, and cotton, and especially woollen, **undershirts**, are coveted, sold at a couple of small shops on **Evripidou St**, *Central Market/Agorà area, opposite Agiou Markou St and Aiolou St*. Loose-fitting, casual **cotton shirts** for men are also sought-after.
* *Shop hours are Mon, Wed, Sat ~9/10am to ~2/3pm, Tues, Thurs, Fri ~9/10am–2pm/5–9pm, but are open longer in tourist areas.*
Sales are twice yearly, in January–February and July–August.

Where to Buy

The main street of Athens is pedestrian-friendly **Ermou St**, which reaches all the way from Syntagma Square through the **shopping district** (clothes and particularly, shoes), down past **Monastiraki Metro station** where the (permanent) **flea market** (souvenirs, trendy clothes, shoes, antiques) is located, especially along parallel **Pandrossou** and **Ifestou sts** and into **Avyssinias Square**, towards **Thissio Metro station**. Pedestrian **Adrianou St** in **Plaka** has souvenirs, including travel-sized and gift-wrapped food products. A temporary **flea market** sets up on *Sunday mornings at 94 Iera Odos* near **Elaionas Metro station** on Line 3. The chicest shopping area in the centre is in the **Kolonaki** district, with many **designer shops** along the streets, particularly **Patriarchou Ioakim St**, pedestrian **Tsakalof St**, and **Skoufa** and **Solonos sts**.

Eat
• Stop for a *souvlàki* or gyros **lunch** in this family-oriented eating area at **Monastiraki Square** and **Mitropoleos St**.
• A place to stop for a cheap lunch in **Thissio/Monastiraki** is the busy *souvlàki* restaurant (**Gyristroula**, tables outside), as well as a sandwich shop (**In Between**), opposite Thissio Metro station.
• In pricey **Kolonaki**, head to **Everest** sandwich shop, on pedestrian Tsakalof and Iraklitou sts, off Kolonaki Square.

Shops (by category)

BAPTISM & CHRISTENING

Buy baptism favours (boubounières) ready-made or DIY with 'charms' bought from bead shops on Praxitelous St

Epitropakis
One baptism shop is Epitropakis. The website shows their **bridal shop** but Epitropakis can handle all baptismal requirements, from the clothes, shoes and undergarments to the *boubounières* or favours, which are elevated to a fine art in Greece.
• *7 Kalamiotou St (bridal shop at no. 9) and Athinaidos St, continuation of Perikleous,* **Monastiraki**, *210-323-8448,* www.angela.gr

Romvis St
Get beautiful clothes and memento items at a shop specializing in this popular church ritual. There are a couple of shops on Romvis St (*off Perikleous St, one block north of central Ermou St,* **Monastiraki***),* including at **no. 26**, and near pedestrian **Kalamiotou St**.

BOOKS & MAGAZINES

Outside the centre, finding foreign press newspapers and magazines is difficult. You can pick up international titles from **kiosks** at **Syntagma Square, Omonia Square, Kolonaki Square,** and the kiosk (*pictured*) at Drakou and Veikou sts (near Syngrou-Fix Metro station), in **Makriyanni/Koukaki.**

Anavasi
Anavasi is the last word in maps, globes and travel books, especially on Greece. Two locations.

• *34 Voulis St, Syntagma Sq.*
• *6A Stoa Arsakiou, Panepistimiou (El. Venizelou) St, **Panepistimio**, 210-321-8104, www.anavasi.gr*

Eleftheroudakis
This bookstore has a good selection of coffee table books, travel, maps and children's books in English on the 1st floor, between the Parenting and Teen fiction sections (the Children's section label is where the Greek books are).
• *11 Panepistimiou (El. Venizelou) and Amerikis sts, **Syntagma**, 210-325-8440, www.books.gr*

Public
Public electronics store also has a selection of children's books in English on the 4th floor, including classics like *James and Giant Peach* and the *Mr Men* series, as well as games, toys and children's DVDs. All kinds of music can be found here, plus gadgets, accessories, computers and mobile phones, and a **café** with a terrace on the 5th floor.
• *Mon–Fri 9am–9pm, Sat 9am–8pm.* • *1 Nikis and 1 Karageorgi Servias sts, **Syntagma Sq**, 210-324-6210, www.public.gr*

Travel Bookstore
If you're over near **Exarchia/Omonia**, the Travel Bookstore has a wide range of... travel books and maps.
• *71 Solonos St, 210-361-6943, **Exarchia**, www.travelbookstore.gr*

CLOTHES, CHILDREN'S

Euro shop
The Euro shop sells kitchen supplies and seasonal toys, but also has a few **Greek-made clothes** (eg shorts) and ceramic items.
• *38 Athinas and Evripidou sts, **Agora/Monastiraki**, 697-712-9148.*

H&M
This popular Swedish chain with many branches around Athens, also has children's clothes at cheap prices.
• *54 Ermou and Kapnikarea sts, **Monastiraki**, 210-323-3858, www.hm.com*

Igglesi

For **traditional Greek costumes** and ancient-style tunics (*pictured*) and *tsarouchia* (pom pom shoes) for parties or events like Halloween or Carnival, Igglesi in the basement has all the getup.

• *100 Adrianou St, Plaka, 210-322-1262, www.iglessi.com*

Lapin House

This local children's clothing chain on the main shopping street has some really nice clothes, but they're pricey.

• *21 Ermou St, Syntagma, 210-324-1316, www.lapinhouse.com*

Pandrossou St

A small shop with **children's T-shirts**, such as cartoon child Alexander the Great or Spartan, (*pictured*) and other clothes that attracts a steady clientele of Canadians (see the collection of business cards—the owner has roots there).

• *Opposite the "Greens" Panathinaikos (Athens sports) club outlet at 47 Pandrossou St near Aiolou St, Monastiraki.*

Prenatal

Italian chain Prenatal has supplies and mid-priced clothes for babies to eight years.

• *4 Nikis St, Syntagma, 210-321-6490, www.prenatal.gr*

Zara

With many outlets around town, you can find a good selection of low-priced kid's clothes in Zara, a popular Spanish chain, and of course women's clothes too.

• *9 Ermou St, Syntagma, 210-325-2579, www.zara.com*

CLOTHES, GENERAL

There are **men's clothing** (tailored, formal) shops along **Stadiou St**—one is **Lentzos** (*9 Stadiou St, Syntagma, 210-322-5113)*—and **casual men's clothes** are available from a slew of international chain stores on **Ermou St**, where you can take your pick from numerous **women's clothing shops** as well.

Hondos Center

You can find **bathing suits** (all ages) from Hondos and other shops here too.

• *39 Ermou St, Monastiraki, 210-372-2900, www.hondos.gr*

Marks & Spencer

British chain M&S has **bathing suits** and clothes for men, women and children.

• *Mon-Fri 9am–9pm, Sat 9am–8pm.* • *33-35 Ermou St, Monastiraki, 210-324-0675, www.marksandspencer.gr*

Men's & women's hats
Traditional Greek **fisherman's caps** and other men's and women's hats can be found at two stores—one is **Pil Poul**; the other is **Polychronopoulos** (*210-321-4510*)—which are beside each other.
• *15 Voreou St, the continuation of Kolokotroni St near Athinas St,* **Monastiraki.**

CLOTHES, GREEK-MADE

Quite a few shops in Plaka on **Adrianou St**, particularly those selling the distinctive and coveted **casual cotton shirts** and cotton knit tops and sweaters, are Greek-made.

Efi's
Fine-quality Greek cotton knit tops and other items are in Efi's, high up on the main pedestrian street in Plaka.
• *150 Adrianou St,* **Plaka***, 210-324-5437.*

Fokas
Two points of purchase of Raxevsky (*see below*) are inside this mini-department store for **casual clothes** and which are centrally located. They offer discounts with the Athens Spotlighted discount card, but at different locations.
• *41 Stadiou St,* **Omonia***, 210-321-5361,* www.fokas.gr
• *Ermou and Voulis St,* **Syntagma***, 210-321-3154.*

Nikorellos
For a wide selection of **Greek-made cotton clothes for babies, children, women and men**, including souvenir T-shirts and baby singlets with slogans, Nikorellos (*pictured*) has a lot to choose from.
• *10 Aiolou St,* **Plaka/Monastiraki***, 210-324-6429.*

Raxevsky
Raxevsky is a reasonably-priced **Athens designer**, and their **children's line** is under the **Mini Raxevsky** (*www.mini-raxevsky.com*) label, with many outlets for these flashy children's clothes, including for **baptism/christening**.
• *30 Ermou St,* **Syntagma***, 210-323-7065.*
• *Raxevsky inside Fokas: Ermou and Voulis sts,* **Syntagma***, 210-323-1050,* www.raxevsky.gr

DEPARTMENT & CHAIN STORES

Athens Heart mall
This small and quieter mall (*pictured*) in western Athens is nearest to the centre but there's no mass transit to it. It has the best kids' entertainment area, however. Shops include **Plaisio** and **Germanos** (electronics and phones), **Sklavenitis** (supermarket, *www.sklavenitis.gr*), **H&M** (clothing), **Mouyer** (children's shoes), and mobile/cell network providers **Wind** and **Vodafone**.
• *180 Piraeos St at Hamosternas Ave, Tavros, 210-341-4105, www.athensheart.gr*
Get there: *Bus nos. 049, 815, 914, bus-stop: Ergon, or suburban train (Proastiakos) Rouf station (journey takes about 10 minutes) or Petralona Metro station on Line 1, then ~15 min walk.*

Athens Metro Mall
This mall is smaller but closer to central Athens and has **Public** and **Germanos** electronics shops, **AB Vassilopoulos** supermarket (*210-976-9556, www.ab.gr*), **H&M**, **Tommy Hilfiger**, **Zara** and many more clothes shops.
• *Vouliagmenis Ave, Agios Dimitrios, 210-976-9444, www.athensmetromall.gr*
Get there: *At Agios Dimitrios Metro station on Line 2.*

Attica Department Store
Attica DS (*pictured*) near Syntagma Square, is a department store which has fashionable designer items in numerous international and local shop-in-shops.
• *9 Panepistimiou St, Syntagma, 211-180-2600, www.atticadps.gr*

Marks & Spencer
The British chain M&S has clothes, a wide selection of underwear, plus house wares and seasonal items.
• *Mon–Fri 9am–9pm, Sat 9am–8pm.* • *33-35 Ermou St, Monastiraki, 210-324-0675, www.marksandspencer.gr*

Plaisio
Around the corner from Public at Syntagma Square, Plaisio also has computers, phones and related accessories.
• *Mon–Fri 9am–9pm, Sat 9am–8pm.* • *3 Voulis St, Syntagma, 210-325-8000, www.plaisio.gr*

Praktiker

A German DIY chain that also sells practical items, right next door to the Athens Heart mall, just west of central Athens.

• *176 Piraeos St, **Tavros**, 210-249-3150, www.praktiker.gr*
***Get there**: Bus nos. 049, 815, 914, bus-stop: Ergon, or suburban train (Proastiakos) Rouf station (journey takes about 10 minutes) or Petralona Metro station on Line 1, then ~15 minutes' walk.*

Public

For electronics, books and some events tickets, Public is right on Syntagma Square and has a **café** upstairs.

• *1 Karageorgi Servias St, **Syntagma Sq**, 210-324-6210, www.public.gr*

The Mall Athens

The Mall is…the biggest shopping centre in Athens, with many chain stores.

• *35 Andrea Papandrou St, **Maroussi**, 210-630-0000, www.themallathens.gr*
***Get there**: At Neratziotissa Metro station on Line 1 and the Proastiakos suburban train line, ~30 min journey.*

FOOD

Buy herbs and spices in bulk on Evripidou St at Athinas St

Central Market/Agorà

The Agorà or Central Market on Athinas St will please your pocket as well as assault your senses. It's a busy area in itself, but the well-stocked market—vegetables, fruit and chicken and sausages on one side, meat, fish and nuts and dried fruit on the other—attracts residents from all over the city.

• *Mon–Thurs 6am–3pm, Fri–Sat 6am–6pm.* • ***Athinas at Evripidou/Sofokleous sts, Monastiraki.***

Herb shop

If you're a foody or want to pick up some dried herbs, you can get packets of Greek **saffron** (*safràn, Kròkos Kozànis*), available in **supermarkets,** and also soothing herbal mountain tea (*tsai tou vounoù*). Get this, as well as prized Cretan wild dittany (*dìktamo*) for yourself or as presents (airport customs are used to seeing them), at Greek products stores, or try the **hole-in-the-wall herb shop.**

• *Corner of Athinas and Evripidou sts, **Agora/Monastiraki.***

The lux-class Grande Bretagne hotel sells own-brand products such as honey, tea, oil and vinegar

ICONS

Apollonos St

Everything church-related, including silver icons and votives (*pictured*) as well as the mediaeval Byzantine art-form of icon-painting, can be found on and around Apollonos St, near the **Metropolitan Cathedral**. Find one that matches your child's name, give one as a gift, or keep for yourself.

• *Behind the Metropolitan Cathedral and Apollonos St,* **Syntagma/Monastiraki**.

JEWELLERY

Adrianou St

Greece is known for its beautifully-crafted gold and silver jewellery, and you can find many shops selling fine pieces all over town, but especially on Adrianou St in Plaka.

• *Adrianou St,* **Plaka**.

Ruby's

One long-established jewellery shop is Ruby's, with a wide selection for every pocket range. They also sell the popular "*mati*" or blue-eye charms to ward off the evil eye, which are used to pin to babies' clothes or around their crib or bed (and thus make unique gifts). They can also quickly resize a ring.

• *105 Adrianou St,* **Plaka***, 210-322-3312.*

PHONES, MOBILE/CELL

Casio

You can get cheap used (from ~€17) or new (from ~€26) **mobile/cell phones** from one of many phone shops around **Omonia Square**, such as Casio.

• *19 Omonia Sq, near Piraeos (Pan Tsaldari) St,* **Omonia***, 210-524-8204, www.e-kotsis.gr*

Check the cash

Shopkeepers may try to pass along badly tattered, torn or taped bills, especially €5 and €10 notes, to foreigners. Hand it back and ask for another one, or coins. The bills are difficult to exchange (which is why they give them to you) as they can only be exchanged at the central **Bank of Greece**

(14 Stadiou St, **Syntagma***, 210-320-1111, www.bankofgreece.gr, Mon–Thurs 8am–2.30pm, Fri 8am–2pm).* Also check for counterfeits. The front face of euro notes have a silver strip hologram along the right side, and a strip down the middle and an image on the left appear when the bill is tilted or held up to the light, among other security features.

Germanos

Germanos electronics chain store (*pictured*), with branches at the airport and many more around town, also sells phones.

• *76 Akadimias St, **Omonia**.*
• *3 Stadiou St, **Syntagma**.*
• *3 Falirou St, **Makriyanni**, 210-921-2603.*
• *26 Kanari St, **Kolonaki**, 210-361-5798.*
• *Frantzi St and Kallirois Ave, **Neos Kosmos**, 210-921-2680, among others, www.e-germanos.gr*

SIM card

You can buy a SIM card with a telephone number (bring your passport), but also increasingly without ID from phone shops. Cost is €5.
• **Cosmote:** *41 Panepistimiou St, opp. the National Library, **Panepistimio**, 801-119-7000, www.cosmote.gr*
• **Wind:** *7 Stadiou St, **Syntagma**, 210-331-6892, www.wind.com.gr*
• **Vodafone:** *3 Stadiou St, **Syntagma**, 210-321-0024, www.vodafone.gr*

SHOES, CHILDREN'S

Admiral

For cheap athletic shoes and sandals, especially if your kids wreck the ones they're wearing, try Admiral. The basement discount part is at **no. 15**, the main shop is across the street at **no. 17**.
• *15 Themistokleous St, **Omonia/Exarchia**, 210-330-1969, www.admiral.gr*

Dee.es

This shoe store is out of the way but has a good selection of quality shoes. Pricey in season but they have good discounts during the sale periods (January/August).
• *145 Elef. Venizelou (Thisseos) Ave and Ifigenias St, **Kallithea**, 210-952-1823.*
Get there: *Trolley nos. 1, 5 from Syntagma Sq to bus-stop: Kallithea, ~20-30 min journey.*

Mouyer

This local chain store makes children's shoes, which are nice but a little pricey.
• *6 Ermou St, **Syntagma**, 210-323-2831, www.mouyer.gr*

SHOES, WOMEN'S

Ermou St

Athenians have a shoe fettish, and there's an exhaustive selection of beautiful, high-quality shoes at a number of shops on pedestrian **Ermou St** heading down from Syntagma Square.
• ***Syntagma** Square to Kapnikareas church, **Monastiraki**.*

Kalogirou
Top-quality shoe store Kalogirou has a stock shop that also sells designer labels (size 38 or 7½ sells out the quickest).
• *12 Pandrossou St, **Monastiraki**, 210-335-6410, www.lemonis.gr*

Spiliopoulos
A well-known stock shop with two branches near each other, apart from shoes, both also carry a large selection of **bags and purses**.
• *63 Ermou St, **Monastiraki**, 210-322-7590.*
• *50 Adrianou St, **Monastiraki**, 210-321-9096.*

SOUVENIRS

Reed slippers are lightweight, enviro-friendly, and great for the beach too. Find them at 5 Pallados St, Psyrri; Lekka and Kolokotroni sts, Syntagma; and on Dexippou St, Plaka

Adrianou St, Pandrossou St
Pedestrian alleys Pandrossou St in Monastiraki and Adrianou St in Plaka are the streets to go for **souvenirs**, with many shops selling unique items, natural products and ever-popular T-shirts, pottery, statues and fridge magnets.
• *Adrianou St, **Plaka**.*
• *Pandrossou St, **Monastiraki**.*

Athinas St
Central Athinas St which runs towards the **Central Market** (**Agorà**) and Omonia from Monastiraki Metro station also has a number of shops selling **traditional products** (*pictured*).
• *Athinas St, between **Monastiraki** and **Omonia** squares.*

Mompso
For something extraordinary, find **bells, brasses** and **horse-related tack** plus riding clothes and accessories at decent prices (whips €15, leather belts with brass buckles €20) at this shop

that also caters to (ahem) pony players.
• *33 Athinas St, Monastiraki, 210-323-0670, www.mompso.com*

Old Prints, Maps and Books
No mistaking what's sold at this shop, where you can get historic old maps, prints and gentle flowers and birds drawings starting at €10.
• *15 Kolokotroni St, Syntagma, 210-323-0923, www.oldprints.gr*

Roussos Art and Jewelry
This shop sells Greek-made products, including beautiful porcelain dolls in traditional costume that start at €43 (*see the website*) that are now collectibles.
• *97 Adrianou St, Plaka, 210-322-6395, www.bestgifts.gr*

Shopping Center Plaka
A well-stocked one-stop shop for souvies and books is Shopping Center Plaka beside the Mitropoleos Cathedral between **Syntagma** and **Monastiraki**.
• *1 Pandrossou St, Monastiraki, 210-324-5405, www.shoppingplaka.com*

SPORTS TEAMS

Kiosks sell Greek and sports team flags

Evrika
At Evrika, sports fans can get official T-shirts and souvenirs of the Greek football (soccer) teams **Panathinaikos** (*210-870-9000, www.pao.gr*), **Olympiakos** (*210-414-3000, www.olympiacos.org*) and **AEK** (*Athletic Union of Constantinople, 210-612-1371, www.aekfc.gr*). Also some souvenirs left from the **2004 Olympic Games** held in Athens.
• *69 Adrianou St, Plaka, 210-325-1935.*

AEK shop
• *Daily 10.30am–8pm.* • *7 Aiolou St, Plaka, 210-323-6750, www.aek-shop.gr (pictured).*

Olympiakos (Olympiacos) official store
• *Daily 10am–9pm.* • *11 Ifestou St, Monastiraki, 210-321-4889, www.redstore.gr*
• *Also a large outlet at Karaiskaki Stadium (Faliro station on Metro Line 1).*

Panathinaikos official store
Apart from the jerseys and merchandise, you can purch
• Daily 10am–8.30pm. • **47 Pandrossou St, Monastiraki**, 210-321-6.
• **The Mall, Maroussi**, Neratziotissa Metro station on Line 1.

Note: See Chapter 15, Spectator Sports section for ticket i

TOILETRIES

Hondos Center
For all kinds of toiletries, perfumes and more, including **swimsuits**, head to a Hondos Center (*www.hondos.gr*) chain store.
• Mon, Wed 9am–8pm; Tues, Thurs, Fri 9am–9pm; Sat 9am–7pm.
• There's a big one (10 floors) at **4 Omonia Sq**, 210-528-2800.
• **39 Ermou St, Monastiraki**, 210-372-2900, near Kapnikarea church.

Pharmacies
Toiletries are available in pharmacies, which also carry baby formula and well-known local natural brands **Korres** (*www.korres.com*) and **Apivita** (*www.apivita.com*).

TOYS, HOBBIES, MUSIC, GREEK-MADE

Syntagma, Kolonaki, Monastiraki

Benaki Museum
There are top-quality gifts at the Benaki Museum.
• Vas. Sofias Ave and Koumbari sts, **Kolonaki**, 210-367-1000, www.benaki.gr

Children's Museum
Museum gift shops often have unique Greek-made items for sale, including here.
• 14 Kydathinaion St, **Plaka**, 210-331-2995, www.hcm.gr

Early Learning Centre
Find toys and educational games and books at branches of Early Learning Centre, a British chain, as well as small beach tents for babies and English-language puzzles, but they are pricey. Download the brochure to see what they have and then call to check availability. There's a small branch of ELC in **Mothercare** (British chain), where you can also get **baby clothes** and **accessories**.
• 44 Ermou St, **Syntagma/Monastiraki**, 210-323-8695; 23 Voukourestiou St, **Syntagma/Kolonaki**, 210-360-1295, www.mothercare.gr, www.earlylearningcentre.gr

...ls made-in-Greece ...mmon (*tàvli*) and chess ...with original pieces, such as ...ose resembling athletes and Greek gods (*pictured*).

• *36 Mitropoleos St,* **Syntagma/Monastiraki**, *210-323-7740,* www.manopoulos.com

Kalyvioti
This is the nearest toy shop to Syntagma Square and has Lego as well as puzzles and other toys.

• *8 Ermou St,* **Syntagma**, *210-323-8392.*

Kefitoys
Kefitoys sells toys including Greek-made plastic diggers and trucks (large) and some Greek-origin puzzles by Epa (www.epatoys.gr) and Remoundo (www.remoundo.gr).

• *30 Evripidou and Athinas sts,* **Agora/Monastiraki**, *210-325-1649.*

National History Museum
The National History Museum also has useful, Greek-themed items (pencils, rulers, puzzles…) for kids.

• *13 Stadiou and Kolokotroni sts,* **Syntagma**, *210-323-7617,* www.nhmuseum.gr

Pegasus
Pegasus is a shop that sells **musical instruments** including bouzouki, small *baglamàs* and *touberlèkia* (bongo drums). They also have a selection of toys and instruments for children, such as recorders and a unique, small Greek-made bouzouki music box (*pictured*) (€15) that plays the tune to "Never on Sunday" (Manos Hadjidakis), from the iconic Greek film (1960) of the same name with Melina Mercouri.

• *26 Pandrossou St,* **Monastiraki**, *210-324-2036,* www.pegasusgreece.com

Praxitelous St, Art & Hobby
To keep your kids busy, there are **art supply and hobby shops** on central Praxitelous St, from **Kolokotroni St** and behind **Klafthmonos Square**, such as Art & Hobby.

• *29-31 Praxitelous St,* **Syntagma (Commercial triangle)**, *210-322-9858,* www.hobby.gr

Public
Public electronic and media store has toys and games (4th floor).

• *1 Karageorgi Servias St,* **Syntagma Sq**, *210-324-6210,* www.public.gr

Toys of the World

This toy shop has the most popular toys: Lego and Playmobil, as well as some Greek-made puzzles by Desyllas (*www.desyllasgames.gr*) that are suitable (ie not in Greek), but Greek language ones would make unique souvenirs. A Parthenon model is popular, plus a large selection of action figures including mythical gods that are only available in Greece, such as Athena in war pose, Poseidon and Zeus.
• *15 Aiolou and Ermou sts, **Monastiraki**, 210-321-3087.*

Waldorf Shop

A tiny shop (***pictured***) in an arcade, has a few small toys and items made in Greece, as well as wooden toys and English books.
• *6 Dragatsaniou St, in the arcade, Klafthmonos Sq, **Panepistimio**, 210-331-1324.*

Makriyanni, Koukaki

Damigos

Damigos is a traditional toy shop that carries some Greek-made toys.
• *40 Dimitrakopoulou St, **Koukaki**, 210-922-0317.*

Environmentally-friendly toys

Shops carrying **Plan Toys** (*24410-25443, www.plantoys.gr*) which are made in Thailand using wood from rubber trees that are no longer productive, include these shops in and around the centre of Athens.

Tip: Old stock is cheaper.
• ***Protoporia*** *bookstore has all the toys from the catalogue: 9-13 Gravias St, between Themistokleous and Em. Benaki sts, **Omonia/Exarchia**, 210-380-7689.*
• ***Public*** *electronics and media department store: 1 Karageorgi Servias St, **Syntagma Sq**, 210-324-6210, www.public.gr*
• ***Hondos Center*** *toiletries and more: 4 Omonia Square, **Omonia**, 210-528-2800, www.hondos.gr*
• ***Ianos*** *bookstore: 24 Stadiou St, **Syntagma**, 210-321-7917, www.ianos.gr*

Greater Athens

Jumbo

This Greek chain store with the most ubiquitous shopping bag in town (***pictured***) is known for its cheap prices and exhaustive selection of toys, crafts, accessories, and baby and children's clothes. Shops alongside (like **Benetton Stock**) usually have shoes. Most of their products are imported from China. A **café-restaurant** may be located near the premises.

• *Mon-Fri 9am–9pm, Sat 9am–8pm.* • *www.jumbo.gr* • *5 Agios Dionysiou St, Piraeus, 210-411-9142, is a large branch near the Metro Line 1 portside terminus.*
***Get there**: At the port exit turn right and keep going to the second traffic light and turn right again. You'll see it a few metres down, about 5 minutes' walk. Or check the website map (Piraeus 2 store in Attica prefecture).*
• *Another branch is located at **Pefkakia** Metro station on Line 1.*

Moustakas

Moustakas is another large, local toy store chain with locations in the suburbs.
• *Mon–Fri 9am–9pm, Sat 9am–8pm.* • *www.moustakastoys.gr*
• *One store is in **River West mall**, **Kifissou Ave, Aegaleo**, 801-222-5050, www.riverwest.gr*
***Get there**: Aegaleo Metro station on Line 3, then bus no. 829 or the mall's free shuttle.*

Girl who ate a balloon in her burger, unfinished, Jan 2013 ☺ 5 yrs
Show off your child's artform—upload talent(s) at www.facebook.com/Mychildartist

Thisseion (Hephaisteion) temple, inside the Ancient Agora, Thissio

Chapter 6: Places to Go, Things to See

Culture is Greece's best-known attraction, and apart from the Acropolis, going to museums and sites is quite cheap. The state encourages visitors with free or low admission to enjoy the vast endowment of treasures first-hand. Don't let children stop you—their presence is expected—while there are also quite a few attractions geared just for them.

While very young children won't appreciate the Acropolis as an adult does, you can bring them to enjoy the sites, but in a different way, or for not as long. Children will have their own experience that will hopefully stay with them as a fond memory of that particular place and time.

Since every child is different—some two-year-olds will happily tag along and enjoy the site while others won't be able to—recommendations and limitations for age ranges are noted only if pertinent, unless specified by the destination.

There are also indications of what to expect, accessibility (strollers or steps), what might pique their (and parents') interest, as well as suggested subject areas noted above each attraction of what children could get out of it as a learning opportunity, for school projects, studies, hobbies or special interests.

Destinations are also rated for "must-sees", eg the Acropolis has four "stars", and whether admission to the point of interest/site is FREE or negligible (€1). Under 18 yrs is usually free admission as well.

Places to go are organized geographically by proximity to the Acropolis and by area.

National museums and sites free entrance days

March 6 (in memory of Melina Mercouri); **June 5** (World Environment Day); **April 18** (International Monuments & Sites Day); **May 18** (International Museums Day); **last weekend of September** (European Heritage Days); **Sundays Nov 1 to March 31**; **first Sunday of the month, except** July, August, September (when the first Sunday is a national holiday, the second is the free admission day); **national holidays***; **Sept 27** (World Tourism Day). *Note: For national holidays and closed days, see chapters 11 and 18.*

Athens Landmarks & Attractions

Geography

Eight hills within the Athens basin are the **Acropolis, Aeropagus, Pnyx, Hill of the Nymphs** and the **Hill of the Muses** in the historic centre, conical **Lycabettus** with a theatre, restaurant and church at the top, **Strefi,** a neighbourhood park, and **Ardittou,** beside the Panathenian Stadium, that attracts joggers through its pine woods. All are within walking distance, with much to see and do on or around them.

ACROPOLIS & AREOPAGUS HILLS

Culture, classics, art, architecture, mathematics, history, mythology

**** Acropolis Hill

The Acropolis (156m/512ft) is deceiving, as the summit of the Sacred Rock where the Parthenon stands can be reached on a gradual path from the well-marked **south slope**. This is the site where the gods Athena and Poseidon vied to become the city's patron. Poseidon produced a salty spring, and the winner, Athena, produced an olive tree.

The perfectly-proportioned, 5th century BC **Parthenon** (*pictured*) was built in Athena's honour during the Golden Age of Athens, under the direction of **Pericles**. The all-marble temple of Athena Parthenos ("Athena the Virgin") was meant to be a masterpiece, built to mathematical precision between 447 and 438 BC, and marks the apex in Doric architecture. The architects, **Ictinus** and **Callicrates**, made curved surfaces appear level, bulging columns appear straight, and inclined columns appear parallel.

Once housing a 12m/40ft gold-and-ivory statue of Athena by **Phidias** (a small Roman copy is in the National Archaeological Museum), thought by some to be the best sculptor ever, the building has been used as Orthodox and Catholic churches, a mosque, and a munitions storehouse, which was its undoing after 2,000 years, when it was bombed by the Venetians during their brief, months' long rule in 1687. It is now undergoing its most extensive restoration to date.

You enter via the Roman built, 267 AD **Beule Gate**, named after the Frenchman who discovered it in 1852.

Before the Parthenon

The Parthenon was not the only temple atop the Acropolis Hill, which served as a citadel and palace of Mycenaean kings in the 14th century BC, as well as being used for religious worship. If you look carefully or do a little research, you can sleuth out the foundations from that era and also from earlier temples, including **temples of Athena Polias** (city guardian) dating from the 7th century BC, the last of which housed an olive wood statue of Athena Polias, the most venerated object at the time.

The 5th century BC Ionic-style **Erechtheion** (*pictured*) is an architecturally unique building, with four different facades. It was a temple to Athena (where the statue was located) as well as other gods, and at one time it was brightly painted, with gilded details, ornate carvings and inlaid multi-coloured glass beads, its imagery and purpose steeped in meaning.

There were also other smaller buildings and shrines dedicated to Athena's cults and various forms, such as Warrior (Promachos), Victory (Nike) and Parthenos (Virgin).

• Get a visual idea of the layout in each era at *www.ancientathens3d.com*

Painstaking restoration

It's still a mystery how the multi-ton blocks of marble were brought from Mt Penteli and erected here, although there are many guesses as to how these buildings, architectural marvels in their own right, were constructed.

The restoration work on the Acropolis buildings may seem never-ending, but it is painstaking work of major proportions.

A civil engineer, Nicholas Balanos, made efforts to restore the monuments between 1894 and 1939 using concrete and iron, which actually damaged the structures. The latest restoration has lasted more than a decade and uses new marble from Mt Penteli and corrosive-resistant titanium.

The Temple of Athena Nike was completely disassembled, restored and reassembled, with hundreds of blocks and beams.

Next is the 5th century BC **Propylaia** columned entrance. To the right (south) is the 244 BC Ionic **Temple of Athena Nike** (Athena Victory) where citizens prayed for success, and to the left (north) is the **Erechtheion**, the tomb of legendary King Erechtheus with its famous caryatid (maiden) columned portal.

Apart from the great view, you can see two ancient theatres. One is the still-used **Herodes Atticus Odeon** (theatre), named after a 2nd century AD benefactor, and the much-renovated **Dionysus Theatre** dating to the 6th century BC and now in ruins.

Take a **virtual tour** (*www.acropolis-virtualtour.gr*) of the site which gives you unprecedented access inside the buildings, which are otherwise cordoned off.

• Canteen opposite entrance. • There is an elevator, but strollers are not allowed. You can leave them at a cloakroom free of charge near the entrance. Toddlers can handle the site itself, but will need help getting up the steps at the entrance. • Winter Mon–Sat 8am–5pm, summer Mon–Sat 8am–8pm, Sun 8am–3pm. • Adults €12, under 18 yrs free. You receive a coupon booklet valid for the Acropolis, Ancient Agora and museum, Theatre of Dionysus, Ancient Kerameikos cemetery and museum, Roman Forum/Hadrian's Library, Roman Agora, and the Temple of Olympian Zeus. • **Entrance off Dionysiou Areopagitou St, Makriyanni**, 210-321-0219, www.culture.gr
Get there: Akropoli Metro station on Line 2, then 10 minutes' walk. Allow ~ an hour.

History, mythology, culture, religion, nature, justice

FREE Areopagus Hill

Exiting the Acropolis, you can reach Areopagus (*pictured*), opposite the entrance to the site, or head to the Acropolis walkway (Dion. Areopagitou St) and cross it into **Pnyx Hill** (*see Filopappou Hill section*). Passing Areopagus continuing north on the path leads you to the north slope and Plaka.

Also known as Mars Hill or Ares Hill, named after the god of war, Areopagι Hill was a "court" in antiquity, the first defendant being mythical Ares himself, on trial for killing Poseidon's son. **Apostle Paul** famously preached here in 51 AD, and the pedestrian street leading here on the west side of the hill is named after him (Apostolou Pavlou). A plaque on the rock face at the entrance to the Acropolis side of the hill commemorates the speech (in Greek).

• Areopagus is not stroller accessible. • Free access from the north slope **(Apostolou Pavlou St at Iouliou Smith St, Thissio)** *and on the path opposite the entrance to the Acropolis, Makriyanni.*

NORTH SLOPE TO PLAKA

Culture, architecture, history

FREE ****** Plaka**

Plaka's mansions, island-village houses and winding pathways stretch up the east and north slopes, which are fun for children to explore in this touristic area. The roads and paths are paved but there are steps, so **strollering** *is possible but challenging.*

Further up the slope, **Anafiotika** (**pictured**) has an island village feel because it was originally settled by islanders from Anafi, who came to Athens in the 19th century to help build the then king's palace. You can walk around to the Acropolis entrance from here (follow the signs).

History, culture

FREE **North slope park**

On the **north slope** there is free roaming into the greenery (**park**), but watch for cliffs and old wells that aren't always marked. Apart from fine views further up, there are other points of interest, such as ancient caves, chapel remains, and

springs, marked by panel signs.
• Stroller accessible.
*Get there: Off a gravel path between **Thissio** and **Plaka** from the west, alongside the **Ancient Agora**'s southern border. Alternately reach here through an entrance (**steps**) near Theorias and Panos sts, Plaka, on the path to the entrance of the Acropolis.*

Children's art

Museum of Greek Children's Art

Close to **Syntagma**, this museum (**pictured**), or gallery, shows the colourful and talented artwork of children in Greece aged 5 to 14, and they often have drop-in programs for parents and children to participate. Some artwork has been made into postcards, and there are other small items for sale in the **gift shop**.

he vicinity. • Steps at entrance. • Tues–Sat 10am–2pm, Sun 11am–2pm,
g. • Adults €2, under 6 yrs free. • **9 Kodrou St, near Voulis St, Plaka,**
ᴵ-2750, www.childrensartmuseum.gr

science, history, music, architecture

FREE **** **Children's Museum**

If you have young children (ages ~18 mos–7 yrs), or from whatever age your baby is engaged in its surroundings, you must take them to the Children's Museum in Plaka, where they can play in various rooms in an old mansion. The rooms are set up for activities such as gymnastics and the body, a market with fruit and vegetable stand, fishmongers, butchers, pharmacy with a medical kit, etc. They can look at books or play with kitchen sets in the "living room," play in a real kitchen, find treasures in the attic, build a wall (*pictured*), draw architectural plans or play in a tree-house in the construction zone, play with instruments, draw on blackboards and play with various blocks, or don an apron and play with water, bubbles and siphons. Also a **gift shop**. There are two outside entrances, so be sure to visit both.
• **Tavernas and cafes** in the vicinity. • Steps to the 1ˢᵗ floors, you can leave a stroller at the entrance.
• Tues–Fri 10am–2pm, Sat–Sun 10am–3pm. • Free entrance. • **14 Kydathinaion St, Plaka,** 210-331-2995, www.hcm.gr

Arts and crafts, culture

Folk Art Museum

If you have time, across from the children's museum is the Folk Art Museum. It appears forlorn and smells a bit musty, but the modern Greek objects on display are worth a look, especially if you're interested in artefacts from the 19th century. Traditional costumes (*pictured*) and large, impressive buckles from various regions and islands are on display upstairs, and a room with frescoes painted by a well-known Greek naïve painter, **Theophilos Hatzimihail**, is a highlight.
• Elevator for strollers. • Tues–Sun 9am–2pm. • Adults €2, under 18 yrs free, students/seniors €1. • **17 Kydathinaion St, Plaka,** 210-322-9031, www.melt.gr

Music, culture, geography

FREE **Museum of Greek Popular Musical Instruments**
Closer to **Monastiraki**, another museum that will intrigue children, especially

those with a musical bent, is the Museum of Greek Popular Musical Instruments. Headphones beside the folk instrument displays let you hear what you see, including drums and tambourines, clarinets, lutes, lyres and many children's instruments (*pictured*). Also a musicology centre where performances are announced on a notice board at the entrance.

If in the area and your **baby needs to feed**, the grassy private courtyard has a bench.

• *Steps up to the 1ˢᵗ floor.* • *Wed noon–6pm, Tues, Thurs–Sun 10am–2pm, closed Mon.* • *Free entrance.* • *1–3 Diogenous St, Plaka, 210-325-0198, www.instruments-museum.gr*

Culture, society, religion, women's studies

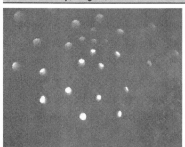

Bathhouse of the Winds

There were many public bathhouses in Athens during Ottoman rule and before plumbing was put in every home in the 20th century. An example is the lovely little 15th-century hamam, Bathhouse of the Winds, or *Loutro ton Aeridon* (Aeolus, god of wind) (*pictured*), which is restored as a museum. Get English info from a brochure (€2), or use the audio guide (23 min). If you don't want to hear the whole thing, skip ahead to the descriptions of room nos. 4 and 5 for charming accounts. About 15–30 minutes to see.

• *Steps to the 1ˢᵗ floor.* • *Summer Wed–Mon 9am–4pm, winter 8am–3pm, closed Tues.* • *Adults €2, under 18 yrs free, students/seniors €1.* • *8 Kyrisstou St, Plaka, 210-324-4340, www.melt.gr*

History, religion, culture

FREE Kapnikarea church

If you need a **break**, head towards the nearby **café/restaurant** street of Kapnikarea, named after the now ill-placed 11th to 13th century Kapnikarea church (*pictured*). Built on the site of a temple to Athena or Demeter, the dome is dedicated to the Virgin Mary. In the middle of Ermou St near Monastiraki, King Ludwig of Bavaria, the first king of Greece's father, saved it from demolition by town planners in 1834.

• *Ermou and Kapnikarea sts, Monastiraki.*

Ceramic Folk Art Museum

A rare physical reminder of 400 years of Ottoman rule is the **Tzisdarakis Tzami** at **Monastiraki Square**, an 18th century mosque which now houses the Ceramic Folk Art Museum. It might be difficult to keep young children away from the exhibits (*pictured*) but worth a look if it's open, it'll take less than half an hour.

• *Restaurants nearby.* • *Steps at the entrance.* • *Wed–Mon 9am–3pm.*
• *Adults €2, under 18 yrs free, students/seniors €1.* • *1 Areos St, Monastiraki Sq, Monastiraki, 210-324-2066, www.melt.gr*

FREE Panagia Gorgoepikoos, aka Agios Eleftherios church
This is a lovely, 12th century chapel dwarfed by the 19th century Metropolitan Cathedral on Mitropoleos St. Dedicated to the Virgin Mary Gorgoepikoos ("She who hears quickly") and St Eleftherios, Empress Irene built the "Little Cathedral" using antiquities from a temple found on the site dating to 400 years earlier, and includes charming flora and fauna in relief (*pictured*). When the Franks and Ottomans expelled Orthodox bishops from the Acropolis, where they had converted the Parthenon into a church, this little chapel became the official Episcopal See of Athens.

• *Mitropoleos and Agias Filotheis sts at Mitropoleos Sq, **Syntagma/Monastiraki**.*

Roman Agora

You'll find the Roman Agora, the market area in use during Julius Caesar's reign with its main landmark, the **Tower of the Winds** (*pictured*), while walking through Plaka towards Monastiraki. The unique, octagonal 1st century BC structure designed by **Andronikos Kyristes** was a water clock topped by a weather vane, and depicts the **eight wind deities**: Zephyros,

Boreas, Notos, Euros, Kaikias, Apeliotes, Skiron and Lips.
Also on site is the beautiful **Fetiye Mosque**, which commemorated Mehmet II's visit to Athens in 1458. Both buildings are closed and the site is fenced, so kids

can run around while you have a break under the trees.

Hadrian's Library, more of a cultural centre, was built in 132 AD and visited by travel-writer **Pausanias**, who described the complex and gardens. There are tavernas alongside for a **lunch** break.

• *Stroller accessible.* • *Daily 8am–3pm.* • *Adults €2 or part of the Acropolis coupon, under 18 yrs free.*
• *End of Aiolou and Pelopida sts, Plaka/Monastiraki, 210-324-5220, www.culture.gr*

History, culture, society, religion, justice, democracy, architecture

Ancient Agora

The Ancient Agora is a good place for little ones to run around. The main sites here are the **Temple of Thisseion**, more accurately but never called the **Hephaisteion (*pictured, beginning of the chapter*)**, after Hephaestos, god of metalwork. It was converted to an  Orthodox church when under religious control, which is why it's in such good condition. Philhellenic Protestants who fought for Greece during the War of Independence were buried here. At the other end of the wooded, natural site is the **Stoa of Attalos (*pictured, background*)** recreated thanks to grants from Rockefeller and the American Archaeological School. As the **Ancient Agora Museum**, it houses unique finds from the site, including pieces relating to early democratic processes, being a place of Assembly in antiquity.

The **Agii Apostoli Solaki church** (Holy Apostles of Solakis) (*pictured, foreground*) within the site dates from 1020 and is a beautiful example of Athenian Byzantine architecture. Decoration includes pseudo-kufic, the oldest Arab calligraphy, and uncommon multiple apses—the semicircular part that protrudes from the church that normally contains the altar. The wall paintings date from the 17th century and are from a demolished church. This one was restored in the 1950s by the Samuel H. Kress Foundation of New York.

• *Stroller accessible, although there are steps in places.* • *Daily 8am–3pm.* • *Adults €4 or part of the Acropolis coupon, under 18 yrs free.* • *Entrance to the site from Adrianou St & Agiou Filippou, Monastiraki, the west end of Polygnotou St in Plaka, or at Thissio Square, Thissio, 210-321-0185, www.culture.gr*
Get there: Monastiraki or Thissio Metro stations on Lines 1 and 3, then 5 min walk.

THISSIO, PSYRRI, KERAMEIKOS, GAZI

Culture, society, history, religion

FREE **** Thissio

Thissio is a very lively and festive **district** especially after nightfall, with street stalls lining **Apostolou Pavlou** (Apostle Paul) St from Thissio Metro station and up towards the square and the **parks** on either side.

Apart from the small **playground**, children also play in the **park** area beside the station—the city's oldest, circa 1868, named after the Thisseion (Hephaisteion) temple across the street—near the top of pedestrian Eptahalkou St on the south side of the tracks.

There are also many outdoor **café-bars** here, and especially down pedestrian **Irakleidon St**, which also leads to **Gazi**. The area is popular with children and people of all ages.

History, society, culture
FREE Open-air museums

Some Metro stations showcase the antiquities found during the dig, as well as ancient foundations left in situ. One of these is at **Syntagma Metro station** along the upper level, where children can see the layers of the ancient city, including a 5th century BC aqueduct that brought water to Athens from distant Mount Hymettus.
• Outside Syntagma station on **Amalias Ave** under a glass roof, the remains of 1,800-year-old Roman baths are exhibited (*pictured*).

Architecture, art, religion

FREE Agii Asomati church
The little Saints of Intangible Spirits (roughly translated) church (*pictured*) appears sunken in the road on Ermou St, beside Thissio Metro station. Dating from the 11th century with an Athenian-style dome, it was altered in the 1950s, and the interior is badly damaged. It's rarely open, but you can sit and have a **break** here (**tavernas, sandwich shops** nearby).
• Agion Asomaton and Ermou sts, **Thissio/Psyrri**.

Art, religion, history
Islamic Art Museum
The Islamic Art Museum is part of the private Benaki museum, and this neoclassical building now houses an important collection of some 8,000 artefacts

from the Islamic world, including India, Persia, the Middle East, Asia Minor, Egypt, Spain and Sicily. The collection was started in Egypt, and includes 8th century Mesopotamian doors, and a 16th century velvet saddle from Malaysia.
• *Stroller accessible* • *Thurs–Sun 9am–5pm, closed holidays.* • *Adults €7, students 25 yrs and under free).* • **Kerameikos Building, 22 Ag Asomaton and 12 Dipilou sts, Psyrri**, *210-325-1311, www.benaki.gr*
Get there: *Near Thissio Metro station on Line 1, heading north towards Piraeos St on Ag. Asomaton St, from Ag. Asomati church.*

Art, history

Museum of Traditional Pottery

For ceramics enthusiasts, the small Museum of Traditional Pottery (*pictured*) is housed in a 19th century building and tasked with preserving and promoting the early 20th century ceramic tradition in Greece. There are examples from each region (Skyros and Sifnos island makes are highlights). The museum is popular with school groups and regularly holds free children's workshops. *Labels in Greek.*
• *Stroller accessible* • *Mon–Fri 9am–3pm, Sun 10am–2pm.*
• *Adults €3, under 18/seniors free.* • **4-6 Melidoni St, Thissio/Psyrri**, *210-331-8491 to 5, www.potterymuseum.gr*
Get there: *one block northwest of Ermou St at Thissio Metro station on Line 1.*

Time out (play, drink, eat, nightlife, photo op)

FREE Thissio Square

Many visitors with young children staying in the centre find their way to the **Thissio playground** (*see Chapter 12*), which is beside Thissio Square. There are countless outdoor **cafes** with a view of the Acropolis here, especially from the far inside of the square where there's also a gravel area that children can play on, just in front of the fenced off Ancient Agora. Stop for a refreshment and a grilled cheese (or ham and cheese) sandwich aka "toast" for the kids.
• *On the Acropolis walkway's pedestrian Apostolou Pavlou St, at the top of Irakleidon, Nileos and Akamandos sts, **Thissio**.*

Art, puzzles

Experience in Visual Arts museum

The Experience in Visual Arts is a small, private museum which has a permanent display of the puzzling drawings and optical art of M.C. Escher with his well-

known optical illusions, and of Victor Vasarely, which might delight and challenge children. They also hold workshops for children and tours in English for groups by appointment. Wide selection to choose from in the **gift shop**.
• *Stroller accessible but with steps • Fri 1pm–9pm, Sat–Sun 11am–7pm. • Adults €6, up to 12 yrs free, students €4. • 16 Irakleidon St, Thissio, 210-346-1981, www.herakleidon-art.gr*
Get there: *Few metres down pedestrian Irakleidon St from Thissio Sq.*

Art, culture, history

FREE Melina Cultural Centre

The Melina Cultural Centre in the landmark, ex-hat-making factory in Thissio has an exhaustive **shadow puppet** (Karagiozis) and paraphernalia (*labels in Greek*) exhibit (*pictured*), including ones that resemble Indonesian puppets. Nostalgic **Olde Athens** is recreated upstairs.

• *Stroller accessible • Tues–Sat 9am–1pm/5pm–9pm, Sun 9am–1pm • Free entrance. • 66 Irakleidon and Thessalonikis sts, Thissio, 210-345-2150, www.cityofathens.gr*

Culture, society, history, time out (shop, eat, nightlife)

FREE Psyrri

This central area was the **tanning district**, and you can still find leather products here, but it also has Greek-oriented **restaurants and café/bars**. The area is not as thumping as it once was, as the latest place to go for nightlife is at nearby **Gazi**.
• *Behind (west) Athinas St towards Monastiraki Metro station, Psyrri/Monastiraki.*

Culture, history, art, religion, mythology

Kerameikos ancient cemetery

Pericles gave his famous funeral oration in 431 BC for soldiers of the Peloponnesian War at this ancient cemetery (*pictured*), where there's a **museum** on site and grounds that are pleasant for wandering with children. It contains statues and monuments dedicated to famous Athenians, the **Sacred Gate** which opened onto the Sacred Way or Iera Odos, the road of the same name that leads to Elefsina (Elefsis in antiquity), site of an important sanctuary to Demeter.
• *Stroller accessible. • Daily 8am–3pm, museum closed Mon. • Museum and site adults €2 or part of the Acropolis coupon. • Entrance on pedestrianized Ermou St near Piraeos St, opposite the Technopolis gasworks complex. • 148 Ermou St, Gazi, 210-346-3552, www.culture.gr*
Get there: *Thissio Metro station on Line 1, then 5 minutes' walk.*

Culture, society, history, time out (eat, drink, nightlife)

FREE **Gazi**

The gay-friendly Gazi district is full of **restaurants and café-bars**, but you can also get a gyros (*souvlàki*) and chips at the "fast-food" **restaurant** (*opposite the Technopolis gasworks plant— hence the area's name—on Persefonis St*). Go for a stroll down pedestrian Ermou St to check it out. It's around where the tall brick smoke stacks are, glowing red at night.
• *At the end of Ermou St and around the Kerameikos Metro station,* **Gazi***.*

History, industry, R&R (time out)

FREE **Technopolis cultural centre & museum**

Gazi is centred around the Technopolis, a former gasworks plant that has a **museum** (*winter daily 10am–8pm, summer daily 10am–6pm, entrance €1, children under 6 yrs free*), small **playground** and **café** on site and is interesting to walk around to see the old equipment. Exhibits, concerts and events, including acrobatics for kids (***pictured***), ice skating in winter, etc are held here, usually free or for a nominal fee.

• *Stroller accessible.* • *Daily summer 9am–9pm, winter 9am–8pm.* • *Free entrance, unless a special event is taking place.* • **100 Piraeos St, Gazi***, 210-347-5518,* www.technopolis-athens.com

Art

Benaki Museum Piraeos St Annex

The spacious Piraeos St Annex, a part of the Benaki, is a few blocks past the Technopolis complex in **Gazi**. It has a rotation of contemporary exhibits (***pictured: children interact at 'Greek Monsters' by Beetroot exhibit***), a great **gift shop** and a pleasant **café**.

• *Stroller-friendly.* • *Wed, Thurs, Sun 10am–6pm, Fri–Sat 10am–10pm, closed Aug and holidays.*
• *Adults €3 to €10, depending on exhibit, €2–€6 students.* • **138 Piraeos and Andronikou sts,**
Gazi/Rouf, *210-345-3111, www.benaki.gr*
Get there: *Bus no. 049 from Athinas St near Omonia Sq, to bus-stop: Kolymvitirio, or 10 minutes'*
walk from Thissio/Gazi area.

SOUTH SLOPE, MAKRIYANNI, KOUKAKI

History, theatre, music

Herodes Atticus Odeon
With its distinctive arched façade,
this 2nd century AD theatre,
known locally as the Iròdion
(*pictured*), was once cedar-
roofed, built by Athens benefactor
Herodes Atticus for his deceased
wife, Regilla. The steeply pitched
marble seating for some 5,000
spectators dates from the 1950s,
as performances are still held at
the open-air venue in summer.
You can reach the Acropolis from
an entrance behind the theatre, through the Theatre of Dionysus site, and get a
good view of the interior from the Acropolis.
• *Open for performances only.* • *Children under 6 yrs not admitted.* • **Dion. Areopagitou St,**
Makriyanni, *210-324-2121, 323-2771, www.greekfestival.gr, beside entrance to Acropolis.*
Get there: *Akropoli Metro station on Line 2, then 10 minutes' walk.*

Art, culture, classics, literature, drama, theatre, history, medicine, religion, mythology

Ancient Theatre of Dionysus
The 6th century BC
theatre (*pictured*) on the
south slope is the oldest
theatre in Athens, having
undergone
reconstructions over 750
years, and had a capacity
of up to 17,000.
  Competitions for the
best drama, which
became a high art form
in the 5th and 4th
centuries BC, took place

here, including those penned by the likes of Aeschylus, Aristophanes, Sophocles
and Euripides, in honour of the god of wine and pleasure, **Dionysus**. The ancient
assembly met here, and in Roman times it was used to hold gladiator competitions
and even sea battles.
  The **Panagia Chrysospiliotissa (Our Lady of the Golden Cave) shrine** is
located in a cave up the hill in this large site, and there are also the remains of the

Asklepion, a clinic and sanctuary dedicated to the god of medicine, **Asclepius,** the **Pericles Odeon,** where musical performances took place, and the **Stoa of Eumenes,** a one-time covered walkway built by the Pergamene king, Eumenes II (198-159 BC) that leads to the **Herodes Atticus Odeon.**

• *You can take strollers and scramble through the hills and paths.* • *Apr–Oct Mon-Fri 8am–8pm, Sat–Sun 8am–3pm. Nov–Mar daily 8am–3pm.* • *Adults €2 or part of Acropolis ticket coupon.* • ***Dionysiou Areopagitou and Thrassylou sts, Makriyanni,** 210-322-4625, www.culture.gr*
***Get there:** Akropoli Metro station on Line 2 and across the Acropolis walkway.*

Enduring drama spectacle

Theatre was as popular in antiquity as sports are today, with theatres having capacities even to some 20,000 seats, such as at that most famous of theatres, the circa 4th century BC, hear-a-pin-drop **Ancient Epidaurus** (Epidavros) (*see Chapter 11 and www.greekfestival.gr for info*) (*pictured*)—enough for an entire town. Athens still has many theatres as the art form remains popular, while in antiquity, the odeons are thought to have developed from the circular threshing floor. Every town had some sort of theatre where people gathered for tragicomic entertainment and to forget their daily cares.
• **Thespis** (hence Thespian) is thought to have come to Athens as a travelling actor and said to be the first to receive an award for his original performance, perhaps on the site of the Theatre of Dionysus, which wasn't yet built in 534 BC when he won his prize.

Art, culture, music, literature, theatre, history

FREE **Lysicrates monument**

The unique Lysicrates monument (*pictured*) is around the corner from the Theatre of Dionysus on Vyronos (Byron) and Selley (Shelley) sts in **Lysicrates Square** surrounded by shops and **cafes**. It is named after the 334 BC winner of the best play performed at the theatre. Monuments like this one lined the connected Tripodon St in Plaka, so-named since the trophies won were displayed on tripods atop the structures. A 17th century Capuchin Franciscan monastery where **Lord Byron** stayed and wrote poetry once surrounded the monument.

• *Stroller accessible.* • **Vyronos, Selley and Lyssikratous sts, Plaka/Makriyanni.** **Get there**: *Off pedestrian Dion. Areopagitou St, then 5 minutes' walk from Akropoli Metro station on Line 2.*

History, culture, society, music, art, games
Athena Apollo Museum

Near Lysicrates Square is a small but interesting display of **reconstructed ancient musical instruments** as well as **ancient toys and games** (recreated **Greek-made** and for sale) above an art gallery, where you can also buy CDs of the music.

• *Building under renovation at time of press; check for accessibility and hours.* • *Adults €4, 6 yrs and up €3.* • **129 Adrianou St, Plaka**, *210-322-8875*, www.athenagames.gr

Art, history, classics, architecture
*** Acropolis Museum

Across from the ancient Dionysus Theatre is the Acropolis Museum, in **Makriyanni.** The large block structure (*pictured*) built over an archaeological site (which you can see underfoot through plexiglass) faces the Parthenon and contains a thoughtfully laid-out collection of some 300 sculptures and fragments found on the Acropolis Hill, including four of the six original **caryatids**—the maiden columns on the portico of the Erechtheion on the hill—which are being cleaned by laser (on display). One was lost during Ottoman rule, and one is in the British Museum.

On the top floor, sculptor **Phidias' famous Parthenon marbles** (mainly copies here) are laid-out as they would have appeared on the temple.

There are two **gift shops** and a **café/restaurant** where you can sit out on the terrace and enjoy the view of the Acropolis opposite. The gift shop at the café has **children's books.** Check for **activities for children** at the information desk, such as finding statues with a map and stickers.

• *Stroller accessible, with elevators and **mother's room.** Active little ones might need to be restrained from touching the displays.* • *Apr–Oct Tues–Thurs/Sat–Sun 8am–8pm, Friday 8am–10pm, Nov–Mar Tues–Thurs 9am–5pm, Fri 9am–10pm, Sat–Sun 9am–8pm, **restaurant** 8am–midnight. Closed Jan 1, Easter Sun, May 1, Dec 25, 26.* • *Adults €5, children 5–18 yrs €3, under 5 yrs and EU students free.* • **15 Dionysiou Areopagitou St, Makriyanni**, *210-900-0900,* www.theacropolismuseum.gr **Get there**: *Beside Akropoli Metro station on Line 2.*

Emotions Museum of Childhood

This small "museum" is down the hill from the Filopappou monument in the area known as **Koukaki** (leads into Makriyanni district). Open weekends only for visitors, it invites family participation with interactive displays focused on children's emotions. The displays are in Greek, but language isn't needed in the downstairs **play area** where children can create and narrate their own stories and themes in a giant story book (*pictured*) using paintings of the most common heroes, villains (wolf, witch, troll, giant, etc), settings (castle, forest, pond, sea, etc), family members, friends, objects of desire and props (golden egg, mirror, sword…) from popular fairytales. Also a dress-up box and "tree" to draw under.

• *It's geared to 4 to 14 yrs; I'd say it was more suited for very young children, ~2 to 6 or 7 yrs.* • *Leave the stroller at the door as there are steps between floors.* • *Sat–Sun 10am–1pm (1–2pm are workshops).* • *€4 per person.* • **7 Karatza and Tsami Karatasou sts, Koukaki**, *210-921-8329, www.mce.gr*
Get there: *Syngrou-Fix Metro station on Line 2, then 10 minutes' walk, or trolley nos. 1, 5, 15, to bus-stop: Zinni.*

FILOPAPPOU HILL

The three historic, pine-covered hills adjacent to the **Acropolis** are collectively known as Filopappou (Philopappos, Philopappus)—a wonderful escape from the city buzz, walking distance from the centre. The light in Greece is famous for its clarity, and there are **great views** of the Acropolis and other landmarks, as well as the sea and sunset from here. Come here for the view, a **nature break** (you could make an activity out of it such as bug collecting, turtle or even owl spotting…), for a walk (*paved and dirt paths, also steps*) or to scramble over the pine-covered hills. Many locals walk their dogs (watch for dog doo) or jog. Bring a picnic **lunch** when the weather is mild, in the spring and fall.

FREE Pnyx Hill

The **Agios Dimitrios Loumbardiaris church** (St James the Bombardier) (*pictured*) is a pretty, 14th century church in the woods along the path *opposite the Acropolis walkway entrance* on Pnyx Hill. It is said that the Ottoman commander, Yusuf Aga, of the Acropolis garrison, planned to use a cannon located at the Propylaia to bombard the church during its name-day celebrations on October 26, 1645. But the night before, lightning struck the gunpowder and killed the commander and his family, except for his Christian daughter.

Often there's a **horse and buggy** waiting near here where you can go on short carriage rides along the Acropolis walkway.

Facing Areopagus and adjacent to the observatory is the site of the **Ancient Assembly**, which moved here from the Ancient Agora, and later was moved to the Theatre of Dionysus. This is where Pericles, Themistocles, and Demosthenes met and debated in the 5th and 4th centuries BC. Signs along the path lead to the outdoor **Dora Stratou Theatre**, where **Greek folk dances** in traditional costume have been staged, accompanied by live music under the stars, for more than 50 years *(see Chapter 10, Venues section)*.

Get there: Reached from Thissio on Dimitriou Aiginitou St alongside the park, or a paved pedestrian flagstone path opposite the entrance to the Acropolis, going past the wood-and-stone, 16th century Agios Dimitrios Loumbardiaris church. • Steps up to the porch. • Public washrooms behind the church. • Dionysiou Areopagitou and Rovertou Galli sts, Makriyanni.

Science, religion, architecture, history, art

FREE Hill of the Nymphs

Lofos Nymphon landmarks are the 19th century, cruciform and domed, old **National Observatory** (1842) *(pictured, background)* designed by one of Athens' best-known architects, Theophilos Hansen, which is located above the multi-domed, pink-hued, circa 1920s **Agia Marina church** *(pictured, foreground)* *(stroller accessible)*. Part of the original 11th century structure is visible inside, where baptisms are performed. The hill

and church were known as the place for women to pray to conceive, continuing from the legacy of the nymphs, who were believed to inhabit the hill and protect women in childbirth. Both of these buildings are visible from the Acropolis pedestrian walkway.

Get there: Reached from streets alongside Agia Marina church in Thissio, or along Akamandos St, Thissio, until you reach the set of steps on the hillside (left) after the fence. • That entrance is more stroller-challenging however, as there are many steps.

History, art

FREE Hill of the Muses

Turning left from the church up the trails is the Hill of the Muses *(Mouseion)*, where you'll eventually reach the Pentelic marble **Filopappou Monument** *(pictured)*, the circa

116 AD tomb of C. Julius Antiochus Philopappus, a grandson of the last Macedonian king and Rome's consul in Athens. The monument, which still contains the partial sculptures of Philopappus on the right and his father, Antiochus IV, on the left, is dramatically lit up at night, together with other Athens landmarks, while during the day you have a 360-degree panorama of the city. It was from here that the Venetians fired cannonballs at an intact Parthenon in 1687 before quitting the city five months later.

Get there: Also accessible from the Acropolis walkway, opposite Agios Dimitrios Loumbardiaris church on the path opposite the entrance to the Acropolis, Makriyanni, and from the ring-road around Filopappou Hill (Koukaki and Ano Petralona). About 10 minutes' walk uphill, stroller accessible with shallow steps.

Roman intrigue surrounds Athenian benefactor

Derek Gatopoulos

Herodes Atticus, a benefactor of Athens, is especially associated with the Herodes Atticus Odeon/Theatre and the Panathenian Stadium, where a memorial tomb (**pictured**) is located (*see 'Ardittou hill'*). He was born in Marathon around 101 AD and educated in Athens in rhetoric, philosophy and law during Roman rule.

He went to Rome where he taught future emperors like Marcus Aurelius, and married Roman aristocrat Aspasia Annia Regilla, bringing her back to Athens to live.

He was a consul of the city from 143 AD, while Regilla was also a prominent benefactor, with monuments attributed to Herodes actually being erected by her. She was a priestess of Tyche and Demeter, and thus the only woman allowed to see the Games in Olympia. Herodes may have killed her in a rage at eight months pregnant with their sixth child in 160 AD due to jealousy.

He was charged with tyranny in 173 AD but acquitted.

He may have dedicated the Odeon to Regilla to quell rumours of her murder, while a street named after her, **Rigillis**, and nearby **Irodou Attikou** (Herodes Atticus) St are located east of the National Gardens.

ZAPPEION, PANGRATI, METS

History, culture, geography/planning, architecture

FREE Hadrian's Arch

This landmark on the busy road opposite Zappeion Gardens and near the Acropolis Museum was built in the 2nd century in honour of the city's patron, Hadrian (76–138 AD), also noted for Britain's Hadrian's Wall. The triumphal gate (*pictured*) faced the new part of the city, which included the Temple of Zeus, that was being built beyond the circa 470 BC Themistoclean Wall that once surrounded Athens.
• *Stroller access.* • *Amalias and Vas. Olgas aves, Zappeio.*
Get there: Akropoli Metro station on Line 2, then 5 minutes' walk.

Architecture, art, history, geography, literature classics

Temple of Olympian Zeus

Just out of Plaka, across Amalias Ave, is this temple, known as *Stì-les* in Greek. Greece's largest temple, the remaining 15 out of 104 colossal, Corinthian capital-topped columns (*pictured*) are 17m/56ft high, and stand in a sanctuary dedicated to Ancient Greece's most powerful god. The temple was started in 515 BC, but the stockpile of materials to make the 96m by 40m (315x131ft) structure were pilfered during its 650-year construction schedule, used to build the Themistoclean Wall and the Capitoline Temple in Rome among other structures. Athenian emperor Hadrian finally completed it in 132 AD, and put a copy of Phidias' famous statue of Zeus, a **wonder of the ancient world**, inside, along with a statue of himself.

• *The grounds here are stroller accessible and good for letting toddlers and children run around (watched though).* • *Daily 8am–3pm.* • *Adults €2, under 18 yrs free, or part of the Acropolis ticket.* • *1 Vas. Olgas and Amalias aves, Makriyanni/Zappeio, 210-922-6330, www.culture.gr*
Get there: Entrance is on Vas. Olgas Ave, opposite Zappeion Gardens. Akropoli Metro station on Line 2, then 10 minutes' walk.

Sports, history, culture

Panathenian Stadium

The *Kalimàrmara* (also Panathenaic) Stadium (*pictured*) was reconstructed in marble by Herodes Atticus in 143 AD where the **original Panathenian Games** took place every four years from 330 BC. A tomb on the side of the track is likely his burial monument, but he's thought to be actually buried under the track. The stadium is one *stade* (hence stadium), an ancient measurement equal to 180m/600ft, and can hold some 50,000 spectators, the same as the Roman Coliseum. This version was rebuilt for the first modern Olympics held in 1896. It marks the **end of the Marathon race**, and was used in the 2004 Athens Olympics.

• *Stroller accessible and kids can run around on the grounds and seating.* • *Daily 8am–5pm winter, 8am–7pm summer.* • *Adults €3, free under 6 yrs, students/seniors €1.50.* • *Entrance to the Panathenian Stadium is from Vas. Konstantinou St, Pangrati, 210-752-2985, www.panathenaicstadium.gr*
Get there: *Syntagma or Akropoli Metro stations on Lines 3 or 2, then 20–30 minutes' walk, including through Zappeion Gardens. Or take trolley bus nos. 2, 4, 10, 11 (a stop is in front of the post office at Syntagma Square) or bus nos. 90, 209 or 550 (northbound from Syngrou Ave) to bus-stop: Stadio.*

History, art, culture

FREE Postal and Philatelic Museum
Stamp enthusiasts can visit the Postal and Philatelic Museum beside the Panathenian Stadium. It has stamps from the first modern Olympics held in Athens in 1896 and other rare examples.

• *Not stroller accessible (steps).* • *Mon-Fri 8am–2pm except holidays.* • *Free entrance.*
• *5 Fokianou St, Stadiou Square, Pangrati, 210-751-9042, www.postalmuseum.gr*
Get there: *Trolley bus nos. 2, 4, 10, 11, bus no. 550 to bus-stop: Stadio.*

Nature, history, literature

FREE Ardittou Hill
This hill (*pictured*) and the **jogging track** around the perimeter of the **Panathenian Stadium** are popular with joggers and walkers for respite from the heat and offers great views of the Acropolis and city, although it may seem a bit neglected. A tomb marks the site where **Herodes Atticus** is said to be buried beside the track, and scant ruins of a **temple to Tyche** (Fortune) are located on the hill, where Herodes Atticus' wife, Regilla, was the first priestess.

• **No food or drink.** • *Stroller with difficulty on the hill; the track is fine.* • *Access to the track and hill is through the green gates into a courtyard on Archemidous St at Agras St (steps), Pangrati/Mets, behind the stadium.*
Get there: *Trolley bus nos. 2, 4, 10, 11, bus no. 550 to bus-stop: Stadio, then 10 minutes' walk.*

History, art, culture, religion

FREE First Cemetery
Just southeast of the hill is the First Cemetery, where the modern city's notables and celebrities are buried. A historical monument in itself, the site is interesting

for its many elaborate tombs and sculptures dating from the 19th century. It's a leafy and peaceful place, not surprisingly, with both wide and narrow paths. The most famous and easily recognizable sculpture is the *Sleeping Lady* (1877) by Tinos islander Yannoulis Halepas (***pictured***), marking the tomb of Sophia Afentaki, a wealthy Athenian's 18-year-old daughter. Christian Orthodoxy only allows burial, so these exorbitantly expensive gravesites are very close together. The more contemporary ones are usually rented for three years, and the remains removed to an ossuary where relatives are meant to rent the boxes in perpetuity. There are separate sections for Protestants and Jews.

• **No food or drink.** • *Stroller accessible.* • *Apr–Oct 8am–8pm, Nov–Mar 8am–5.30pm.* • *Free entrance.* • **Anapafseos and Trivonianou sts, Mets**, 210-923-6720.
Get there: *Bus A3, A4, 103, 108, 111, 155, 206, 208, 237, 856, 057, or 227 to bus-stop: A' ("Proto") Nekrotafio.*

LYCABETTUS, KOLONAKI, EVANGELISMOS METRO STATION AREA

Geography, technology, religion, culture

FREE **Lycabettus Hill**
Northeast of the Acropolis is the highest of the city's eight hills, Lycabettus (Lykavittos), the conical (saddle-shaped from the back) hill rising up 277m/909ft from the fashionable **Kolonaki** district. In mythology it is said to have been dropped by the goddess Athena by mistake.

There are **two summits**, the highest being the site of the circa 1780 **Agios Georgios (St George) church** (***pictured***), which is the best spot to see the city in its enormity. **Café Lycabettus** (*210-721-0700*) has outdoor terraces serving drinks and ice creams here, where you pay more (€10 ice cream) for the privilege. There is also a seafood **restaurant, Orizontes** (*210-722-7065, www.orizonteslycabettus.gr*), run by the same company, **Kastelorizo** (*210-898-3840, www.kastelorizo.com.gr*), which also runs the enclosed **cog railway/funicular**, which brings you behind the church to the entrances of the café and restaurant.

There are easy paths down the hill if you prefer a nature stroll. It's a bit of a hike to walk up the trails to the top, and even to get to the point where the short funicular begins.

It's about a 10-minute walk through the pine-covered paths from the café and church to the open-air **Lycabettus Theatre** (*210-722-7233, www.greekfestival.gr*) which is also reachable by car, but taxis are loathe to drive up here—you could try and lure one with the promise of a fare back down.

• *Stroller accessible but hard-going uphill.* • *Teleferik (funicular) every 30 minutes, 9am–3am.*
• *€7 round-trip, half-price one-way and 4–8 yrs, under 4 yrs free; tickets can be bought with a credit card.* • **Aristippou and Ploutarchou sts, Kolonaki/Lycavittos**, 210-721-0701.
Get there: *Bus nos. 022, 060, or 200 bring you near the cog railway start, which you can get from Akadimias St, Kanari St or Kolonaki Sq to bus-stop: Loukianou or Marasli (sts), then 10 min walk.*

Culture, history, art

FREE THURS Benaki Museum

The renowned Benaki Museum, housed in a neoclassical building near Syntagma and Kolonaki, contains art and exhibits from the Neolithic period to the 20th century, with ancient art and sculpture, costumes, paintings including by **El Greco**, and memorabilia from the 19th century War of Independence, including of **Lord Byron**, who sparked Romantic notions of liberation and joined the Greek cause. The folk art collection is remarkable, with rooms decorated as they were in the 18th century. The collection and house of the benefactor, Anthony Benakis, were bequeathed to the state in 1931. They often have **programs for children** on weekends—check the website. The **gift shop** includes reproductions in silver and terra-cotta, jewellery, books and icons. There's a roof-garden **café** here.

• *Stroller accessible with notice (call ahead to open the back door).* • *Wed, Fri, Sat 9am–5pm, Thurs 9am–midnight, Sun 9am–3pm.* • *Adults €7, adult accompanying a child €5, Thursdays free or €1 donation.* • *Vas. Sofias Ave and 1 Koumbari sts, Kolonaki, 210-367-1000, www.benaki.gr*
Get there: Syntagma Metro station on Lines 2 and 3, Parliament/National Gardens exit, then 5–10 minutes' walk. Allow at least an hour there.

History, culture, art

Cycladic Art Museum

A private museum with a grand entrance, the Cycladic Art Museum (*pictured*) has a notable collection from various benefactors of the stylish, modern-looking art from the Cycladic islands and other areas dating from 3200 to 2000 BC. The small galleries are well-organized, and there are **workshops for children** on weekends (check the website). **Café, gift shop** and **book shop.**

• *Stroller accessible from 4 Neophytou Douka St entrance.* • *Mon, Wed, Fri, Sat 10am–5pm, Thurs 10am–8pm, Sun 11am–5pm, closed national holidays.* • *Adults €7, half-price on Monday, under 18 yrs free.* • *1 Irodotou St at Vas. Sofias Ave (Stathatos mansion entrance), and 4 Neophytou Douka St, Kolonaki, 210-722-8321 or 210-722-8323, www.cycladic.gr*
Get there: Between Syntagma and Evangelismos Metro stations on Line 3.

Religion, art, history, mythology

Byzantine and Christian Museum

The Byzantine and Christian Museum is located on the grounds of a 19th century aristocrat, Sophie de Marbois, duchess de Plaisance (1785–1854). The history of the early Christian church is chronicled with noteworthy artefacts, including 5th–8th century leather shoes for adults and children, and the transition from the worship of gods to Christianity, such as Christ metamorphosing from the animal-loving Orpheus (*pictured*).

• *Stroller accessible.* • *Tues–Sun 8am–3pm, last entrance 2.30pm.* • *Adults €4, children under 18 yrs free.* • **22 Vasilissis Sofias Ave, Rigillis**, *210-721-1027, www.byzantinemuseum.gr*
Get there: *Evangelismos Metro station on Line 3, Rigillis park exit, then 5 minutes' walk.*

Military history, culture, social studies

War Museum

Military aficionados, historians and children too will appreciate the War Museum (***pictured***), which has a collection of military objects ranging from antiquity to the 20th century. Exhibits include machinery and weapons, battle plans and etchings, uniforms (including a samurai outfit) and aircraft. Also memorabilia from foreigners fighting alongside Greeks during the 19th century War of Independence against Ottoman rule, and from those who cheered Allied Europe's first land battle victory in WWII, when Greece routed Italy.

• *Stroller accessible with some steps.* • *Tues–Sun 9am–2pm. Adults €2, under 18 yrs free.*
• **2 Rizari St at Vas. Sofias Ave, Rigillis**, *210-725-2974, www.warmuseum.gr*
Get there: *Evangelismos Metro station on Line 3, Rigillis park exit. Allow ~an hour there.*

SYNTAGMA SQUARE, STADIOU ST

History, culture, architecture

**** Syntagma Square

Syntagma is the city's heart. Major rallies and protests take place here opposite **Parliament**, where two Metro lines also intersect. On it is the **Tomb of the Unknown Soldier** and the changing of the guard, luxury hotels, a McDonald's, media department store (Public), banks, a post office, ministry offices and all kinds of shops. The square

itself (***pictured, facing west down central Ermou St***) has grass, trees and benches around a fountain (*free wifi zone*), and is flanked by a couple of **cafes**.

The square was named after the populace demanded a constitution (*sýntagma*) in 1843 from the installed German monarchy when the modern state was first formed in the 19th century. King Otto had been stalling on his promise to provide one.

History, society, architecture

FREE Parliament

Athens' biggest landmark (*pictured*) in the centre is the Parliament building, the one-time palace of the Bavarian King Otto (1833–62) when a monarchy was installed by the European powers of the time. Designed by architects from Munich and completed in 1842, the building has housed parliament since 1935, as Greece flip-flopped between a monarchy and a republic until the monarchy was abolished in 1974.

• *Syntagma Sq*, 210-370-7000, www.hellenicparliament.gr, **library** 210-370-7275, Mon-Fri 9am-1.30pm/6-8.30pm, Sat 9am-1.30pm.

History, culture

FREE Changing of the guard

Children will enjoy seeing the changing of the guard (*pictured*) at **Syntagma Square**, in front of Parliament. A flock of pigeons will wait with you as two elite Presidential Guard soldiers known as Evzones in traditional costume (*foustanèlla*) stand before the **Tomb of the Unknown Soldier** (circa 1932). The guards step away from their posts and engage in a short exercise *at the top of the hour. The duty-rotation ceremony is more elaborate and takes place at 11am on Sunday.*

• *Amalias Ave. & Vas. Georgiou 'A St*, **Syntagma Sq.**

Religion, history, arts and crafts

Jewish Museum of Greece

Jewish communities are thought to have existed since Hellenistic times in Greece, and more since the Spanish Inquisition. Some 8,000 remnants from 4,000 years have been collected at the Jewish Museum of Greece, including 600-year-old textiles, displayed on various small levels that are *stroller accessible* in this neoclassical building (*pictured*) near Syntagma Square.

• *Mon–Fri 9am-2.30pm, Sun 10am-2pm.* • *Adults €6, 6–15 yrs €3, under 6 yrs free.* • *39 Nikis St, Syntagma*, 210-322-5582, www.jewishmuseum.gr

Royalty, history, religion, culture, art

FREE Sotira Likodimou church

Aka St Nicodemus church (*pictured*) with the tall bell tower on Filellinon St at Syntagma is also known as the **Russian church**. The largest mediaeval church in the city was founded before 1031 by Stefan Likodimou, and is a copy of the Hosios Loukas monastery near Delphi. It was bought and restored in the mid-19th century by the Russian Orthodox church. The bell, which has a wonderful resonance, was a gift from the czar, while the interior was painted by artists Nikiforos Lytras and Bavarian Ludwig Thiersch.

• *Services on Sundays from 7.30am.* • *21 Filellinon and Souri sts, Syntagma, 210-323-1090.*

History, culture, literature, religion

FREE SUN National History Museum

Going towards Omonia Square, the National History Museum is located behind the bronze statue of the man (War of Independence leader Theodoros Kolokotroni, 1770-1843) on the horse near Syntagma. Housed in the old Parliament (*Palaia Vouli*, 1875-1935), it contains artefacts dating from the Fall of Constantinople (1453) to World War II. Most memorabilia dates from the 19th century and is connected with Greece's fight for independence. Lots of mediaeval gear (*pictured*), swords and guns, paintings and costumes, ship figureheads and models, and "treasure chests" for pirate-mad children. A blink-or-miss corridor (no. 8), contains **Lord Byron's** helmet, pistol and sword, camp bed, a portrait of Teresa Makri, the "Maid of Athens" immortalized in poetry, and the urn of Napoleon's nephew, Paul Bonaparte (1808-1927), who also died for the cause. The **gift shop** has unique, Greek-themed items for children.

• *About 20 shallow steps at the entrance.* • *Tues–Sun 9am–2pm.* • *Adults €3, free under 18 yrs.*
• *13 Stadiou and Kolokotroni sts, Syntagma, 210-323-7617, www.nhmuseum.gr*

History, commerce, mythology, culture, art, architecture

Numismatic Museum

Visit the central Numismatic Museum (*pictured*) located near Syntagma inside the lavishly decorated Iliou Melathron (Troy Mansion)—a 19th century villa and one-time residence of Troy and Mycenae sites discoverer **Heinrich Schliemann**, if ancient coins (hoards, treasure chest booty) also pique your interest. Some 600,000 coins are displayed dating from 700 BC, when the earliest coins were said to be minted on the island of Aegina, the *chelòne* (turtle) coins of circa 700–550 BC, by the king of Argos. Other sources say the honour goes to the Lydians (but no coins have been found), or to Kyme, ancient Greece, struck by Demodike, wife of King Midas himself.

The ancient Greeks spread the practice of exchanging coins for commerce and trade throughout the Mediterranean, Near East and the Balkans. Also a **gift shop**. At the back of the pretty courtyard is a secluded **café**, a little oasis in this business district area. The iron gates and fence in the front are in the design of the swastika, which at the time, and still today, is a symbol of happiness in Asia.

• *Steps at the entrance.* • *Tues–Sun 9am–4pm.* • *Adults €3, free under 18 yrs.* • **12 Panepistimiou St, Syntagma,** *210-363-2057, www.nma.gr*

Get there: *Syntagma Metro station on Lines 2 and 3, then 5 minutes' walk to Panepistimiou (El. Venizelou) and Voukourestiou sts.*

Architecture, religion

FREE Agii Theodori church

This church (***pictured***) on Evripidou St just east of Klafthmonos Square on Stadiou St is one of the most beautiful. According to inscriptions on marble tablets over the lintel, it was rebuilt in the 12th century, after an earlier structure that had also been renovated in 1065 was perhaps damaged beyond repair by an earthquake. It was damaged during the 19th century War of Independence but restored in 1840.

You can stop for a *souvlàki* or drink at the **café** (***Alpeis**, 7 Palaion Patron Germanou St, **Klafthmonos Sq,** 210-331-0384*) on the square surrounding the church.

• *Evripidou & Aristidou sts at **Klafthmonos Sq, between Omonia and Syntagma squares**.* **Get there:** *From Panepistimio Metro station on Line 2 or from the Central Market (Agorà) on Athinas and Evripidou sts, then 5 minutes' walk.*

History, art, culture

City of Athens Museum

The stately mansion that the first king and queen of Greece, Otto and Amalia, lived in while the palace (now Parliament) was being built in the 1830s, houses the sleepy City of Athens Museum (***pictured***), which showcases royal and contemporary artefacts from mainly 19th century travellers. Noted items on display in the elegant rooms are **Louis XIV chairs**, a painting of mad King

Ludwig (the teenage Otto's father), and art by **Edward Lear**, **Edward Degas** (*Dancer holding a fan*) and **Edward Turner**. Impressive pieces include an enormous (2.6x5.2m), circa 1674 painting that shows the Parthenon 13 years before its roof was exploded by the Venetians, an oil of Greek pirates, a painting of an intent **Lord Byron** with the Acropolis in the background, and a charming, circa 1892 painting of Carnival by

renowned Greek painter **Nikolaos Gyzis**, as well as beautiful lithographs and watercolours of this once pastoral Levantine town.

• *The ground floor is stroller accessible, then stairs to the first floor. Displays are only cordoned off. •* *Mon, Wed, Thurs, Fri 9am–4pm, Sat–Sun 10am–3pm. • Adults €3, up to 13 yrs free, students €2. • 7* ***Paparigopoulou St, Klafthmonos Sq**, 210-323-1397, www.athenscitymuseum.gr* ***Get there**: Off **Stadiou St**, from Panepistimio Metro station on Line 2, Korai exit, then 5 minutes' walk.*

Architecture, history, culture, society

FREE Academy of Athens
The first of three notable neoclassical buildings on Panepistimiou St, marked as Eleftheriou Venizelou St after an important Greek statesman, is the Academy of Athens (*pictured*). With columns topped by Athena and Apollo, it was designed by Theophilos Hansen, who along with his brother, designed many buildings for the modern capital when it was established in the 19th century. There's also a reference **library** (*210-366-4790*).
• *28 Panepistimiou St, **Panepistimio**, 210-360-0207, www.academyofathens.gr* ***Get there**: Panepistimio Metro station on Line 2, Akademia exit.*

Architecture, history, culture, society

FREE University of Athens
The next building is one of the campuses of the University of Athens, designed by Theophilos's brother, Christian Hansen, and features frescoes of ancient Greek authors in the portico.
• *30 Panepistimiou St, **Panepistimio**, telnos by dept, www.uoa.gr* ***Get there**: Panepistimio Metro station on Line 2, Akademia exit.*

Architecture, history, culture, society, religion

FREE National Library

The National Library, also designed by Theophilos Hansen, is a reference library containing early **illuminated gospels**.

• *Stroller accessible from the back entrance.* • *Mon–Thurs 9am–8pm, Fri–Sat 9am–2pm. Manuscripts Mon–Fri 9am–1.45pm, 210-360-2422; Call one or two days ahead to see particular manuscripts.*

• *32 Panepistimiou St, Panepistimio, 210-360-8597, www.nlg.gr*

Get there: *Panepistimio Metro station on Line 2, Akademia exit.*

OMONIA SQUARE, VICTORIA, EXARCHIA

Forming part of the commercial triangle of central Athens, **Omonia Square** is the scruffiest, edging into a down-at-heel shopping and commercial area. All kinds of characters populate the square, which has undergone countless transformations in a bid to make it more attractive and hospitable, but to no avail. There is, however, a well-stocked kiosk that sells all kinds of magazines. Between Omonia and Victoria Metro stations is the **National Archaeological Museum**, ~10 minutes' walk from Omonia.

Historis, culture, automotive industry

Hellenic Motor Museum

Not only car enthusiasts will enjoy the Hellenic Motor Museum, a thoughtfully laid-out modern space where an array of shiny autos (*pictured*) from mainly around Europe are showcased, so a very different experience from exhibits across the Atlantic. All are said to be in working order and are from a single  collector. Apart from the cars themselves, 111 on display at a time of the more than 300 in his collection, included are important "firsts," and some unique hood ornaments. The cars are shown with wall-sized photos of models in their era, often with celebrities.

See the history of the wheel on your way up the ramp entrance, and buy a model or photo of your favourite from the **gift shop** at the top. Also a F1 simulator (€10) and a **cafe**.

• *Stroller accessible.* • *Tues–Sat noon–9pm, Sun 11am–6pm.* • *Adults €8, students and seniors €5, under 6 yrs free.* • *33–35 Iouliannou and Patission sts, Museo, 210-881-6187, www.hellenicmotormuseum.gr*

Get there: *From Victoria Metro station on Line 1, then 5 minutes' walk, inside the Athenian Capitol mall complex opp. the National Archaeological Museum (north and west one block).*

History, art, mythology, culture

*** National Archaeological Museum

The National Archaeological Museum should not be missed, since it contains the greatest finds from throughout the country, referenced in classical as well as archaeology and history studies.

Highlights from the Neolithic, Mycenaean, Cycladic, Thera, Sculpture, Vase and Minor Objects, Metals, and Egyptian collections include the *Mask of Agamemnon* unearthed in Mycenae, the rare, circa 2nd century BC bronze *Jockey of Artemision* statue (*pictured*) and the older bolt (or trident) throwing *Zeus (or Poseidon) of Artemision*, modern-looking 4,000-year-old Cycladic statues, quaint frescoes circa 1700 BC, and well-known mythical scenes depicted on red-figure and black-figure Attic pottery, as well as finely-crafted jewellery.

The museum also holds important temporary exhibitions: until August 31, 2013 is the "Shipwreck of Antikythera" that includes the Antikythera Mechanism "computer", circa 150 BC.

There is a small **cafe** on site and a few cafes circling the museum front garden.
• *Not recommended to take very young, active children, unless in a stroller.* • *Mon 1.30pm–8pm, Tues–Sun and holidays 9am–4pm. Check for seasonal changes.* • *Adults €7, under 19 yrs free.*
• **44 Patission (28ᵗʰ Octovriou) St, Museo**, *210-821-7717, www.namuseum.gr*
Get there: *Victoria Metro station on Line 1, or trolley nos. 2, 3, 4, 5, 6, 7, 8, 9, 11, 13 or 15 north-bound to bus-stop: Polytechnio.*

Nature, time out, play

FREE Strefi Hill

The last hill is Strefi—a small, wooded hill with a local neighbourhood feel in the bohemian **Exarchia** district, which has a lot of students and associated trendy shops and **cafes**, especially around **Exarchia Square**. A place to bolt if you're in the area behind the National Archaeological Museum. There's a small **playground** near the entrance.
• *Em. Benaki and Anexartisias sts, **Exarchia**.*

Aphaia temple, excursion or DIY day-trip to nearby Aegina island

Chapter 7: City Tours

Bicycle Tours

Acropolis Bikes
This outfit rents bicycles and also does organized tours. Charges are €3 an hour, €10 for four hours, €15 for 24 hours, €25 for two days, €7 per day for longer. Helmets, locks, etc, also tools for longer tours are included. Children's bikes available but rented at owner's discretion.

• *Mon–Fri 9am–2.30pm or by appointment.•* **10–12 Aristidou St, near Klafthmonos Square** *off Stadiou St, near Panepistimio Metro station, 210-324-5793, 694-430-6130, www.acropolisbikes.gr*

Athens by Bike
One-hour tours (Mon–Fri 11am) by regular (€7.50) or electric (€11.50) bike and bicycle rental specials from Friday 2pm until Sunday 11am for €17 as well as other discounts. Regularly €5 for three hours, €8 for 3–6 hours, and €12 for 6–24 hours. Seats, chariot, and a limited number of small-sized bicycles and helmets are available with advance notice. Helmet, lock and map included.

• *Tues, Thurs, Fri 1pm–8.30pm, Sat–Sun 9am–8pm, Mon, Wed by request.* • **16 Tzireon and 117 Athanasiou Diakou sts, Makriyanni**, *213-042-3922, www.athensbybike.gr*

Cyclists meet-up
Join in with tle locals, as cyclists meet outside **Thissio Metro station** for evening

rides on Fridays except at Easter, Christmas and in August. (Updates in Greek at *www.podilates.gr*).

Funbike

For something completely different, ride a four-wheeled bicycle carriage (*pictured*) with pedal-assist (motorized), that also has two seats in

front for small children. Two-seater +2, four-seater can fit six +2.
• *2-seater €10ph, €7 per half-hour. 4-seater €16ph, €13 per half-hour.* • **1 Lebesi and Makriyianni sts, Akropoli/Makriyanni,** *210-922-7722, 694-846-9749, www.funbike.gr*

Funky Ride

Funky Ride charges €9 for eight hours, €12 for 24 hours and offers discounts for more days and groups. Currently has one smaller bike of 20 inches (for ~ eight yrs old). Helmets, locks, maps included.
• *Mon–Sat 10am–3pm, Tues, Thurs, Fri 10am–3pm/6–9pm.* • **1 Dimitrakopoulou St, Makriyanni,** *211-710-9366, www.funkyride.gr or call 693-765-3363 for bookings.*

Coach Tours

Many travel agencies around town offer **city sightseeing tours** as well as day excursions to **Delphi, Ancient Corinth** and **Mycenae, three-island day cruises** to **Aegina, Poros** and **Hydra, three-day** or more **Aegean cruises (Variety Cruises,** *214-216 Syngrou Ave, 210-691-9191, www.varietycruises.com* has yacht cruises starting at €150pp), and tours to other well-known locales but for longer durations. Check for deals. In August 2012 for example, **Majestic Travel** offered the **three-island day cruise** for €25 (normally around €95) including lunch.
• *3 Kydathinaion St,* **Syntagma/Plaka,** *210-322-3891, www.majestictravel.gr*

Two well-known travel agency operators:
• **Chat Tours:** *9 Xenofontos St,* **Syntagma,** *210-323-0827, www.chatours.gr*
• **Key Tours:** *4 Kallirois and Lebesi sts,* **Makriyanni,** *210-923-3166, www.keytours.gr*

Athens Open Tour

This open-top coach leaves every 30 minutes and does 14 stops in Athens, starting from **Syntagma Square.** They also do a tour leaving from the cruise-ship terminal in **Piraeus.** Check for online deals.
• *Adults €18, 5–15 yrs €8, 24 hours plus a day free, or 22 stops including Piraeus for €20, 5–15 yrs €8.* • *210-881-5207, www.athensopentour.com*

City Sightseeing Bus

Another open-top double-decker (*pictured*), has a 15-stop tour that's 90 minutes (ticket good for 24 hours plus a day free), and leaves every 30 minutes from **Syntagma Square**. *Adults €18, 5–15 yrs €8.* They also do a **port of Piraeus and Athens** tour for 70 minutes.
• *Adults €22, children €9.*
• *210-900-2600, see www.citysightseeing.com for map and info.*

Mini-trains

A couple of **mini-trains** do tours around the main Athens sites, which is a fun ride for kids as well as saves tired legs.

Happy Train

Happy Train (*pictured*) runs hourly 9am–9pm. You can also hop in at the Acropolis Museum and at the Roman Agora in Plaka, near Monastiraki.
• *Adults €6, children 6–12 yrs €4, 5 yrs and under free, discounts for groups.* • ***Ermou St at Syntagma Sq**, 210-725-5400, www.athenshappytrain.com*

Sunshine Express

This one starts at Areos and Adrianou sts in Monastiraki and has two tours, taking approx 40 minutes and an hour-and-40 minutes. They run from 11am till dusk on weekends and holidays in winter, and until midnight in summer, except between 2.30pm and 5pm.
• *Adults €5, children under 10 yrs €3.* • ***Areos St, Monastiraki**, 210-881-9252, www.sunshine-express.gr*

Walking Tours

Athens Walking Tour

Hotels often offer guided walking tours, but one that's proved popular is the Athens Walking Tour which also has tours tailored to cruise-ship passengers, and food tours.
• *From €29 for an Acropolis Museum guided tour and €36 for a city and Acropolis tour. Discounts available for families.* • *210-884-7269, www.athenswalkingtours.gr*

Trekking Hellas

Trekking Hellas also does Athens walking tours of 3-4 hours, among others.
• *Snack included for €39.* • *210-331-0323,* *www.trekkinghellas.gr*

Segway

If you don't mind the odd looks, consider a tour on a Segway rider (***pictured***). There is a knack to it but it's handy, especially if you want to do a lot of sightseeing in a day.

• *Children must be at least 12 years old and weigh 100lbs (46kg).* • **9 Frinichou and Eschinou sts, Plaka**, *210-322-2500,* *www.athenssegwaytours.com, near Akropolis Metro station on Line 2.*

You can also ride along the Acropolis walkway by horse and carriage. Waiting for customers outside the entrance to the Acropolis, Dion. Areopagitou St, Makriyanni

It's all Greek

Αα Ββ Γγ Δδ Εε Ζζ Ηη Θθ Ιι Κκ Λλ Μμ Νν Ξξ Οο Ππ Ρρ Σς Ττ Υυ Φφ Χχ Ψψ Ωω

The Greek language is a source of pride, having endured for thousands of years. It was the **lingua franca** or common language throughout the Mediterranean and into western Asia for trade and intellectual pursuits, especially following the conquest of **Alexander the Great** more than 200 years before Christ. It was the language used to write the **New Testament**, and why **Apostle Paul** knew it and was understood in his sermons throughout the Roman Empire that followed.

Ancient Greek was not superseded by Latin, as it was considered the language of culture and studied by educated Romans, and remains part of the curriculum in schools offering degrees in the Classics.

The "alpha and omega" are also studied in divinity classes, and of course endures in countless English words (angel, astronaut, aroma...), being especially useful in medical terminology, due to the ease with which it can transform, from **root words** (*haema* = blood), **prefixes** (*auto–* = self, *aero–* = air) and **suffixes** (*–ectomy* = incision, *–osis* = disease, *–pathy* = suffering...).

Many areas to explore at the G. Averof Battleship Museum, Flisvos

Chapter 8: Field Trips—Indoor

Places to Go (by proximity to central Athens)

These attractions in Greater Athens are organized according to distance from the historic and commercial centre—Syntagma Square.

History, railway industry

FREE Railway (Train) Museum, Kato Patissia *5km/3.1mi*
See steam engines, trams, carriages, including one given as a gift to the sultan of the Ottoman empire, and other historical items of the Greek railway.
• *No food or drink available.* • *Stroller accessible.* • *Tues–Fri 9am–1pm.* • *Free entrance.* • *4 Siokou St, opp. 301 Liosion Ave, Kato Patissia, 210-512-6295.*
Get there: Kato Patissia Metro station on Line 1, then 10 minutes' walk west to the railway track. Journey takes ~20 minutes.

Natural sciences, environment

Natural history museums, Panepistimioupoli, Zografou *5.2km/3.2mi*
If you've had enough of statues and pottery, **four natural history museums** are located in the Geology and Biology building of the University of Athens, Panepistimioupoli (University Town). They follow the academic calendar and are closed over Christmas and Easter holidays, and a month or so in August.
• *Entrance is free or token.* ***No food or drink available.***

FREE Botanical Museum

There's a Botanical Museum here of mainly Greek flora. The extensive Herbarium is for researchers only, but the "Attica Landscape and Environment" exhibit is open to the public.

• *Stroller-accessible from the back entrance (elevator), furthest entrance to the bldg (after the "flag" entrance), ground floor steps.* • *By appointment (can check while there), Mon–Fri 10am–2pm.* • *€1 per person.* • ***Geology and Biology building, Panepistimioupoli,*** *210-727-4356, http://emuseums.cc.uoa.gr*
Get there: *Bus no. 250 from Evangelismos Metro station on Line 3 (bus-stops on Vas. Sofias Ave or Rigillis St) to bus-stop: Geology. Journey ~20-30 min. Allow ~2 hours for all museums.*

FREE Museum of Mineralogy and Petrology

Don't miss the Museum of Mineralogy and Petrology at the separate entrance to the building, which has an impressive collection of crystals and unique rocks from the ancient quarries of Lavrio in Attica, fluorescent stones (***pictured***) that will delight children, precious gems, industrial-use rocks alongside common consumer products, meteorites, and finds from the Santorini volcano. Child-friendly for school groups, with *many labels in English.*

• *Steps at entrance, left of "flag" entrance.* • *Mon–Fri 8am–2pm, closed mid–July, Aug.* • *Free entrance.* • ***Geology and Biology building, Panepistimioupoli,*** *210-727-4112, http://museums.geol.uoa.gr/mineralogy*
Get there: *Bus no. 250 from Evangelismos Metro station on Line 3 (bus-stops on Vas. Sofias Ave or Rigillis St) to bus-stop: Geology. Journey ~20-30 min. Allow ~2 hours for all museums.*

FREE Paleontology and Geology Museum

The pre-historic museum collection on two levels has fossils and shells, many from the Pikermi, Attica site—one of the first ever to be excavated in the 19th century—and includes a display of dwarf animals— elephant, hippo, deer, otter (***pictured***)—that evolved on flora-limited islands (Crete), enormous tusk fossils, a giant turtle model, and a hanging cast skeleton of the enigmatic mosasaurus. *Some labels in English.*

• *Steps at the entrance (with overhead flag) at the zebra crossing.* • *Mon–Fri 9am–2pm, €2 or free for individuals.* • *Ground floor, basement,* ***Geology and Biology building, Panepistimioupoli,*** *210-727-4086, http://paleo-museum.uoa.gr*
Get there: *Bus no. 250 from Evangelismos Metro station on Line 3 (bus-stops on Vas. Sofias Ave or Rigillis St) to bus-stop: Geology. Journey ~20-30 min. Allow ~2 hours for all museums.*

Zoological Museum

The Zoological Museum has been used for studying since the 19th century, with the largest collection of stuffed, pickled and pinned creatures in the country. Lots of floor space between the exhibits (*pictured*) of some 500 mammals, including a tiger, lions, moose, ostriches, some 2,500 birds and nests (spot the tiny Athenian owl), 1,000 reptiles and marine life as well as insects and shells. Notable are a lyre bird and freaks of nature, such as a calf with heads at both ends and an eight-legged sheep, as well as fish that look like ducks. Most specimen display cases are old-fashioned, but DD5 gave it a thumb's up. *Some displays are cordoned or open*, so keep an eye on toddlers. *Labels in Greek and Latin.*

• *Steps (outside, inside) at the entrance (with overhead flag) at the zebra crossing.* • *Mon–Fri 9am–1pm, adults €2, up to 18 yrs free.* • **Geology and Biology building, Panepistimioupoli**, 210-727-4609, 693-222-8569, *http://old.biol.uoa.gr/zoolmuseum*
Get there: *Bus no. 250 from Evangelismos Metro station on Line 3 (bus-stops on Vas. Sofias Ave or Rigillis St) to bus-stop: Geology. Journey ~20-30 min. Allow ~2 hours for all museums.*

Child-oriented history, science
Hellenic Cosmos, Tavros *5.4km/3.3mi*
See a 45-minute interactive 3D tour of Ancient Greece, hosted in English on a dome screen at the child-oriented Hellenic Cosmos, a short bus ride from central Athens. Also a 3D projection of Ancient Olympia and interactive, "scientific principle" exhibits for children, but these are geared to Greek school-children, so most descriptions are in Greek with a short English version, but they are engaging. Films (one on Darwin) are shown as well, but they are also in Greek.

• **Café** *on site.* • *Stroller accessible.* • *June 1–Sept 30: Mon–Fri 9am–4pm, Sun 10am–3pm, closed August 10–27. Oct 1–May 31: Mon, Tues, Thurs, 9am–2pm, Wed–Fri 9am–8pm, Sat 11am–4pm, Sun 10am–4pm.* • **Dome projections**: *Adults €10, 5–18 yrs €8, under 5 yrs €1.* • **Daypass** *(dome projection, 3D Ancient Olympia projection, interactive exhibit) adults €15, 5–18 yrs €12.*
• **254 Piraeos St, Tavros**, *212-254-0000, www.hellenic-cosmos.gr*
Get there: *Kallithea Metro station on Line 1 then 10 minutes' walk west, or bus no. 049 to bus-stop: Ifantiria, or bus no. 914 to bus-stop: Skoli Kalon Technon.*

Natural sciences, astronomy
Planetarium, Paleo Faliro *5.9km/3.6mi*
Athens has a world-class Planetarium with a 25m/82ft iWerks (like IMAX) 360-degree dome screen that shows 40-minute shows, and some are geared to young children. It's a short bus or taxi ride from the centre, but during weekends the shows are often sold out. You can book online and if you really want to see a show here, book ahead. Getting through by phone is difficult—wait for an operator.

• **No food or drink available**, *but tavernas nearby.* • *Stroller accessible.* • *Programs Sept–July.* • *Adults (18–65 yrs) €8, under 5 yrs free, children, students, 65+ yrs €5 (and residents with multiple children and unemployed, with a card). Little Prince adults €5; children, students, 65+ yrs €3. Some shows (not documentaries) adults €6, children, students, 65+ yrs €4.* • *Advance tickets Mon–Tues*

9am–2pm, Wed–Sun 10am–8pm. • **Eugenides Institute, 387 Syngrou Ave, Paleo Faliro,** *210-946-9600, www.eugenfound.edu.gr*
Get there: *Bus nos. B2, 126 (from Piraeus), 550 to bus-stop: Evgenideio. Journey takes ~15 min.*

Play, eat, shop

ᖴᖴᓍᓍ Ikea & River West Mall, Aegaleo *7km/4.3mi*

Get your **breakfast, lunch** or **dinner** at this child-friendly haven in western Athens, where you can also leave children 3–10 yrs at **Ikea's** free-entrance Smaland, the **supervised play area,** while you eat and shop. Also a **play area** for children under 3 yrs inside the **cafeteria.**
• *Mon–Fri 10am–9pm, Sat 10am–8pm.* • **96-98 Kifissou Ave (west side of the highway), Aegaleo,** *801-11-22-722, 210-354-3403, www.ikea.gr*

The **River West Mall** is next door, with chain stores, including Moustakas toy store, Carrefour supermarket, large, free **play area (*pictured*)** that's unsupervised but may have directed activities suitable for toddlers and older, and a roomy **mother's room.**

• *Same hours as Ikea.* • **Kifissou Ave, Aegaleo,** *801-222-5050, www.riverwest.gr*
Get there: *Egaleo Metro station on Line 3, then bus no. 829 or the mall's free shuttle. Or take a taxi, around €7–8 each way.* **Driving:** *You must go from Iera Odos Ave and then left on Kifissou Ave, as there's no left-turn on the highway (Kifissou) from the other direction (Petrou Ralli Ave). Plenty of underground parking (shared).*

History, maritime, industry, weaponry

ᖴᖴᓍᓍ G. Averof, Velos museums, Flisvos, Paleo Faliro
7.4km/4.6mi

The *Averof* (*pictured*), docked at Flisvos Marina, was at one time the most modern and powerful ship in both the fleets of Greece and its then rival, Turkey, and is the only example of a **heavy-armoured cruiser** from its time. The warship has been impressively **restored to circa 1913,** with much brass, copper and steel, antiquated eye-openers like manual wheels to raise the anchor, speaking tubes, cannon-cleaning brushes and trumpets (no loudspeakers).

The 10,200 ton, steel-plated warship was launched on February 27, 1910, and headed the Greek Navy fleet in the Balkan War of 1912. It has served in WWI, patrolled the seas off Bombay in WWII, brought the exiled government in Cairo back to the port of Faliro in 1944, and been to England twice for special appearances. It was decommissioned in 1952.

Named after the benefactor whose funds were used to purchase the made-in-Italy ship, it has Italian engines (19,000hp), French boilers, German generators, and English Armstrong cannons (190 and 234 millimetres).

Top speed was 23 knots.

The lower decks comprise cramped quarters and low ceilings, plus many compartments, hazardous areas that are cordoned off but not blocked, steep steps with leg-grazing, non-slip adhesives, and reachable, do-not-touch displays, so *not friendly for strollers or children under 5 yrs*. A **gift shop** has mementos, with t-shirts, caps, brass and ship-model key chains, worry beads, pens and pencils.

* **Velos Museum**. Near the *Averof* is the **DD** *Velos*, a **circa 1942 Boston-made, Fletcher-class destroyer**.

• *Same hours as the Averof but with free entrance.*

Two more ships docked here may also be open: the *Eugenios Eugenides*, a Scottish-origin, **1929 schooner** built for Sir Walter Runciman, and *Thalis O Milisios* (Thales of Miletus), a circa **1909 Greek cable-laying ship** rescued by the Aegean Maritime Museum of Mykonos (*22890-22700*).

• *No food or drink: the machines were empty during a Sunday visit in Oct 2012.* • *Not stroller-accessible; very young children need to be carefully supervised.* • *Mon–Fri 9am–2pm, Sat–Sun, holidays 10am–5pm, closed Jan 1, Dec 25, Easter Sat, Easter Sun.* • *Adults €2, up to 6 yrs free, 6–18 yrs €1.50.* • *Averof, Flisvos Marina, 210-988-8211, www.bsaverof.com*
Get there: Tram-stop: Trocadero (SEF line), ~a 30 min journey, then 10 minutes' walk to the ship. • *Allow an hour-and-a-half or more for the 'Averof'.*

History, electric railway industry

FREE Athens Piraeus Electric Railways Museum, Piraeus
8.5km/4.3mi

Located in what was the station post office inside Piraeus Metro station (*pictured*), the **Athens Piraeus Electric Railways Museum** has objects and books relating to one of Europe's oldest Metro railways, with Piraeus station inaugurated in 1869. It includes a wooden carriage (Baume & Marpent/David Desouches & Cie) circa 1904. Rolling stock was also manufactured by Thomson Houston. Since that time, the trains have been made by Siemens and/or consortia with them.

• *Cafes and restaurants nearby.* • *Stroller accessible.* • *Mon–Fri 9.30am–2pm.* • *Free entrance.*
• *Inside Piraeus Metro station, Piraeus, 210-414-7552, www.isap.gr*
Get there: Piraeus Metro station, terminus Line 1, ~15 minutes' journey from Monastiraki.

History, natural earth sciences

Goulandris Natural History Museum, Kifissia *15km/9mi*
To see a private collection of stuffed animals (real ones), minerals, shells, fossils, plants, insects and a Triceratops model skeleton (*pictured*), head up to the Gaia Centre—Goulandris Natural History Museum. The **gift shop** here has the most beautiful prints of Greek wild flowers as well as some toys. Also a **café**.

• Stroller accessible with some steps.
• Mon–Sat 9am–2.30pm, Sun 10am–2.30pm, closed on national holidays. • Adults €6, up to 18 yrs €4. • **13 Levidou St, Kifissia**, 210-801-5870, www.gnhm.gr
Get there: Kifissia Metro station (terminus) on Line 1 (journey takes ~40 min), then 10–15 minutes' walk east, exit through the park, one block beyond Kifissias Ave and turn left on Levidou (north) to the corner of Othonos St.

Play

Playmobil Funpark, Kifissia *18km/11mi*
Playmobil Funpark has 500m2 (5,382sq ft) for Playmobil models, in king size. There are separate rooms where children 18 mos–4 yrs can play separately from older children, to about 11 yrs. Also a **gift shop** and a **café**.
• Mon–Thurs 10am–8pm, Fri–Sat 10am–9pm, Sun 10am–8.30pm. • Parents free, Mon–Fri children €8, Sat–Sun children €12. • **9 Matsa St, Kato Kifissia**, 210-807-5404, www.playmobil.com
Get there: Long ride on bus no. B9 from Halkokondyli St, near Omonia Square to bus-stop: Kalyftaki.

The Midas Touch

King Midas was real, living centuries before his mention by **Aristotle** and **Herodotus** (4th and 5th centuries BC). The myth goes that he gave hospitality to the disoriented and drunken foster father of the god of wine, **Dionysus**, and in return, Dionysus granted Midas his wish, which was that whatever he touched would turn to gold. The gift became a curse, however, as he could not even eat, and turned his own daughter into a golden statue. Midas asked the god to reverse the power, so Dionysus said that if Midas put his hands in the **Pactolus River** (in fact rich in gold dust), it would stop whatever he touched from turning to gold.
• Midas is also said to be the son of Gordias (who made the **Gordian Knot**—another famous myth), as well as discovered lead.
• Midas got donkey ears from the god **Apollo**, after Midas said that a lesser god, **Pan,** was a better lyre player than Apollo following a contest.

The Attica Zoo near the airport in Spata is popular and easy to get around

Chapter 9: Field Trips—Outdoor

Places to Go (by proximity to central Athens)

These destinations in Greater Athens and Attica are listed according to their distance from the historic and commercial centre—Syntagma Square.

Kaisariani Monastery,
Kaisariani *5km/3mi*
It's an effort to reach Kaisariani Monastery (***courtyard, pictured***) if you don't have a car, as the public transport stops some way down the hill, but if you can make the journey, you'll find an abandoned 11th century monastery on the shady slopes of **Mt Hymettus** (Ymittos), and

there are blink-or-miss views if you're able to drive along the mountain rood. Mythical Aphrodite's sacred spring is also the source of the **Ilissos River** which begins here. Best time to go is in the wild-flower-resplendent spring, when you can have a **picnic** on the grounds.

• No food or drink available, apart from spring water. • Stroller accessible only to the church. • Tues–Sun 8am–3pm (2.45pm last entrance). • Adults €2, free under 18 yrs, EU students free, other students half-price. • Continuation of Ethnikis Antistaseos Ave, Kaisariani, Ymittos, 210-723-6619. Get there: Bus no. 250 from Evangelismos Metro station on Line 3 (bus-stops on Vas. Sofias Ave or Rigillis St) to bus-stop: Grammateia, takes you closest, then a long walk (15–30 min) uphill to the monastery and grounds. Journey takes ~an hour.

Natural sciences, environment, agriculture

FREE Antonis Tritsis Park, Ilion *8km/5mi*

If you want to experience and learn about farming and insects as well as reptiles, make the journey to the Antonis Tritsis Park, the largest park in Greater Athens, located in Ilion, north-western Athens.

Once owned by Englishmen and then Queen Amalia in the 19th century, the park covers 120 hectares (300 acres).

This important bird habitat attracts

some 180 varieties that include resident ducks (bring bread), and is rich in biodiversity, with six artificial lakes connected by a small canal, and numerous trails and open spaces to run and play (distances are long—you may want to bring bicycles), plus orchards, a **playground**, small amusement park, and **shops** and **cafes** inside the **Naturashop** complex, which is part of the **Queen's Tower** (Pyrgos Vassilissis) section of the park. In here is a **shop** (*10am to sunset, closed 2pm–5pm in summer and if very hot, open evenings only*) selling wooden toys, natural lotions, bio-clothes, even natural hair dye, a natural food products shop, cafes, and next door is an old **winery**, where you can buy wine from the private estate that still operates alongside the park.

There's also an outlet (*open weekends*) for the **Hellenic Ornithological Society** which sells caps—welcome if you forgot yours on a hot day.

• 23 Spyrou Moustakli St, Ilion, 210-231-6977, www.ornithologiki.gr

Organization Earth is next door, and has a large **gift shop** with toys and a display area where children can learn all about insects. Children (and their parents) can also try their hand at agriculture with volunteers (*pictured*), planting or tending crops to the sounds of classical music from speakers throughout the cultivation site. A "**talking garden**" where the trees tell stories (in Greek) beside the Queen's Tower will have the little ones wondering who's talking. There are stables here with privately boarded show horses, but they are out of bounds.

• *Tues–Sun 10am–8pm.* • *Adults w/ a guide €5.50, 4–18 yrs €3.50. Adults w/o a guide €3.50, 4–18 yrs w/ parents €3.* • *67 Dimokratias Ave, Ilion, 210-232-5380, www.organizationearth.org*

Further along the canal to the main *platèia* or square, near the playground, is the **Greek Reptile Centre**, which has one of the largest collections of reptiles in Europe, comprising snakes, lizards and other reptiles, including the indigenous poisonous viper, six-metre-long pythons, boa constrictors, rattlesnakes, cobras, black mambas and anacondas. Children are allowed to handle the snakes, with the assistance of a handler.

• *Daily 10am–10pm, call if you want to make sure someone's there to assist you, it's the small white building marked "Elliniko Kentro Erpeton".* • *Adults €4, under 3 yrs free, 3 yrs and up €3.* • *Reptile Centre, 210-231-2057, www.erpeta.org*

• *Stroller accessible.* • *Tritsis park open 24 hours.* • ***23 Spyrou Moustakli St, Ilion***, *210-232-3163, www.parkotritsi.gr* • *Entrances on Hasias Ave. (west) and Dimokratias Ave. (east), Ilion.*
Get there*: From Attiki Metro station, bus no. B12 to bus-stop: 6ᵗʰ Hasias; bus no. 704 to bus-stop: Dodekanisou; bus nos. A10, B10 to bus-stop: Proti Polikation (Dimokratias Ave side). Suburban rail Ag. Anagryri or Pyrgos Vassilissis stns. Journey takes 30–60 min. Also info on www.parkotritsi.gr*

History, religion, art, architecture, culture

FREE **Dafni Monastery, Haidari** *10km/6 mi*

An important site near Athens is Dafni (Daphni, Daphne) monastery, which is west of Athens at the end of Iera Odos road. Now in ruins, the main draw here are the remarkable **11ᵗʰ century mosaics**, with charming biblical depictions that include the baptism of Christ, and a Pantocrator said to be the best Byzantine example. But you need to climb ladder steps to see them, so parents will have to take it in turns if caring for little ones. There is also a small **museum** here.

Founded in the 6ᵗʰ century on the site of an ancient temple of Apollo, Ionic columns had been used in its construction, removed by **Lord Elgin** in the 19ᵗʰ century. Originally a three-aisled basilica, which is rare in these parts, it was dedicated to the Dormition of the Virgin in the 11th century (depicted in mosaic) and used as a monastery for Frankish Cistercian monks. By 1458, the then Turkish rulers had returned it to the Orthodox church. During the 19ᵗʰ century Greek War of Independence, it was used as a garrison, and Bavarian troops accompanying the first king of Greece stayed here. It housed psychiatric patients from 1883 to 1885. It was first excavated in 1892 following earthquake damage.

There are two **playgrounds**, one beside the monastery and another in the nearby **Botanical Gardens** (*see Chapter 12*), which has a **canteen**.

• ***No food or drink in the vicinity****.* • *Grounds stroller accessible, but steps and ladder to mosaics.* • *Tues and Fri 9am–2pm.* • *Free entrance.* • ***Dafni Monastery, Haidari***, *210-581-1558, www.culture.gr*
Get there*: Buses leave from Koumoundourou (aka Eleftherias) Sq, near Omonia, heading west on Piraeos (Panagi Tsaldari) St. Bus nos. B16, Γ16, 801, 836, 845, 865, 866 to bus-stop: Moni Dafniou. Journey takes ~45 min.*

History, maritime, environment, industry, society

FREE **Port of Piraeus** *10km/6mi*

The ancient port of Piraeus is the busiest passenger port in Europe and one of the busiest in the world, serving some 20 million passengers a year. The pretty harbour at **Mikrolimani** is lined with seafood tavernas and **café/bars** in front of sailing yachts, but the most impressive is the **main port** at the end of the line for

Metro Line 1 and the suburban rail. It's busy and scruffy, but if your children love boats and if you get the timing right, you will both marvel at the skill of the captains, especially in heavy traffic, who can seemingly turn their lumbering crafts on a dime and "park" in tight spots alongside other equally large ferries (*pictured*). It makes you wonder about all the fuss to catch a boat elsewhere.

• *Stroller accessible on the streets; the overpass elevator outside Piraeus Metro station rarely works. There is an escalator.* • **Port of Piraues, Piraeus**.
Get there: *Piraeus Metro station (terminus) on Line 1. Journey takes ~20 minutes.*

Sports/Olympics history, architecture, society

FREE Olympic Stadium (OAKA), Maroussi *11km/7mi*

Also known as the Olympic Stadium, OAKA was completed in 1982 and named in honour of Greece's first modern Olympics marathon winner, Spiros Louis (1873–1940). Located in Maroussi, some 11km/7mi northeast on arterial Kifissias Ave, the distinctive, arched and braced roof by Spanish architect Santiago Calatrava was added, along with more buildings in the complex, for the 2004 Summer Olympic Games. Closed inside unless an event is taking place.

For 15 or more people, **guided tours** can be arranged at €3 per person, under 12 yrs free. Contact the stadium (210-683-4777) for details.

• *Olympic Centre of Athens, **Maroussi**, 210-683-4060, www.oaka.com.gr*
Get there: *Irini Metro station on Line 1. Journey takes ~30 minutes.*

History, architecture, natural sciences, society

FREE Syngrou Estate park, Maroussi

13km/8mi
Located north of Athens in Maroussi and running alongside Kifissias Ave, is Syngrou Estate park, a large, 97-hectare (240-acre) park of trails through olive groves and pistachio and almond orchards (*pictured*), as well as woodland that includes the Aleppo pine, the sap of which is used to make *retsìna*.

It was the estate of a Greek banker, Andreas Syngros, best known for completing the Corinth Canal.

Bought from an Englishman in 1875, it includes greenhouses (one contains a collection of **cactuses and succulent plants**, *open by appointment*) and buildings designed by Ernst Ziller of Bavaria, the architect of many Athenian buildings, a circa 1880 tower, the country's only Greek Orthodox **Gothic-style chapel** dedicated to St Andrew, and a **mansion** *(open by appt)*. Also a **beekeeping museum** *(open by appt)*.

The park was bequeathed to the state in 1921, upon the death of Syngros's wife, Iphigenia, and is run by the **Institute of Agricultural Sciences**, which holds seminars on topics such as bee-keeping, medicinal plant uses and viticulture.

On the way here, you'll pass the **Olympic Stadium** (OAKA), the outstanding roof of which was designed by Spanish architect Santiago Calatrava and used during the 2004 Olympics.

There's plenty of tree-shade, so suitable in all seasons, and is a nice setting for a picnic, but in summer it's probably too hot during the day.

*• No facilities, food or drink. • Stroller accessible. • Year-round dawn to dusk, except hot and windy days due to fire risk. • The park is fenced but entrance is free (open gates). There are three entrances on Kifissias Ave, as well as entrances on Androu, Efkalypton, and Voreou Epirou sts. • Also **free** **parking** (off Kifissias Ave, Kat hospital traffic light). • 182 Kifissias Ave, Kifissia, 210-801-1146, www.ige.gr*
Get there: Maroussi or KAT Metro station on Line 1 (journey takes ~30 min), then 10 min walk east and across Kifissias Ave; or bus no. 550 (many stops) from Syngrou Ave or Vas. Sofias Ave in town, to "Ktima Syngrou", bus-stops: Aggeioplastiki or KAT.

Play

Balux Café (the House Project), Glyfada   *14km/8.5mi*

This is a popular meeting place (**restaurant/café**) for foreign mothers in Athens of toddlers and young children, as there is also a **playroom**, small **playground**, rides and bouncy castle at the beachside location, with comfy rooms and **pool**.

• Daily. • Pass for games and rides €10. • 58 Poseidonos Ave, Astera Glyfada, 210-898-3577, www.baluxcafe.com
Get there: Bus nos. A2 or E22 from Akadimias St, Panepistimio, or from bus-stops at the top of Syngrou Ave (Makriyanni, Temple of Zeus (Stiles) to bus-stop: Asteria (Glyfada). Tram-stop: Metaxa Aggelou or Kolymbitirio, Asteria. Journey takes 30-60 min.

Natural sciences, environment

FREE Mt Parnitha gondola, Aharnon

18km/11mi

This excursion takes in a 10-minute, free **gondola** ride up Mt Parnitha, perhaps for a buffet **lunch** *(weekends only)* or **dinner** *(daily)* with a view over the city, a short walk, or to hit the **casino** without the kids.

The **Teleferik** gondola *(pictured)* is in Aharnon, north of central Athens, or drive the entire journey (30km/19mi).

There are steps involved at every leg once you get to the Teleferik station, so it's *not stroller-friendly but not impossible.*

At the top, one of you could try the one-armed bandit at the **Regency Casino Mont Parnes** *(Aharnon, 210-242-1234, www.regency.gr)*, which is where you arrive through swank, indoor corridors leading past washrooms to **1055 Café-Restaurant,** where the pleasant grass and panoramic view does not face the fire-damaged hillsides.

• *Buffet €15 per person, under 6 yrs half-price.* • *Daily 8pm–2am, Sat–Sun 1–6pm/8pm–2am.* • *210-242-1055.*

From the hallway you can go downstairs to the **National Forest**, and if you're lucky, spot some deer (check out the window, just before you arrive at the Teleferik entrance on the way back).

It's not much of a walk around the vicinity since the devastating fires of 2007. You'd basically come up here for the gondola ride and views, and the buffet lunch or dinner, which includes salads, hot dishes such as sole and beef, and desserts.

There is *nowhere else to buy food or drink* while here, so if you don't plan on eating at the restaurant buffet or it's closed, at least bring a couple of bottles of water.

FREE While here, check out the environmental exhibits at the **Little Museum of Parnitha.**

• *Daily 10am–6pm.* • *Free entrance.* • *At the main building of the Teleferik (not up the mountain), 210-244-5226.*

• *Gondola takes ~10 minutes, cable-car every 1.5 minutes for 15 persons.* • *Stroller accessible/easy to get on and off.* • *Free entrance.* *Parnitha Teleferik, Aharnon.*

Get there: *There's a bus leaving from the Hilton to the Teleferik daily 2.30pm, arrival at the Teleferik 3.40pm, and leaving from Lavrio Sq (Omonia) at 6.15pm, arrival at the Teleferik 7.10pm. Bus to the Hilton leaves from the Teleferik at 10.30pm and 11.30pm, and bus for Omonia leaves 1.30am. There are also* **taxis** *at the Teleferik station.*

Public bus: *Take bus A10 or B10 to Menidi (Acharnes), bus-stop: Karavos, then by* **taxi**.

Driving: *Take National Road No. 1 (Lamia-bound) to the Metamorfosi exit, then keep left and follow the signs for Parnitha (turn left, over the highway), and straight, along Tatoiou, which turns into Karamanlis and Parnithos aves, following the signs for Parnitha and the Teleferik (gondola cable-car, brown sign). Journey takes ~30 min.*

Natural sciences, zoo

Attica Zoological Park, Spata
22km/13mi

If a zoo is a must-see, come to this popular park on the Attica plain, which covers 47 acres (19 hectares) near the airport. There are about 2,000 birds and many animals, including giraffes, zebras, pygmy hippos, lions, bears, monkeys, and a lemur "cage" you can walk in (*pictured*), plus pony rides. Also a **marine park** with dolphin shows. A **dinosaur museum** is in the works. **Café** on site.

• *Stroller accessible.* • *Daily 9am–sunset.* • *Adults €15, 3–12 yrs €11, family (2+2) €48, family (2+3) €58.* • *Yalou, Spata.* 210-663-4724, www.atticapark.com

Get there: Bus no. 319 from Doukissis Plakentias Metro station on Line 3, Christoupoli-bound, to bus-stop: Irodotou. **Driving**: Take Attiki Odos toll-road (www.aodos.gr) from the airport to exit 18 (Spata) or from Elefsina to exit 16P (Rafina). Journey takes ~an hour.

History, nature, culture, society

FREE Tatoi Royal Estate, Parnitha foothills
27km/16mi
Royalists and history buffs might want to make the journey out to Tatoi, northwest of Athens. Currently it's a rather sad, rundown place since the core 1,800 hectare estate of some 40 buildings

(*pictured*) dating to the 19th century have been closed and neglected since 1967, when King Constantine II and his family made a hasty exit following a military coup.

Some pieces of machinery, including cars, remain in situ, as if time stopped decades ago. Apart from the closed main residence—the grand but modest summer palace in the foothill pine forests of Mt Parnitha—there are also smaller buildings of charming architecture, and a long-empty swimming pool down what would have been a stately set of steps to the bottom of the garden.

Following the abolition of the monarchy in 1974 and after a long legal battle, the European Court of Human Rights finally awarded the estate to Greece in 2003, with monetary compensation given to the former king and his family.

Typically, many agencies are responsible for different areas of the 4,700-hectare (11,600-acre) site; many of the buildings are listed for preservation and are the purview of the culture ministry, which reportedly intends to turn it into a museum, or sell it, given the nation's protracted economic woes.

There is free entrance to the grounds and the **cemetery** of early royalty on Paleokastro Hill, including the tomb of King Alexander located inside the mausoleum and who, most unusually, died of infection from a monkey bite.

There are also the simple graves of Paul and Frederika, Constantine's parents, and other members of the royal family.

The paths are *easy to walk or stroller*, and there are **toddler swings** here, where the path begins to the hilltop cemetery and chapel.

• **No facilities, food or drink.** • *Daily until sunset.* • *Free entrance.* • **Tatoiou St, Parnitha.**
Get there: *Driving (no public transport): Take National Road No. 1 northbound, across Attiki Odos to Tatoi exit and onto Tatoiou St. Many entrances to the estate, which are not signed. Journey takes ~an hour.*

Play activities

Adventure Park, Malakasa *39km/24mi*

Pretend to be Indiana Jones or another action hero, climbing or swinging through the trees on various apparatuses at Adventure Park. Also bungee jumping, trampoline, archery.

• *Activities for 3 yrs and up.* • *Bring a picnic lunch with you, or visit a nearby taverna.* • *Wed–Sun 10am to sunset, and daily during school holidays, including the summer, unless weather is bad. Call beforehand.* • *Entrance €2, but activities such as flying routes, bungee jumping, trampoline and archery run from €6 to €25 for combined activities, including the entrance fee.* • **Adventure Park, Malakasa**, *210-3329-0985, 22950-98335, www.adventure-park.gr*
Get there: *From Victoria station on Metro Line 1, 5 minutes' walk east on Heyden St to Mavromataion St, the terminus for the* **KTEL long-distance bus** *(210-880-8000, www.ktelattikis.gr), destination Skala Oropou, leaves every two hours and stops outside the park. KTEL bus tickets €3.70, under 6 yrs free.*
Driving: *National Road No. 1 Athens–Lamia, Malakasa, 2nd exit after Markopoulo-Oropou exit and along the side-road heading north, there are signs for the park. Journey takes ~ hour.*

History, architecture, culture, mythology

Temple of Poseidon, Sounion *69km/43mi*

The Temple of Poseidon at the end of the promontory at **Sounion**, south of Athens, is on the excursion map and worth a visit, especially at sunset, when it's also busiest. What remains of the 5th century BC temple are columns, famously grafitti'd by **Lord Byron**. In mythology, this is the place where King Aegeus waited for his son, Theseus, to return from killing the Minotaur in Crete. If he lived, the sail would be white, if not, it would be black. A victorious Theseus forgot to change the sail and his father, upon seeing it black, fell to his death in sorrow. The Aegean sea is named after him.

• **Restaurant** *near the site.* • *Stroller with difficulty to get up to the site.* • *Daily 9.30am–sunset, last entrance a half-hour before sunset. Closed national holidays.* • *Adults €4, under 18 yrs free. Organized tours are ~€40.* • **Nao, Sounio**, *22920-39363, www.culture.gr*
Get there: *KTEL buses (210-880-8080, www.ktelattikis.gr, €6.30) ply the route along the coast, which leaves from Patission St at Aigyptou Sq near the National Archaeological Museum, leaving hourly from 6.30am to 6.30pm; departing Sounion from 5.40am (from 8am Sun) to 9pm, or get on at KTEL bus-stops along the route through town. Journey is ~2 hours.*

Activities, natural history, natural sciences, aquatic

DIVING EXCURSION, LESSONS

If here for a few days or longer, take advantage of the warm seas and numerous diving sites around Attica by taking a couple of lessons or going on a dive. All offer PADI and other courses, including for beginners.

Athina Diving

This outfit on the south coast offers shore dives for €20 and wreck dives for €50 among others. Starter courses include skin diving, discover scuba, and a two-day scuba diving license course.

• *38th klm Athens–Sounion Road,* **Lagonissi**, *22910-25434, www.athinadiving.gr*

Aqua Divers Club
ADC on the south coast regularly teaches ex-pat children from 8 yrs.
• *P. Fokea, **Anavyssos**, 22910-53461, www.aquadiversclub.gr*

Divers Club
This one is in the Marathon/Nea Makri (east coast) area.
• *417 Marathonas Ave, **Nea Makri**, 22940-69196, www.diversclub.gr*

Paralos Diving Academy
Paralos is located in the northern suburbs.
• *40 Agiou Konstantinou St, **Maroussi**, 210-610-5202, www.paralos.net*

Sotiriou Diving Centre
This one is located in town.
• *33 Taxilou St, **Ilissia**, 210-770-5470, www.scubagreece.gr*

Drawing (card for cousin Lazaros), Dec 2012 ☺ 5 yrs

Disney on Ice is a spectacle for pre-schoolers, Tae Kwon Do Centre, Faliro

Chapter 10: Leisure & Entertainment

Greeks love **theatre**, and there are many playhouses around the country. Most performances are in Greek but there are also shows for children, and some where language is no barrier. They usually take place in the winter season, from October to May or June.

To see what's on, check *www.ellthea.gr* and *www.viva.gr*.

Arts and entertainment events, exhibitions and programs for kids are also noted in the weekly *Athinorama* listings magazine (in Greek, ask your hotel for assistance) or see *www.athinorama.gr*.

The daily *Kathimerini* inside the *International Herald Tribune* lists some events of interest to **English-speaking** readers, including for kids. Check the Cultural Diary in *www.ekathimerini.com*.

For **music acts and concerts**, check *www.rockpages.gr, www.qubo.gr* (click "events"), Ticket House *(42 Panepistimiou St, Korai Square area, 210-360-8366; www.tickethouse.gr)*, and *www.ticketshop.gr, 211-955-2300*.

• *On the calendar **sample*** in autumn 2012 (ie check organizers and venues):

Red Hot Chili Peppers at OAKA stadium (*Irini Metro station on Line 1*) (*www.didimusic.gr*), Dead Can Dance at the open-air Lycabettus Theatre (*www.didimusic.gr*); Cirque Du Soleil at OAKA basketball stadium (*www.lavris.gr*); Disney on Ice at the **Tae Kwon Do Centre**, Faliro (*tram-stop: Agia Skepi), (www.abcd.gr)*; Coldplay at the Concert Hall (*www.megaron.gr*).

Live Shows, Events, Exhibitions

VENUES

Badminton Theatre

This playhouse in **Goudi** (6km/3.5mi) hosts many international acts (*pictured, Denmark's 'Flying Superkids'*) and concerts.

• Badminton Theatre, **Goudi**, 210-884-0600, www.abcd.gr, www.badmintontheatre.gr
Get there: Katehaki Metro station on Line 3, exit for Katehaki (Kanellopoulos) Ave towards the hospital, then ~10–15 minutes' walk. After the second traffic light (from Messogion Ave), enter the pedestrian entrance of Goudi Park alongside the fence, walk straight through the gate, where signs lead after 300 metres to the theatre.

Coronet Theatre

The **Coronet** in **Pangrati**, in the area behind the Panathenian Stadium, often has children's performances, such as foreign magic acts.

• 11 Frinis and Ymittou sts, **Pangrati**, 210-701-2123, www.coronet.gr
Get there: Trolley no. 11 to bus-stop: Pl. Pangratiou.

Dora Stratou Theatre

From Pnyx Hill, signs along the path (*but you can't take a stroller through this entrance*) lead to the outdoor **Dora Stratou Theatre**, where samples of **Greek folk dances to live music** (*pictured*) have been performed for more than 50 years.

The elderly singer, Yiota Pantazi, also has an astonishingly beautiful voice.

This unique event under the stars lasts about an hour and is also something to enjoy with older kids, while younger ones (any age) are also welcome.

• Stroller accessible from the main entrance. • Performances June–Sept (closed a few days in August—check the website), Tues–Sun ~8.30pm. • 210-324-4395 (**office: 8 Scholiou St, Plaka**), 210-921-4650 (theatre), www.grdance.org • Tickets €15, under 5 yrs free, 5–15 yrs €10; ▓FREE▓ may offer free entrance in late summer: check at the office. **Dora Stratou Theatre, Pnyx Hill, Ano Petralona**.

Get there: You can reach the theatre via a path on Pnyx Hill, or by going along the road around the hill if you have a stroller. Or Petralona Metro station on Line 1 and trolley no. 15, bus-stop: Filopappou, or bus no. 227, bus-stop: Dryopon, then 15 minutes' walk.

Megaron Mousikis (Concert Hall)

The Megaron Mousikis or Athens Concert Hall (*pictured*), holds **Sunday morning performances** that give priority to children, to familiarize them with **music and classical** performances, and gives them the opportunity for interactive play (€8). They also offer reduced rates or ticket sales on the day of regular performances. Check the events list on their website, or call 210-728-2333 for information.

• *Vas. Sofias Ave and Kokkali St, **Embassy district**, 210-728-2000, www.megaron.gr*
Get there: Megaron Mousikis Metro station on Line 3 (two stops from Syntagma), Parko (Park) Eleftherias exit, then few minutes' walk past the park heading north/east.

Michael Cacoyannis Foundation

All kinds of performances (opera, concerts, theatre, children's plays, cinema…) as well as art exhibits take place at one of the city's newest venues.

• *206 Piraeos St, near Hamosternas Ave, **Tavros**, 210-341-8550, www.mcf.gr*
Get there: Bus nos. 049, 815, 914 to bus-stop: Tavros, or Tavros Metro station on Line 1, then 10–15 minutes' walk.

National Opera

The **National Opera** (Olympia) has a children's stage, putting on performances such as the "Nutcracker" **ballet** over the holidays and "Little Red Riding Hood" through the end of April 2013.

• *59–61 Akadimias St, **Omonia**, 210-366-2100, www.nationalopera.gr*

Onassis Cultural Centre

Music, dance, art, theatre and other events take place at another new venue in Athens.

• *107–109 Syngrou Ave, **Neos Kosmos**, info/tickets 210-900-5800, admin 213-017-8000, www.sgt.gr.*
Get there: Trolley no. 10, bus nos. A2, B2, E22, E90, 040, 550 to bus-stop: Panteios or tram-stop: Kasomouli, then 5 minutes' walk.

Parnassos Concert Hall

Classical piano music lovers can also see concerts at reasonable prices right in central Athens in the **Piano Forte** series.

• *Tickets from €5, and include an €20-ticket for families of five. Tickets available at Eleftheroudakis bookstore, 11 Panepistimiou (El. Venizelou) St, call 13855, or book online at www.viva.gr*
• *Karytsi Square, near Kolokotroni and Stadiou sts, **Syntagma**, www.pianostaforte.com*

Theocharakis Foundation

International art exhibits, music performances and other events take place at the Theocharakis Foundation in central Syntagma. Also a **café** and **gift shop** with child-friendly items.

• *9 Vas. Sofias Ave /1 Merlin St, **Syntagma**, 210-361-1206, www.thf.gr*

SHADOW PUPPET PLAYS

Unique and popular with children are the shadow puppet theatre performances (*Karagiòzis*). Poking fun at current or historic events, the main character, poor Karagiozi, is seen alone or with friends in either heroic or ridiculous situations, such as flying in space (***pictured***), skiing down a mountain, or taking part in the Olympics. **Unima Hellas** (*www.unimahellas.org*) has info on the theatres.

Koukles kai Figoures (*pictured*) is a theatre located in Plaka: call or drop by for show times.
• *30 Tripodon St, **Plaka**, 210-322-7507.*

Sunday performances (in Greek) take place at the **Michael Cacoyannis Foundation**.
• *206 Piraeos St, near Hamostemas Ave, **Tavros**, 210-341-8550, www.mcf.gr*
Get there: *Bus nos. 049, 815, 914 to bus-stop: Tavros, or Tavros Metro station on Line 1, then 10-15 minutes' walk.*

Bowling

Blanos Bowling

Down the south coast in Glyfada, Blanos is suited for older children (bumper rails), as well as **disco roller skating**, billiards and arcade games.

• *Mon–Fri 5pm–1am, Sat–Sun 10am–1am. Mon–Fri €3 per game, Sat–Sun €4; **roller skating** €7 includes rental. • **Dousmani and 81 Vas. Georgiou sts, Glyfada**, 210-898-0159, www.blanosbowling.gr*
Get there: *Bus nos. A2, A3, E22 from Akadimias St, Panepistimio to bus-stop: Plateia Glyfadas; tram-stop: Agg. Metaxa, then 5 minutes' walk.*

Odeon Starcity Planet Bowling

This alley (*pictured*) and game arcade is near the Intercontinental and Ledra Marriott hotels but it's not for small children (under 5 yrs) as the balls are large for 10-pin bowling. They carry small shoe sizes and have gutter bumpers (never a gutterball).

• *Mon–Thurs 4pm–2am, adults €3, children/students €2.50; Fri–Sun 10am–2am, adults €4, children/students €3.50.* • **Odeon Starcity, 111 Syngrou Ave and Leontiou St, Neos Kosmos**, *210-610-1400, www.starcity.gr*
Get there: *Bus nos. 2, 22, 90, 040, 550, 106, 126, 134, 135, 136, 137, trolley no. 10 to bus-stop: Panteios; tram-stop: Kasomouli, then 5–10 minutes' walk. ~10 min from the centre.*

Cinema

See what's playing through the English-language websites *athens.angloinfo.com* or *www.xpatathens.com*, or have someone help you find out by looking up *www.athinorama.gr*, the authority in up-to-date listings. Adult-oriented (I mean for grown-ups) movies are normally in English with Greek subtitles, but nearly all the children's movies are **dubbed into Greek**, unless stated otherwise—you need to scour the listings. These films usually play at the multiplex cinemas.

Odeon Starcity

Odeon Starcity is near the Intercontinental and Ledra Marriott hotels, on arterial Syngrou Ave that leads to the south coast. Order tickets online, adults €7.50, 3D movies €10. They also have 3D and interactive theatre for children in winter.

• *English-language programs (films or interactive) info: Mon–Fri 10am–1pm, 210-678-6581, www.cinemapark.gr* • **111 Syngrou Ave and Leontiou St, Neos Kosmos**, *801-116-0000, www.odeon.gr*
Get there: *Bus nos. 2, 22, 90, 040, 550, 106, 126, 134, 135, 136, 137, trolley no. 10 to bus-stop: Panteios; or tram-stop: Kasomouli, then 5–10 minutes' walk. About 10 min journey from the centre.*

Village

Two multiplexes are within striking distance of central Athens, and this one is in a mall (Athens Metro Mall) on a Metro line. Order tickets online, adults €7, students €5, 3D movies are adults €12 and children €11.

• *276 Vouliagmenis Ave, **Agios Dimitrios**, tel 14848, www.villagecinemas.gr*
Get there: *Agios Dimitrios Metro station on Line 2, Ioannou Metaxa St exit (front of the train).*

OPEN-AIR CINEMA

Experience watching a film under the stars in summer—a unique, now protected part of the Mediterranean heritage. *Tickets are ~€9 for adults.*

Aegli, Zappeio

The oldest (circa 1903) of the outdoor theatres is Aegli in Zappeion Gardens.

• *Beside Zappeion Hall, **Zappeio**, 210-336-9369, www.aeglizappiou.gr*

Cine Paris, Plaka

A rooftop open-air cinema is in **Plaka**, **Cine Paris** (*pictured*).
• *22 Kydathinaion St, **Plaka**, 210-322-2071.*

Thission, Thissio

Thission (circa 1935) screens classic and contemporary films in two showings, usually around 9pm and 11pm, which is quieter (volume turned down). Sit under the stars in the garden, which has a canteen, small tables and chairs.
• *7 Apostolou Pavlou St, **Thissio**, 210-347-0980.*

Golf

Glyfada Golf Course is an 18-hole, par-72 course is on the south coast in Glyfada. The Municipality of Glyfada manages the course.
• *Mon 1pm–sunset, Tues–Sun from 7am or 8am-sunset. On weekends you must book a time with the municipality.* • *9 holes €50, 18 holes €62, both courses €90, no discounts for children.* • ***Glyfada Golf, Glyfada**, 210-894-6820, www.glyfada.gr*
Get there: *Bus nos. A2, A3, B3 to bus-stop: 3rd Glyfadas; or tram-stop: Plateia Vergoti. ~30–40 min journey, then 10–15 minutes' walk.*

Ice Skating

During the winter months small temporary ice rinks set up at some malls, where you can rent skates and equipment such as double "bladed" ones for children and chair supports. Cost is free to €10, including skate rental and often, lessons. The surface quality varies, with more imperfections and ice shavings than would be found at a permanent rink.

Athens Heart Mall

The mall sets up a large, 1,000m2 covered rink (*pictured*) (*Ice Arena, 694-066-5707, www.icearena.gr*) from end-October to end-April. Entrance from "0" floor inside the mall, opposite Sklavenitis supermarket.
• *Daily 11am–11pm.* • *Skate rental and entrance €10, no time limit.* • ***180 Piraeos St at Hamosternas Ave, Tavros**, 210-341-4105, www.athensheart.gr*
Get there: *Bus nos. 049, 914 (from Athinas or Piraeos sts), 815 (from Vas. Sofias, Panepistimiou or Piraeos sts) to bus-stop: Ergon, suburban train (Proastiakos) to Rouf station. Journey takes ~10 min.*

Athens Metro Mall

A small rink may be set up beside the **Volta Fun Park** (*210-975-0630*, *www.voltafunpark.gr)* indoor play area on the 2nd floor. Small support chairs with handles for young skaters available.

• *276 Vouliagmenis Ave,* ***Agios Dimitrios****, 210-976-9444,* _www.athensmetromall.gr_
Get there*: Agios Dimitrios Metro station on Line 2, Vouliagmenis/Metaxa St exit. Journey ~15 min.*

Blanos Sports Park

This complex has an **indoor ice-skating rink, bowling alley, children's play area** (includes bouncy slide), bar, and other enticements.

• *Mon–Fri 5pm–midnight, weekends/holidays 10am–2am.* • ***Bowling*** *Mon–Fri €3 per game, Sat–Sun €4.* • ***Ice skating*** *Mon–Fri €6 includes skates, Sat–Sun €9.* • ***Paidotopos*** *(children's play area): 210-663-5825.* • *Mesogeia, on the 1ˢᵗ klm of the Pikermi–Spata road,* ***near the town of Spata and Athens International Airport****. 210-663-5835,* _www.blanospark.gr_
Get there: *Bus nos. 304, 316 from Nomismatokopeio stn on Line 3 or 319 from Douk. Plakentias on Line 3 to bus-stop: Strophi, then taxi 1km on Pikermiou Rd. Journey ~1+ hours.*

Technopolis cultural centre

Gazi may also have a temporary rink set up in December/January. Support chairs with handles for young skaters.

• *€4, skates included.* • ***100 Piraeos St, Gazi****, 210-347-5518,* _www.technopolis-athens.com_
Get there*: Walking distance from Thissio (10 min) and Kerameikos (5 min) Metro stations on Lines 1 and 3 respectively.*

White Fantasy, Marina Alimou

A 500m2 temporary rink (*pictured*) is set up under a white tented structure beside Alimou Park, between the seaside promenade and Poseidonos Ave. Support chairs with handles for young skaters. There's a **canteen** nearby, or go to **Ostria Cafe**.

• *Nov–March Mon–Fri 4pm–11pm, Sat–Sun, holidays 10am–midnight.* • *€8 skates included, unlimited time, €7 for a 15-min lesson.* • ***Beside Alimos Park, Alimos****, 210-531-0819,* _www.whitefantasy.gr_*. On the waterfront next to Ostria Café on Poseidonos Ave, end of Kalamakiou Ave.*
Get there*: 10 min by taxi down Syngrou Ave or 45 min by tram to stop: Kalamaki. Bus nos. E22, A2, B2 from Akadimias St to bus-stop: 4ᵗʰ Kalamaki.*

Ash Monday kite-flying at Filopappou Hill. See what's on during your trip

Chapter 11: Events & Holidays

Many festivals, religious festivities and special events take place throughout the year, many offering an unexpectedly welcome dimension to the trip, such as Christmas, Easter, and Carnival in Athens and around Greece.

Museums and sites closed days

Museums may not be open during public holidays, or else have reduced hours. The hours of operation usually change in April/May and October, staying open longer during the summer months. Check www.culture.gr or call ahead.

State-run sites and museums are **closed**: January 1, March 25, Orthodox Good Friday morning (*April 18, 2014; April 10, 2015*), Orthodox Easter Sunday (*April 20, 2014; April 12, 2015*), May 1, December 25–26, and occasionally when there is a strike.

State-run sites and museums observe their **Sunday schedule**: January 6, Orthodox Ash (Clean) Monday (*March 3, 2014; February 23, 2015*), Orthodox Easter Saturday (*April 19, 2014; April 11, 2015*), Orthodox Easter Monday (*April 21, 2014; April 13, 2015*), Orthodox Whit Sunday (*June 24, 2013; June 9, 2014; June 1, 2015*), August 15, October 28.

National Holidays

JAN 1: New Year's Day. New Year's Eve celebrations at main city squares; Agios Vassilis (name day) is the Greek version of Santa Claus.

JAN 6: **Epiphany**. People gather to celebrate blessing of the water at a holy spring or by the sea. The water is taken home and sprinkled in the house to bless it. In **Piraeus**, near Athens, and elsewhere, people dive in to retrieve a cross.

FEB OR MAR: **Clean (Ash) Monday (*Katharà Deftèra*)**. People traditionally prepare a Lenten picnic of pickles, beans, *dolmades* (rice stuffed vine leaves), salads and seafood, and go to a park to fly kites on the first day of Lent. **Filopappou Hill (*pictured, beginning of the chapter*)** in Athens is the most popular site with Greek dancing and singing, and kites (often flimsy) can be bought from itinerant sellers near the hill. *(March 3, 2014; February 23, 2015)*.

MAR 25: **Independence Day** and the **Feast of the Annunciation**. The day commemorates Bishop Germanos of Agia Lavra monastery in the Peloponnese's gesture of raising the Greek flag in 1821 in defiance of 400 years of Ottoman rule, marking the beginning of the fight for independence, achieved in 1829. Parades take place on central Amalias Ave in Athens.

MARCH, APRIL OR MAY: **Orthodox Easter (*Pàscha*). Easter Sunday, Easter Monday**. Usually takes place a week later than Western Easter, this is Greece's most celebrated holiday, and Holy Week, the week before Easter Sunday, has its own traditions.

On **Tuesday** homes and pathways in the countryside are whitewashed, on **Wednesday** holy oil is brought home to bless the house, on **Thursday**, scriptures are read about the Last Supper, people take communion, there is an all-night vigil, and the souls of the dead, including Christ's, are believed to descend. Eggs are boiled and dyed red symbolizing the blood of Christ and rebirth, and sweet Easter bread (*tsourèki*) is baked. On **Good Friday**, church bells toll solemnly throughout the day, and at around 8pm, parishioners join a procession of the funeral bier (*epitàphios*) around the neighbourhood (*pictured, in Thissio*).

Agia Marina church in Thissio is popular as it meets up with nearby **Agios Athanasios church** parishioners on pedestrian Apostolou Pavlou St, and then turn around and continue on their way.

On **Saturday**, any remaining spirits are scared away that might hinder the Resurrection (*Anàstasi*) which takes place at midnight, signaled by a peeling of bells and the priest's words that Christ is Risen (*Christos Anèsti*). Candles are lit from a flame brought from Jerusalem and passed around, and people bring the flame home to draw a cross with the smoke on their doorframes to bless the household. Youths usually set off a lot of firecrackers near the church, so bring earplugs or stuff your baby's/toddler's ears with tissue. At home, people break the Lenten fast by eating soup made of lamb's innards, and the lamb is roasted on a spit (normally) on **Sunday**, with much celebration. The church service celebrates the Resurrection in many languages, symbolizing unity (*agàpi*). **Easter Monday** is a **national holiday**. *(April 20&21, 2014; April 12&13, 2015).*

MAY 1: Labour Day, May Day (*Protomaià*). International Labour Day commemorates the strike in the US and Canada when six people died in a crackdown in Chicago on May 1, 1886, still remembered in Europe. Flower wreaths are hung on the doors, and people go on picnics.

MAY OR JUNE: Whit Monday. *(June 24, 2013; June 9, 2014; June 1, 2015).*

AUG 15: Assumption of the Virgin. Most Greeks go on their annual holidays during this feast day, celebrated at namesake churches around the country and especially on the island of Tinos, where pilgrims head to the church dedicated to the Panagia Evangelistria in droves.

OCT 28: Ochi (No) Day. Commemorates the day the Greek prime minister denied Italy's "request" to enter the country during WWII. Greece handed the Allies their first land victory after routing the Italians. Parades take place in Thessaloniki.

Nov 17: Unofficial holiday marking the student uprising against the American-backed 1967–74 junta, commemorated by a march to the US Embassy. Many businesses stay closed, expecting violence, especially along the route.

DEC 25 and 26:
Christmas. Christmas in Athens can be magical, as trees lining roads and street lamps are festooned with lights. **Christmas trees** are decorated at central squares, especially Syntagma, which also may host a free carousel, free ice skating, and seasonal street stalls. There are many events, including a children's display and

activities inside the **National Gardens (*pictured*)** There may also be children's events at **Technopolis** (*check the City of Athens site at www.cityofathens.gr*) Look for **special packages**, as luxury hotels and restaurants offer tantalizing menus on Christmas Eve and New Year's Eve. *Check the City of Athens website www.breathtakingathens.com for events, and www.all-athens-hotels.com for luxury hotel special menus during events and holidays.*

Other Annual Events in Greece

JAN 30: **Nationwide**. Churches dedicated to **Trion Ierarchon** (Basil, Gregory, John—the three hierarchs) celebrate. Religious trinkets and items are sold in stalls that open near the church, one of which is on Trion Ierarchon St, near Thissio.

FEBRUARY: **Nationwide**. **Carnival** (*Apòkri-es*) takes place for the three weeks preceding Lent. Children dress up in costumes for their Sunday outings, many villages celebrate in unique ways, and in Athens, the **Plaka** district is fair game for head-bopping with plastic bats, amid the confetti and streamers. The port city of Patras has the best-known parades and displays. The last weekend is the most intense.

MAR-MAY: **Athens**. **Fun runs** around the city organized by the **City of Athens** includes a ▮FREE▮ **3km/2mi run** open to children 9+ yrs, as well as a half-marathon (21km/13mi) and one that's 8km/5mi. Start is at the Panathenian Stadium. Check for these and other exhibitions and events through *www.breathtakingathens.com*.
• *63A Athinas St, **Agora**, 210-372-2001, www.cityofathens.gr, or SEGAS, 137 Syngrou Ave, **Nea Smyrni**, 210-933-1113, www.segas.gr or www.athinahalfmarathon.gr*

MID-MAY: **Athens**. An **international art fair** of modern art, with paintings, sculpture, installations, video art and photography, **Art-Athina**, takes place at the Faliro Pavilion (*210-330-3533, www.art-athina.gr*).

MAY-OCTOBER: **Athens and around Greece**. **Athens and Epidaurus Festival** events, with ancient Greek dramas staged plus a roster of concerts and dance performances in the ancient, open-air Irodion Theatre (*pictured*), aka **Herodes Atticus Odeon** (*210-324-2121 or 210-323-2771*) in Athens (*no children under 6 yrs*); at the **Ancient Epidavros Theatre** (*27530-22026, 27530-22666 or 27530-23009*) in the Peloponnese (*same-day transport arranged, no children under 6 yrs*); and many other venues around the country. **Tickets** can be bought at the venue, by phone, online, at **Public** department store (*1 Karageorgi Servias St, **Syntagma Sq**, 210-324-6210, www.public.gr*) and

Papasotiriou (book stores, *www.papasotiriou.gr*), and at the **Athens Epidaurus Festival's central box office.**
• *39 Panepistimiou St (sign-posted El Venizelou) in the arcade, Panepistimio, 210-327-2000 or 210-928-2900, www.greekfestival.gr*

MAY 21: **Crete** commemorates the WWII **Battle of Crete** with the Allies. In villages such as Agia Eleni in **Thrace**, northwestern Greece, and Langada **near Thessaloniki**, northern Greece, **fire-walking**, a throw-back to pagan times, takes place on **St Constantine and Helen** day.

MAY-JULY: **Rhodes.** A **mediaeval fair** takes place around historically mediaeval venues with plays, team games, costumes, music, sports including sword fights and treasure hunts, arts and crafts and more.
• *22410-74405, www.medievalfestival.gr*

JUNE: **Rhodes. Rhodes Rock** (*www.classicrocktours.com*) does a **classic rock music festival** at St Paul's Bay in Lindos on the island of Rhodes each year in June, with bands playing old favourites, including Jimi Hendrix, ZZ Top, Queen, Pink Floyd and many more.

JUNE 17: **Nationwide. Agia Marina church** in **Thissio**, Athens, has its saint's day festival, with many icons and street food for sale at the **evening outdoor fair** that lines Agia Marinas St until the Acropolis walkway at Apostolou Pavlou St, opposite Thissio Square.

SUMMER SOLSTICE: **European Music Day.** The year's best new artists perform at public squares.

JUNE/JULY: **Athens.** Summer **Rockwave Festival** (*210-882-0426, www.rockwavefestival.gr*)—big name international line-up plays over three days at Terra Vibe venue in **Malakasa**, 37km/23mi from Athens. In 2012, Ozzy Osbourne, Slash, The Prodigy and Lynrd Skynrd featured.
• *3 Eptanissiou and 2 Pipinou sts, Kypseli, 210-882-0426, www.didimusic.gr*
Get there: *Malakasa, 37th klm Athens-Lamia National Road, or from Sfendali rail station, chartered bus also available.*

JUNE: **Nafplio.** Cultural events take place in venues such as the mediaeval **Palamidi fortress** and Agios Georgios church courtyard.
• *27520-27153, www.nafplionfestival.gr*

AUGUST: **Nationwide.** FREE During the **full moon**, many archaeological sites are open at night and events take place, such as live music and orchestras, discounted performances at Dora Stratou (Greek dance) theatre, or the dolphin show at the Attica Zoo. Events at state-run sites are announced by the culture ministry (*www.yppo.gr*); whose staff are likely working for free on the night. Ask at your hotel for the latest events (announced close to the day), or check *www.breathtakingathens.com*.

SEPTEMBER 8 (NEAREST SATURDAY): **Spetses.** The role of the island in the Greek War of Independence is commemorated by re-enacting a Greek warship heading off the Turkish flagship in the island's harbour, known as the **Spetses Armata.**

EARLY SEPTEMBER: **Thessaloniki**. The prime minister makes his annual economic speech at the **International Trade Fair**.
• *2310-129111, www.tif.gr*

OCTOBER 26: **Thessaloniki**. Much celebration for **St Demetrius**, the northern port city's patron saint.

NOVEMBER, SECOND SUNDAY: **Athens**. **Athens Classic Marathon**, the original, commemorating Pheidippides' fatal journey over 42km/26 miles to announce "Nike" (victory) against the Persians' at the 490 BC Battle of Marathon. It starts from the city of Marathon 42km/26mi from Athens to the Panathenian Stadium. There are parallel races of 5km, 10km, power-walking, and a 420metre/yard **children's marathon** for 4–12 yrs.
• *SEGAS Marathon office, 137 Syngrou Ave, Ag. Sostis, **Nea Smyrni**, 210-933-1113, www.athensclassicmarathon.gr*

EARLY NOVEMBER: **Thessaloniki**. **International Film Festival** has been running since 1960.
• *2310-378400, www.filmfestival.gr*

Santa delivering presents, Dec 2012 ☺ 5 yrs

Playgrounds (here Thissio) can be full at 9pm in summer (10pm dinner hour)

Chapter 12: Parks, Playgrounds & Indoor Play Areas

The location of a playground is usually one of the most important considerations for young families, yet is often absent from travel guides.

In Athens there are a few green spaces here and there, but not all are child-friendly, and there are only a few **playgrounds** in central Athens, with none in the historic or commercial centre.

Maps are often out-dated and show playgrounds that are closed, non-existent, or else turn out to be tiny basketball courts. On the plus side, when you do find them, they are fenced, safe places to go well into the night in summer. Some close from 3pm to 5pm due to the heat, but are open until 9.30–10pm to compensate, with even very young children enjoying the playground when the temperature is cooler, especially after being pent up in apartments (or hotel rooms). Parents bring their children to these and to local squares from around 7pm in summer, since the daytime heat is too intense.

Note that all references to "winter" include spring and autumn, ie when daytime temperatures are bearable, in the following descriptions.

Play areas are also **rated** from 1 to 5, with an explanation of why they lose points.

Paidòtopos are **indoor or outdoor child activity places** and soft play areas with bouncy castles, slides or other equipment. In Greece they are **supervised**, so you can leave your child from 3 yrs and up (go in with your child if younger), and sit at the **café** (always licensed!), or even go off shopping if the place is located in a mall. Selected **amusement (aka Luna) parks** are also mentioned below.

The locations of the following playgrounds are plotted on a Google map: *http://goo.gl/maps/IEnSh*

Playgrounds (by area)

MONASTIRAKI, THISSIO, ANO PETRALONA

Thissio Square playground, Thissio

Rate: 4 (small)
Location: Central Athens, west border of the Ancient Agora.
Nearest areas: Thissio, Monastiraki, Psyrri.
Nearest hotels: O+B, Phidias, Jason Inn.
Nearest sites: Ancient Agora, Acropolis, Pnyx Hill.
Better for summer or winter (shade/shelter): Shade from trees; good year-round.
Equipment: Two bucket swings, two regular swings, see-saw, small slide, and a makeshift "sandpit" by the tree.
Toilets: No, but there are many cafes in the vicinity.
Fenced: Yes.
Stroller accessible: Yes.
Age appropriate (eg bucket swings for babies): Babies to 10 yrs.
Details: The Thissio Square playground is nearest for those staying around Monastiraki and Thissio. This is a small, friendly park with a view of the Acropolis (great photo opportunities) on the pedestrian walkway that's handy for getting some playtime, fresh air, and letting off energy. It can get quite busy.

Hours: Gates are always open.
Where: *Thissio Sq*, Apostolou Pavlou St, beside entrance to the Ancient Agora, at the top of Nileos, Akamandos, and Irakleidon sts.
Get there: Thissio Metro station on Line 1, then 5 minute's walk; or Monastiraki Metro station on Lines 1, 3, then 10 minutes' walk. On the pedestrian walkway from the Acropolis or from Thissio station, it's just north of Thissio Sq, beside the small football/soccer court and Thissio Park.
Geotag: @37.974921,23.720341

Kymaion St playground, Thissio, Ano Petralona

Spacious, old-fashioned, and sadly, under-used

Rate: 4 (short open hours)

Location: West side of central Athens.

Nearest areas: Thissio, Ano Petralona, Psyrri, Gazi.

Nearest hotels: Jason Inn, Phidias.

Nearest sites: Nymphon Hill, Pnyx Hill, Dora Stratou Theatre, Gazi.

Better for summer or winter (shade/shelter): Shade from trees, good year-round.

Equipment: Toddler swings, two regular swings, see-saw, slide.

Toilets/facilities: Toilet (squat) available but filthy. 4yo didn't want to go in.

Fenced: Yes.

Stroller accessible: Yes, but over a gate.

Age appropriate (eg toddler swings for babies): Babies to 10 yrs.

Details: This is a nice grassy park with a lot of space close to Filopappou Hill. It's a pleasant, shady area used mainly by locals but is run by an elderly woman with a large dog (fenced in but barking) who lives on site. The land was bequeathed for children's use but the caretaker adheres more to the letter than the spirit of the largesse, with very limited opening times. Children finish school ~1pm (when it closes). The park was temporarily closed in April 2013.

Hours: Winter: 9am–1pm/4pm–6.30pm. Summer: 9am–12.30pm/6pm–8.30pm. Closed Sundays.

Where: Thissio, near Pnyx and Nymphon Hills, Akamandos St to the ring-road around Filopappou Hill (Stisikleous Ave).

Get there: Thissio Metro station on Line 1, then 10 minutes' walk; or Kerameikos Metro station on Line 3, then 10 minutes' walk. From Thissio station walk along the pedestrian walkway to Akamandos St (opposite Thissio Sq) and walk along it until you see the preschool. The steep road in front of it is Kymaion St. Follow it down and the park will be on the left.

Geotag: @37.973297,23.71474

Ring-road (*Periferiakò*) playground (Alsos Petralona), Thissio

Rate: 3 (unkempt, not much equipment)

Location: West side of central Athens.

Nearest areas: Thissio, Ano Petralona, Psyrri.

Nearest hotels: O+B Hotel, Phidias, Jason Inn.

Nearest sites: Nymphon Hill, Pnyx Hill, Dora Stratou Theatre.

Better for summer or winter (shade/shelter): Shade from trees; good year-round.

Equipment: Chained seat swings, regular swings, see-saws, merry-go-round, slide, basketball courts.

Toilets/facilities: Yes, and a caretaker during the day.

Fenced: Yes, but gate entrances are open.

Stroller accessible: Yes.

Age appropriate: Toddlers and up.

Details: This quiet playground is on the beginning of the ring-road around Filopappou Hill from Thissio. It's a pleasant, shady place with equipment spread across the area amongst the trees, and used mainly by locals (and since it's always open, anyone can come and go). It's not that well-kept—careful of broken glass in empty "sandpits" (more like foundations)—and the equipment is old-fashioned, so no bucket (baby) swings. There is a caretaker in a small building that includes a bathroom. There are plenty of benches. No signs are posted saying no motorbikes, consequently some who use the basketball courts bring theirs inside the playground rather than leaving them in the parking lot.

Hours: Always open.

Where: ***Thissio****, near Pnyx and Nymphon Hills, Akamandos St to the ring-road around Filopappou Hill (Stisikleous Ave).*

Get there: *From Thissio Metro station on Line 1, walk ~10 minutes along the pedestrian walkway to Akamandos St (opposite Thissio Sq) and continue until you see a small pedestrian road on the right (Troon St) that has a school on one side and the park on the other. There's a gate where you can go up the steps, or keep going on the ring road and follow the fenced park around to the next entrance veering right, which is more level (for strollers). This entrance opens up from Evg. Antoniadou St, which starts as a dirt path along the fenced perimeter of the park from the ring-road, just beside Kallisthenous St.*

Geotag: *@37.972392,23.716307*

Filopappou Hill (Apollonia Sq) playground, Ano Petralona

Filopappou: Busy, baby-friendly

Rate: 2 (small, little shade, out of the way)
Location: West side of central Athens.
Nearest areas: Ano Petralona, Koukaki, Thissio.
Near hotels: No.
Nearest sites: Nymphon and Filopappou Hills, Dora Stratou Theatre.

Better for summer or winter (shade/shelter): Although within a park there is little shade, so better in the early evening in summer, anytime in winter.
Equipment: Four bucket swings, two regular swings, two slides, rocking horses.
Toilets/facilities: No.
Fenced: Yes.
Stroller accessible: Yes.
Age appropriate (eg bucket swings for babies): Babies to 10 yrs.
Details: This is a small, fenced-in playground within a park in a residential area opposite **Nymphon Hill** and **Dora Stratou Theatre** on the ring-road, and therefore convenient if you're in a car (parking). Not for a special trip but if you're in the area...

Hours: Gate open during the day, year-round.
Where: Apollonia Sq, Ano Petralona, opposite Nymphon Hill and Dora Stratou Theatre, ring-road (periferiako) around Filopappou Hill.
Get there: From Petralona Metro station on Line 1, then ~10 minutes' walk, or trolley no. 15 (Petralona station terminus) to Merkouri Sq, walk up Antaiou to Gkika St, which fronts the playground.
Geotag: @37.967174,23.714697

Technopolis play area, Gazi

Small toddlers play area is beside a café at Technopolis, Gazi

Details: Within the Technopolis complex, **Gazi** (entrance on Persefonis St), there's a small plastic slide and cubby hole play area (up to ~4 yrs) set up near the **café** (*Café to Dimou Gaz a L'eau, 100 Piraeos St, Gazi, 210-347-0981, www.technopolis-athens.com*) nearest Persefonis St.

Hours: Daily summer ~9am–9pm, unless there's a ticket entrance event. Winter ~9am–5pm.
Where: Piraeos and Persefonis sts, Gazi, end of Ermou St, west Athens.
Get there: Kerameikos Metro station on Line 3, trolley no. 21, bus nos. 035, 049, 227, 815, 838, 914
to bus-stop: Fotaerio.
Geotag: @37.977593,23.713539

SYNTAGMA, ZAPPEION

National Gardens playground, Syntagma Square

National Gardens 'maypole' ride

Rate: 5
Location: Central Athens
Nearest areas: Centre, Plaka, Kolonaki, Makriyanni.
Nearest hotels: Those around Syntagma Sq, Plaka, Kolonaki, Monastiraki.
Nearest sites: Parliament, Plaka, Acropolis, shopping district.
Better for summer or winter (shade/shelter): Shade from trees, good year-round.
Equipment: Bucket and regular swings, merry-go-rounds, see-saws, slides, sandbox.
Toilets/facilities: Yes.
Fenced: Yes.

Stroller accessible: Yes.
Age appropriate (eg bucket swings for babies): Babies to 12 yrs.
Details: Along with adjacent Zappeion playground, this is the closest to Syntagma Sq and Makriyanni, and the easiest to get to. Once the royal gardens, the **playground** is well-shaded in the southwest corner of the park. The paths are a bit difficult to follow but it's near adjacent Zappeion Gardens—listen for the sound of children. Also popular with expats, it has a sandbox, a picnic table as well as plenty of benches, and child-sized toilets. The 15.5 hectare (38-acre) National Gardens has many paths and places to sit, with ponds, small waterfalls, and a little "**zoo**" of chickens, ducks, peacocks, rabbits and wild goats, as well as a quaint **Children's Library** (*210-323-6503, Tues–Sat 8am–2.30pm*). It has a few English books and tables to draw or play chess, and the librarian will babysit if the children (3+ yrs) can do their activity on their own.

Hours: Park open daily sunrise to sunset.
Where: National Gardens, **Syntagma Sq.**
Get there: Syntagma Metro station on Lines 2, 3, then 5-10 minutes' walk. From Syntagma station, walk south along Amalias Ave to the gate near the kiosk with the children's toys and follow the signs along the paths. Other entrances at Zappeion Gardens on the south side of the gardens, the east where there is a small **café** (4 Irodou Attikou St, 210-723-2820), and north (Vas. Sofias Ave).
Geotag: @37.972231,23.738548

Zappeion playground, Syntagma, Makriyanni

Rate: 4 (no swings, but nice grassy areas and a trampoline)
Location: Central Athens.
Nearest areas: Centre, Plaka, Kolonaki, Makriyanni, Kalimarmara (Pangrati).
Nearest hotels: Those around Syntagma, Plaka, Makriyanni, Koukaki, Neos Kosmos (Kinosargous).
Nearest sites: Parliament, Plaka, Panathenian (Marble) Stadium, Temple of Olympian Zeus, shopping district (Syntagma Sq)
Better for summer or winter (shade/shelter): Shade from trees, good year-round.
Equipment: Slides, "trampoline", merry-go-round, rocking horses, green area.
Toilets/facilities: Yes, but sometimes locked. Nearby is a **café**.
Fenced: Yes.
Stroller accessible: Yes.
Age appropriate (eg bucket swings for babies): Toddlers to 10 yrs.
Details: This is a very nice, large and shady park on the southwest corner of Zappeion Gardens, opposite the car park for Aegli **café** (*210-336-9363, www.aeglizappiou.gr*), towards Vas. Olgas Ave. The park, with its broad boardwalk, tree-lined entrance, fountain area and winding paths through the greenery, was described as the "quintessence of park" in 1939 by American author Henry Miller, and the 19th century Zappeion building is historic in its capacity to revive the Olympic movement (first modern Olympics held at the Panathenian Stadium in 1896). It does not have swings, but it does have a sandpit with little wooden playhouses that young children will enjoy, and the trampoline.

Hours: Park open daily.
Where: Zappeion Gardens, **Syntagma/Makriyanni.**
Get there: Syntagma Metro station on Lines 2, 3, then 5-10 minutes' walk.
Geotag: @37.9701,23.73726

MAKRIYANNI, KOUKAKI

Kallisperi St playground, Makriyanni

Swing-set and benches on a secluded pedestrian street near the Acropolis Museum

Rate: 1 (small, little and old equipment, not fenced in)
Location: Makriyanni.
Nearest areas: Akropoli, Makriyanni.
Nearest hotels: Divani Palace Acropolis, Filippos, Herodion, Art Hotel, Hera.

Nearest sites: Acropolis Museum, Acropolis, Ancient Theatre of Dionysus, Temple of Zeus.
Better for summer or winter (shade/shelter): Shade from trees, good year-round.
Equipment: Four old-fashioned toddler swings, see-saw.
Toilets/facilities: No.
Fenced: No.
Stroller accessible: Yes.
Age appropriate: Toddlers to 4 yrs.
Details: I hesitate to call this a playground as it's just an old swing set and see-saw in the small pedestrian street beside the school, but it is also just off the Acropolis walkway. If you're in the area (Acropolis Museum) and desperate to give your child some "swing" time or to eat/feed, you can come to this little-known, discreet place and rest on plenty of seating.

Hours: Open 24 hrs.
Where: Makriyanni, one block south of Dion. Areopagitou (Acropolis walkway) St on Kallisperi St between Karyatidon and Mitsaion sts, beside the primary school.
Get there: From Rovertou Galli St turn off on Kallisperi, Karyatidon or Mitsaion sts. From Akropoli Metro station on Line 2 walk up Dion. Areopagitou St one block to Mitsaion (beside the Acropolis Museum), and down one short block to Kallisperi St.
Geotag: @37.969096,23.726872

Paidiki Hara playground, Koukaki

Entrance to the playground is beside the court, where parents also gather to throw balls to toddlers

Rate: 3 (little shade, closed 3–5pm)
Location: Southwest side of central Athens, near Panteion University, Nymphon Hill (Filopappou Hill).

Nearest areas: Ano Petralona, Koukaki, Kallithea.
Nearest hotels: Tony Hotel, Marble House, Ilissos Hotel.
Nearest sites: Nymphon and Filopappou hills, Dora Stratou Theatre.
Better for summer or winter (shade/shelter): Shaded benches. Open year-round but better in the early evening in summer.
Equipment: Eight bucket swings, two regular swings, slide, rocking horses, see-saw. **Basketball/volleyball court** is available for anyone to kick a ball around, including toddlers.
Toilets/facilities: Toilet in the basketball court, but rarely open.
Fenced: Yes.
Stroller accessible: Yes.
Age appropriate (eg bucket swings for babies): Babies and up.
Details: This is a well-used, fenced-in playground (*paidiki harà*) at a busy intersection in a dense residential area. It has a large basketball/volleyball court, so a magnet for kids playing with balls. Where to take your children when they need some space to run.

Hours: Daily 8.30am–2.30pm/5pm–9.45pm.
*Where: **Kountouriotou Sq, Koukaki**, at the west end of Veikou and Dimitrakopoulou sts, just before the overpass into Kallithea suburb.*
Get there: Syngrou-Fix Metro station on Line 2, then 15 minutes' walk; or trolley bus nos. 1, 5, 15 (no. 15 also from Petralona Metro station) along Veikou St from Syntagma Sq to bus-stop: Paidiki Hara.
Geotag: @37.96176,23.719182

Flowers, fairies, Feb 2012 ☺ 4.5 yrs

KOLONAKI

Dexameni Square playground, Kolonaki

Dexameni Sq is busy and handy

Rate: 3 (small, not much equipment)
Location: (Uphill) from central Athens.
Nearest areas: Centre, Kolonaki, Exarchia.
Nearest hotels: Periscope, St George Lycabettus.
Nearest sites: Lykabettus Hill, Kolonaki shopping district, Parliament.

Better for summer or winter (shade/shelter): Shade from trees, good year-round.
Equipment: Bucket and regular swings, see-saw, slides, monkey bars.
Toilets/facilities: No.
Fenced: Yes.
Stroller accessible: Yes.
Age appropriate (eg bucket swings for babies): Babies to 10 yrs.
Details: This is a small park on the square where children also play ball. It's a convenient place to let children play and let off steam, such as after a trip up Lycabettus Hill. The surrounding area is steep.

Hours: Park open daily.
Where: **Dexameni Sq, Kolonaki**, near the centre, Lykabettus, Syntagma Sq.
Get there: From Evangelismos Metro station on Line 3, then 5–10 minutes' walk uphill from the station. Walk north up Ploutarchou St to Haritos St and go left (east). The square will be on your right, before you reach Irakleitou St.
Geotag: @37.978794,23.741616

Kitsiki Square playground, Kolonaki

Lots of nannies at hillside Kitsiki Sq playground

Rate: 3 (small, hard to get too—uphill)
Location: Lycabettus/Lykavittos, east side of central Athens.

Nearest areas: Kolonaki, Lykavittos, Megaron Mousikis (Concert Hall), Embassy.
Nearest hotels: Athens Lycabettus, Periscope, St George Lycabettus, Hilton.
Nearest sites: War Museum, Byzantine and Christian Museum, Lycabettus Hill.
Better for summer or winter (shade/shelter): In a pine wood at the foot of Lycabettus Hill, so shade in summer.
Equipment: Bucket and regular swings, slides, see-saw, rocking horses. Gravel and rubber mats.
Toilets/facilities: No.
Fenced: Yes.
Stroller accessible: Yes.
Age appropriate (eg bucket swings for babies): Babies to 10 yrs.
Details: A busy little park where anything goes (balls, skates, etc) from the paucity of playgrounds around this hilly area, many of the kids are accompanied by nannies. Shaded by pine trees, located in a small park.

Hours: Park open daily, closes late.
*Where: **Kolonaki**, behind the Gennadiou Library, at the top of Xenokratous St, entrance on Deinokratous (up the ramp) and also entrance from Kleomenous St (down a path with steps).*
Get there: Bus no. 060 on Kleomenous St to bus-stop: 3ʳᵈ Lykavittos; or bus nos. 022, 060 on Souidas St to bus-stop: Evangelismos.
Geotag: @37.980545,23.747678

ILISSIA, EMBASSY

Ilissia Park playground, Ilissia

Ilissia: Fenced off for toddlers

Rate: 5
Location: East of central Athens.
Nearest areas: Ilissia, Zografou, Kaisariani, Kolonaki, Megaron Mousikis (Concert Hall), Embassy, University.
Nearest hotels: Hilton, Ilissia Hotel, Crowne Plaza, Divani Caravel.
Nearest sites: War Museum, Art Gallery, Byzantine and Christian Museum, Kolonaki shopping, Ambelokipi shopping, nightlife.
Better for summer or winter (shade/shelter): In the woods, so plenty of shade.
Equipment: Bucket and regular swings, rocking horses, slides, monkey bars, see-saws.

Toilets/facilities: No, but there is a portable toilet at the end of the path leading from the other side of the church (Stenon Portas St entrance).
Fenced: Yes.
Stroller accessible: Yes.
Age appropriate (eg bucket swings for babies): Babies to 10 yrs.
Details: This is a really nice park and pleasant place to pass the time for young children, babies and toddlers, in a quiet area that's cool in summer inside the pine woods. Divided into two levels: one for older kids (3 yrs and up), and an area fenced off for babies and toddlers.

Hours: Park open daily.
Where: *Ilissia*, inside Ilissia park near Haralambos church, end of Dimitressa St.
Get there: From Megaron Mousikis Metro station on Line 3, then ~10 minutes' walk from the station. Turn left on Papadiamantopoulou St and first right on Alkmanos St, then all the way up (hill), till you're in front of the park (where the street veers left) and turn right on the path. **Alternate entrance**: From Iason Dragoumi St into the church courtyard, where there's a ramp up to the porch on the far (south) side of the church front, then a few steps up along the path beside the bell tower leads to the playground.
Geotag: @37.975809,23.755006

Kaisariani Park playground, Ilissia

Small but easy access Kaisariani

Rate: 1 (small, unkempt, far away, not much shade, closes mid-day)
Location: East side of central Athens.
Nearest areas: Ilissia, Kaisariani, Pangrati, University, Evangelismos.
Nearest hotels: Divani Caravel, Hilton, Ilissia Hotel, Crowne Plaza.
Nearest sites: War Museum, Art Gallery, Byzantine and Christian Museum.
Better for summer or winter (shade/shelter): Winter and evenings as the trees don't offer much shade.
Equipment: Bucket, chain and regular swings, see-saws, slides, rope climb.
Toilets/facilities: No.
Fenced: Yes.

Stroller accessible: Yes.
Age appropriate (eg bucket swings for babies): Babies to 10 yrs.
Details: This is a rather unkempt little playground where the locals come to chat and give the children a chance to let off steam. Little ones like the swings and slides. The trees don't really offer shade during the mid-day heat, which doesn't really matter since the park is closed from 3pm–5pm daily. While I wouldn't make a special trip here, the walkway is pleasant.

Hours: Daily 9am–2pm/5pm–9pm.
Where: Ilissia, at the beginning of a pedestrian park pathway that continues from Vas. Alexandrou Ave where Efroniou, Theologou and A. Dimitrou sts intersect. Gate is from the path.
Get there: From Vas. Alexandrou and Vas. Sofias aves, head south past Syngrou Hospital and past the Divani Caravel hotel, which has a nice, grassy park in front. When the straight road ends and veers left and right, continue straight into the grassy pedestrian area where there are paths. The gate to the playground is on your left, beside the parking lot and in front of a gas station.
Geotag: @37.971927,23.752753

Zografou playground, Ilissia

*Paths to play areas
at Zografou*

Rate: 3 (bit unkempt and out of the way)
Location: East side of central Athens.
Nearest areas: Ilissia, Zografou, Megaron Mousikis (Concert Hall), Embassy.
Nearest hotels: Michalakopoulou St hotels such as Crowne Plaza, Hilton.
Nearest sites: Megaron Mousikis Concert Hall, Lycabettus/Lykavittos Hill, Kolonaki shopping, Art Gallery, War Museum, Byzantine and Christian Museum.
Better for summer or winter (shade/shelter): Shade and shelter from pine trees and structures.
Equipment: Bucket and regular swings, see-saws, slides, rolling "log", monkey bars, bridges, picnic tables.
Toilets/facilities: No.
Fenced: Yes.
Stroller accessible: There are some six to eight stairs at the gate entrance.
Age appropriate (eg bucket swings for babies): Babies and up.
Details: This is a nice, quite roomy playground and meeting place that attracts all ages from the surrounding neighbourhood. It's on a hillside in a quiet residential area that forms a triangle bound by Sevasteias, Nymfaiou, and Semelis sts. Equipment and picnic tables are spread over different levels, which give a feeling of "privacy," or at least your own spot.

Hours: Park open daily.
Where: *Ilissia/Zografou*, gate is on Sevastias St at the end of Ozolon St.
Get there: From Megaron Mousikis Metro station on Line 3, then ~10 min walk. Take Vas. Sofias exit and turn right on Dion. Aiginitou St, at the end cross and turn left on Michalakopoulou St, and right on Nymfaiou. It'll be on your left. Semelis St is blocked from the playground's southeast border.
Geotag: @37.977678,23.758675

Neapolis Square, Neapoli, Alexandras Ave

Neapolis Square has shade and a couple of swings

Rate: 2 (small, little equipment, out of the way)
Location: Northeast of central Athens.
Nearest areas: Alexandras Ave, Lycabettus Hill.
Nearest hotels: Proteas, Zafolia.
Nearest sites: Lycabettus Hill, Exarchia.

Toilets/facilities: No.
Fenced: No.
Stroller accessible: Yes.
Age appropriate: Toddlers to 4 yrs.
Details: A few toddler swings and a see-saw in a small, shady spot.
Hours: Not enclosed, freely accessible.
Where: *Neapoli*, Asklipiou and Fanariotou sts, Alexandras Ave area.
Geotag: @37.987437,23.746401

NEOS KOSMOS

Heldraix (Heldreich) Square playground, Neos Kosmos

Lots of space to throw a ball, but little shade

Rate: 4 (area)
Location: South of central Athens, east of Syngrou Ave.
Nearest areas: Neos Kosmos, Kinosargous, Kallithea, Koukaki.

Nearest hotels: Athenaeum Intercontinental, Ledra Marriott.
Nearest sites: Filopappou Hill, on the main road to south coast beaches.
Better for summer or winter (shade/shelter): No or little shade in the playground, so better in the winter or summer evenings.
Equipment: Swings, bucket swings, slides, monkey-bars, and large court area (no shade).
Toilets/facilities: At the **café** on site.
Fenced: Yes.
Stroller accessible: Yes.
Age appropriate (eg bucket swings for babies): Babies and up.
Details: This is a large playground area serving the surrounding densely built-up, residential, mainly immigrant neighbourhood. Enclosed playground, plus separate fenced-in area to play ball, plus grassy places to sit near the municipal-run **café** (*Café tou Dimou, concession of same operators as the Technopolis café, 210-347-5518, 9am-9pm*) that has tables outside and inside; snacks, drinks, coffee and ice cream. Area is safe during the day but may get a bit rougher after nightfall.

Hours: Daily.
*Where: **Neos Kosmos**, behind Athenaeum Intercontinental hotel, bound by Evrydamantos St between Lagomitzi and Heldreich sts.*
Get there: 10 min on the tram, 4th stop from Syntagma (stop: Kasomouli), then 10 minutes' walk behind Atheneum Continental on Filinou St and cross Lagomitzi St (main road).
Geotag: @37.956941,23.722237

Kallirois playground, Ag. Panteleimonos, Kinosargous, Neos Kosmos

Small Kallirois has a lovely tree

Rate: 4 (small)
Location: Near Akropoli and Syngrou-Fix Metro stations, south side of central Athens.
Nearest areas: Kinosargous (Neos Kosmos), Makriyanni, Plaka (south-east slope), Mets.
Nearest hotels: Those near the beginning of Syngrou and Kallirois aves, in Makriyianni, near the Temple of Olympian Zeus.
Better for summer or winter (shade/shelter): Shade from a large tree year-round.
Nearest sites: Temple of Olympian Zeus, Ancient Dionysus Theatre, Acropolis Museum and Acropolis.
Equipment: Slide, regular swings, baby/toddler swings, rocking horses, see-saws, monkey bars.

Toilets/facilities: No.
Fenced: Yes.
Stroller accessible: Yes.
Age appropriate (eg bucket swings for babies): Babies to 10 yrs.
Details: This is a small, pleasant park that's convenient for those staying in the vicinity. Nice equipment, but the main feature is the beautiful shade tree.

Hours: Park open daily.
*Where: **Ag. Panteleimonos Sq, Neos Kosmos**, beside Kallirois Ave opposite Petmeza St, **Makriyanni/Kinosargous**. Entrance on Menaixmou St.*
Get there: Akropoli Metro station on Line 2, then 5 minutes' walk; Tram-stop: Fix.
Geotag: @37.964983,23.730597

Lambraki Hill playground, Vouliagmenis Ave, Neos Kosmos

Lambraki Hill is great if you're in the area

Rate: 4 (not easy access)
Location: Near the top of Vouliagmenis Ave, west side, opposite the First Cemetery, Mets, south of central Athens.

Nearest areas: Kinosargous (Neos Kosmos), Mets, Makriyanni.
Nearest hotels: Those near the beginning of Vouliagmenis, Syngrou and Kallirois aves.
Better for summer or winter (shade/shelter): Shade from pine trees year-round.
Nearest sites: First Cemetery, Temple of Olympian Zeus, Panathenian Stadium.
Equipment: Slide, regular swings, baby and toddler swings, rocking horse, see-saws, monkey bars, basketball court, open space for skating, trails for bicycle riding, walking in the woods.
Toilets/facilities: Yes, at the municipal café on site.
Fenced: Yes.
Stroller accessible: Yes.
Age appropriate (eg bucket swings for babies): Babies to 10 yrs.
Details: This is a lovely, good-sized park and playground sandwiched between schools up on a hill, with a basketball court, square, trails, and places near the park to eat, including an on-site **café**. It is uphill however, and you'd get here on foot or by bus.

Hours: Park open daily.
*Where: **Neos Kosmos**, near the beginning of Vouliagmenis Ave (south side), entrance off Pithiou Ave, south side of the park.*
Get there: From Kallirois and Vouliagmenis aves, ~10 minutes' walk. Bus nos. A3, A4, B3, 227, 856 on Vouliagmenis Ave, bus-stop: Varioti; or bus no. 202, bus-stop: Lefka.
Geotag: @37.962547, 23.732593

NEA SMYRNI

Nea Smyrni Alsos playground, Nea Smyrni

Nea Smyrni Alsos is shady and spacious, plus has a café on site

Rate: 4 (out of the way)
Location: About 4.5km/3mi south of central Athens.
Nearest areas: Neos Kosmos, Kallithea.
Nearest hotels: Athenaeum Intercontinental, Ledra Marriott.
Better for summer or winter (shade/shelter): Shade year-round.

Equipment: Slides, regular swings, toddler swings, sand pit, merry-go-rounds (roundabouts), see-saws.
Toilets/facilities: Yes, beside the cafe.
Fenced: Yes.
Stroller accessible: Yes.
Age appropriate (eg bucket swings for babies): Older babies to 10 yrs.
Details: This is a nice playground surrounded by trees in a wooded area with trails and a central square (*plateìa*) with a **café** selling snacks, drinks and ice cream.

Hours: Park open daily.
*Where: **Nea Smyrni**, Ag. Foteinis area, south-east of Syngrou Ave, bound by Efesou, Kordeliou, Patriarchou Ioakeim and Elefth. Venizelou sts.*
Get there: From Syntagma to 7th tram stop: Aigaiou, then 5 minutes' walk along the tram line heading south to the main entrance, just before Patr. Ioakeim St.
Geotag: @37.949138,23.716006

CHILDREN'S HOSPITAL, GOUDI

Paidon Square playground, Paidon children's hospitals, Goudi

Handy location opposite the children's hospitals

Rate: 3 (out of the way, small)
Location: About 4.5km/3mi northeast of central Athens.

Nearest areas of interest: Lycabettus Hill.
Nearest hotels: President, Elizabeth, hotels near Mavili Sq, Megaron Mousikis and Ambelokipi Metro stations, ie Alexandras Ave, Vas. Sofias Ave and surrounding area.
Better for summer or winter (shade/shelter): Trees near the benches, better for winter (mild weather) and evenings.
Equipment: Slides, regular swings, toddler swings, rocking horses, see-saw, small climbing apparatus.
Toilets/facilities: No. Ask at the hospital across the street, or inside the adjacent pay parking lot.
Fenced: Yes.
Stroller accessible: Yes.
Age appropriate (eg bucket swings for babies): Older babies to 10 yrs.
Details: This is a small playground with some shade trees near the benches that's convenient if for any reason you need to go to the hospital. **Ice cream and snacks** are available at nearby kiosks and **cafes** (there's one beside the Agia Sofia hospital chapel near the entrance, no seating) in the hospital grounds, which also has a small, busy **playground** (swings, slide, see-saw) opposite, inside the site.

Hours: Park open daily.
Where: Goudi, opposite Agia Sofia and Aglaia Kyriakou Children's Hospitals, on the corner of Thivon and Papadiamantopoulou sts, entrance from Igimonos St behind the park.
Get there: Bus no. 815 from Piraeos St, Akadimias St, or Vas. Sofias Ave near Evangelismos Metro station on Line 3 to bus-stop: Nos. Paidon.
Geotag: @37.983547,23.768379

VOULIAGMENIS AVE, AGIOS DIMITRIOS (ATHENS METRO MALL STATION)

Agios Dimitrios playground, Agios Dimitrios Metro station, Vouliagmenis Avenue

Ag. Dimitrios Metro station playground also has toddler slides

Rate: 2 (out of the way, gravel ground, busy)
Location: About 4.5km/3mi south of central Athens.
Nearest areas of interest: Athens Metro Mall.
Better for summer or winter (shade/shelter): Trees near the benches, better for winter (mild weather) and evenings.
Equipment: Slides, regular swings, toddler swings, merry-go-round (roundabout), see-saw.
Toilets/facilities: Yes, at the cafe.
Fenced: No, there are low walls separating the areas.
Stroller accessible: Yes.
Age appropriate (eg bucket swings for babies): Older babies to 10 yrs.
Details: If your child needs to let off steam after you've been shopping at the mall, this is a convenient place to get their play-time in. It's near busy Vouliagmenis Ave so not very peaceful, but there's a high screw slide here that will appeal to older children. Also a **café**.

Hours: Park open daily.
Where: **Agios Dimitrios**, *on the south side of Athens Metro Mall, on the west side of Vouliagmenis Ave, the main street going to southern Athens.*
Get there: *Agios Dimitrios Metro station on Line 2, then 5 minutes' walk.*
Geotag: *@37.938258,23.74079*

Amusement Parks, Indoor & Supervised Play Areas

Many amusement parks and indoor play areas, called "*paidòtopos*" here, have areas that are both supervised and (liquor) licensed—an attractive combination for harried parents after a hot day to relax with a coffee or drink. They will take your mobile/cell phone number and call if they need you, typically if the child wants to go to the washroom or is thirsty.

Athens Heart Mall, Tavros

Athens Heart Mall has a supervised play area and trampoline

Rate: 4 (not easy access, unless driving)
Location: west of central Athens.
Details: There's a large **supervised play area** (*Volta Fun Park, 210-341-2019, www.voltafunpark.gr*) located in this mall on the 3rd floor that has been transformed into a mini-amusement park, with **mini-bumper cars** (€3) and many rides, including an eight-mat **trampoline** (€3 for 10 min), arcade, mini-train and **inline skating**/roller-blading (€5 unlimited time). Supervised from 3 yrs and up, parent accompanies younger children.

Hours: Year-round daily 10am–10pm.
Entrance: €5 per child, waived for mall purchases €50+.
Where: 180 Piraeos St at Hamosternas Ave, **Tavros**, 210-341-4105, www.athensheart.gr
Get there: Bus nos. 049, 815, 914 to bus-stop: Ergon, or suburban train (Proastiakos) to Rouf station (journey takes ~10 minutes); or via Petralona Metro station on Line 1, then ~15 minutes' walk.
Geotag: @37.969711,23.700707

Athens Metro Mall, Agios Dimitrios

It's a jungle in there: supervised play area and adult seating (more seating and rides on the other side of the glass), Athens Metro Mall, Ag. Dimitrios Metro station

Rate: 5
Details: A **supervised play area** (you can have a coffee or

drink, read, go shopping, etc) for children 3 yrs and up, **Volta Fun Park** (*210-975-0630, www.voltafunpark.gr*) is located on the 2nd floor in this mall. From 3 yrs supervised, parent accompanies younger children.

Hours: Year-round daily 10am–midnight.
Entrance: €5 per child.
*Where: 276 Vouliagmenis Ave, **Agios Dimitrios**, 210-976-9444, www.athensmetromall.gr*
Get there: Located at Agios Dimitrios Metro station on Line 2, Vouliagmenis Ave/Ioannou Metaxa St exit (front of the train), ~10-15 min journey from Syntagma.
Geotag: @37.939815,23.740361

Mikres Istories, Koukaki

Whimsical waiting area at Mikres Istories (Short Stories)

Rate: 4 (set times for drop-ins)
Location: south side of central Athens, near Filopappou Hill and Syngrou Ave.
Nearest areas: Filopappou, Makriyanni, Neos Kosmos.
Nearest hotels: Tony Hotel, Marble House.
Nearest sites: Acropolis Museum, Acropolis, Ancient Theatre of Dionysus, easy access route to south coast beaches.
Better for summer or winter (shade/shelter): Indoor. Closed for drop-ins July to mid-September.
Equipment: All kinds of activities, from drawing and painting to exercising.
Toilets/facilities: Yes.
Fenced: Gated and doors closed.
Stroller accessible: Few steps at the front entrance and to the 2nd floor.
Age appropriate: Babies to 8 yrs.
Details: A place specially suited for children aged 3-6 yrs, **Mikres Istories** or "Short Stories," is an excellent **supervised play area** that also has craft activities.

Hours: Winter: daily 9am–9pm; summer: 9am–11.30pm. Drop-ins (drop-off your child) Tues/Thurs 6pm–7.15pm, Sat 11am–noon.
Entrance: €5 for drop-in or €35-45 a month.
*Where: 70 Dimitrakopoulou St, **Koukaki**, 210-922-7730, www.mikresistories.gr*
Get there: Metro Syngrou-Fix (within walking distance from the Acropolis Museum), or take trolley nos. 1, 5 or 15 from Syntagma Square (first bus-stop on the street in front of Public and McDonald's) or from Syngrou Ave, and alight at bus-stops: Gargaretta or Zinni on Veikou St and walk down a block to Dimitrakopoulou St.
Geotag: @37.964585,23.724117

Playgrounds & Supervised Play Areas, Greater Athens

SOUTH COAST, NEAR ATHENS/PIRAEUS (PALEO FALIRO, FLISVOS, KALAMAKI, ALIMOS)

Flisvos Marina, Paleo Faliro

Flashy Flisvos Marina attracts throngs for the evening 'stroll'

Rate: 4 (no shade)
Location: About 7km/4mi south of Athens.
Nearest areas: Faliro, Piraeus, Nea Smyrni, Alimos, Kallithea.
Nearest hotels: Arma, Avra.

Nearest sites: Piraeus port, Glyfada shopping, beaches.
Better for summer or winter: Winter or evenings in summer, when the heat of the day is past.
Toilets/Facilities: Yes.
Fenced: No.
Stroller accessible: Yes.
Age appropriate: All ages, but *be careful with toddlers* along the marina (it is an open wharf).
Details: At Flisvos Marina you can get an ice cream and gawk at the mega-yachts, and blend in with the yacht-y set. People come here to stroll and the kids love looking for fish (but carefully, as there is no barrier at the edge of the quay). Underwater lights at night attract some rather large specimens. An **amusement park** with children's rides, trampolines and a bouncy castle and **cafe** (*Volta Fun Park, Marina Flisvos, Paleo Faliro, 210-985-0340, www.voltafunpark.gr*, free entrance, pay per ride) is behind the row of shops and cafes interspersed with public washrooms. The bouncy castle is a **supervised play area** (3 yrs and up). It's a 10–15 minute walk along the waterfront promenade (southeast) to **Flisvos Park playground**, although there's also a small **playground** here, on the way to the promenade (southeast end).

Hours: Not enclosed; shop hours Mon–Fri 10am–9pm, Sat 10am–8pm.
*Where: **Marina Flisvos, Paleo Faliro**, 210-987-1000 to 2, www.flisvosmarina.com*
Get there: 10 min by taxi down Syngrou Ave; 20 min by bus no. 550 from Akadimias St, Panepistimio area in town, to bus-stop: Terminus (end of the line, behind the marina); 45 min by tram to tram-stop: Trokadero. Allow 1–2 hrs there.
Geotag: @37.930727,23.686244

Flisvos Park playground, Faliro

Playground paradise: Giant Flisvos on the waterfront has many play areas that kids will love, as long as it's not too hot

Rate: 4 (no shade)
Location: 6km south of Athens, near the end of Syngrou Ave.
Nearest areas: Faliro, Kallithea, Piraeus, Glyfada.
Nearest hotels: Avra, Coral, Poseidon Hotel.
Nearest sites: Piraeus port, Glyfada shopping, beaches.
Better for summer or winter (shade/shelter): There's little shade here, so best in the winter or evenings.
Equipment: Swings, bucket swings, many slides, monkey-bars, "rope tree", sandbox, rocking horses, green areas.
Toilets/facilities: Yes.
Fenced: Yes, but with open walkways.
Stroller accessible: Yes.
Age appropriate (eg bucket swings for babies): Babies to 10 yrs.
Details: This is touted as the "biggest and best playground in Greece." Children will love all the "slide-houses" that have been put up in two adjacent play areas surrounded by grass, with the promenade and the sea on the south side. Also a **café** (licensed, with snacks and light lunches: *Parko Flisvou, 210-988-5140, www.floisvospark.gr*) is nearby on the way towards **Flisvos Marina** with a very handy, **fenced-in tykes playground**: slides, trampoline, swings, and washroom facilities.

Hours: Winter daily 9am–9pm; summer 9am–11.30pm.
Where: Flisvos Park (Parko Flisvou), Paleo Faliro, on the waterfront beside Poseidonos Ave.
Get there: From Syntagma to tram-stop: Parko Flisvou; bus no. 550 from Kifissias, Vas. Konstantinou or Syngrou aves to the Terminus (end of the line), then ~15 minutes' walk.
Geotag: @37.927545,23.688412

Loca Fun Park, Alimos

Derek Gatopoulos

Rate: 4 (closed in winter)
Location: About 10km/6mi south of Athens, towards Glyfada.
Age appropriate: From 3 yrs; accompany babies and toddlers on the mini-train.
Details: Large **amusement park** beside the landmark **Ostria Café** (*10 Poseidonos Ave, Alimos, 210-985-2350, www.ostria.gr*) on the seafront has all kinds of rides to tempt little ones, including swan-boats, mini-train (*pictured*), trampolines, bouncy castle (**supervised play area**) and electric cars as well as refreshments and snacks.
Marina Alimou Park playground is behind it.

Hours: Winter: Mon–Fri 11am–6pm, Sat–Sun 11am–8pm. May–June daily 11am–10pm, July–Aug daily 5pm–11pm.
Entrance: Rides €1–€3, bouncy castle (supervised) €5.
Where: 18 Poseidonos Ave, *Alimos*, 697-002-2775, www.locafunpark.gr

Get there: 10 min (10km/6mi) by taxi down Syngrou Ave; or 45 min by tram to tram-stop: Kalamaki; or bus nos. E22, A2, B2 from Akadimias St, Amalias or Syngrou aves to bus-stop: 4th Kalamaki.
Geotag: @37.910236,23.709826

Marina Alimou playground, Alimos

Rate: 5
Location: About 10km/6mi south of Athens, towards Glyfada.
Nearest areas: Alimos, Faliro, Piraeus, Glyfada.
Nearest hotels: Avra, Coral, Marina Alimos Hotel Apartments, Poseidon Hotel.

Nearest sites: Piraeus port, Glyfada shopping, beaches.

Better for summer or winter (shade/shelter): There's plenty of tree-shade so summer or winter, day or evening.

Equipment: Swings, bucket swings, many slides, rope-climbing, monkey-bars, running "log", green areas. Also a bicycle "pit" beside the Ostria cafe.

Toilets/facilities: At Volta Fun Park next door, in summer. Porto-potties beside ice rink (tented building) next to the park in winter.

Fenced: Yes but with open walkways.

Age appropriate (eg bucket swings for babies): Babies to 12 yrs.

Details: Easy to reach if driving, this really nice seaside playground has lots of trees, grass, shade, space and equipment, an upscale **café** (Ostria) on one side with parking, and an **amusement park** (*Loca Fun Park, 18 Poseidonos Ave, 697-002-2775, www.locafunpark.gr, see separate listing*) in front of it, as well as the peaceful and waterfront promenade, a bicycle-riding "pit" for young learners, and an ice rink next to it in winter. The playground activities are unusual and appealing for children of all ages.

Hours: Daily.

Where: Alimos Park, Alimos, on the waterfront beside Ostria Café on Poseidonos Ave, end of Kalamakiou Ave.

Get there: 10 min by taxi down Syngrou Ave; 45 min by tram to stop: Kalamaki; bus nos. E22, A2, B2 from Akadimias St, Amalias or Syngrou aves to bus-stop: 4th Kalamaki. Allow 1–2+ hrs there.

Geotag: @37.910496,23.710181

RENDI & DAFNI, HAIDARI, WESTERN ATHENS

Allou Fun Park and Kidom, Rendi

Fantastically ornate, two-tier carousel at Kidom, Rendi

Rate: 4 (out of the way)

Location: About 7km/4mi west of Athens.

Nearest areas: Tavros, Aegaleo, Nikea (Nikaia) suburbs.

Nearest sites: Piraeus, routes (National Road) to north or south Greece.

Better for summer or winter (shade/shelter): Winter and summer evenings.

Toilets/facilities: Yes.

Fenced: Yes.

Age appropriate: Toddlers and up.

Details: A large **amusement park** some 20 minutes from the centre by bus is divided into two areas. The bigger **Allou** has many rides, including a huge Ferris wheel and a 40m-drop Shock Tower for bigger kids and teens. **Kidom** across the road has rides and games for children 3 to 9 yrs (and younger when accompanied by an adult on some rides), such as a smaller Shock Tower (which kids will love), a roller coaster, flying elephants, trampolines and a great play area, where kids go up a ramp with an inner-tube and are assisted down a "hill".

*Hours: **Kidom** (210-425-2600, www.allou.gr): (3–9 yrs) Mon–Thurs 5pm–11pm, Fri 5pm–midnight, Sat 10am–midnight, Sun 10am–11pm.*
***Allou** (210-425-6990, www.allou.gr): Mon–Thurs 5pm–midnight, Fri 5pm–1am, Sat 10am–1am, Sun 10am–midnight.*
***Entrance**: Free. Rides €1–€10, or €23 for unlimited rides (we managed ten rides/activities in about two hours in Kidom).*
***Where**: Kifissou & Petrou Ralli aves, **Agios Ioannis–Rendi**.*
***Get there**: From Piraeos Ave, trolley no. 21, bus nos. B18, Γ18 to bus-stop: Kan Kan or Fix.*
***Geotag**: @37.973331,23.672984*

Diomidis Botanical Gardens, Dafni, Haidari

Little visited Diomidis Botanical Gardens has much biodiversity

Rate: 4 (distance from town)
Location: About 11km/7mi west of Athens.
Nearby sites: Dafni Monastery (*see Chapter16, Excursions to Monasteries section*) is a few minutes' walk further west, which also has a larger, shaded **playground** beside it.
Better for summer or winter (shade/shelter): Both.
Toilets/facilities: Yes.
Stroller accessible: Yes.
Age appropriate: All ages.
Details: Some 20 hectares of cultivated, botanical gardens amid 186 hectares on the mountainside is one of the largest and oldest in the Eastern Med. The grounds are pleasant for strolling (**and strollering**, *for the most part*). Founded in 1952 as part of the University of Athens, the garden has among the greatest range of biodiversity, containing some 3,700 species of plants, including a medicinal herb garden, and most are labelled. There are many ponds so bring a **picnic** lunch, or have a skewer of meat and soft drink at the **canteen** opposite. This is an excursion or day-trip in its own right, on the western outskirts of Athens (half-hour to 45-minute drive: you can easily spend two hours here). It's easy to reach but isolated.

There is also a small **playground** (bucket swings, regular swings, see-saw, rocking horses) inside the Gardens.

Hours: Mon–Fri 8am–2pm, Sat–Sun 10am–3pm. Gates close promptly. Free guide by appointment. Closed July 15–Aug 31.
Entrance: Free.
Where: **Haidari, Dafni,** at the top of Iera Odos, 210-581-1557, www.diomedes-bg.uoa.gr
Get there: Buses from Koumoundourou/Eleftherias Sq, Omonia Sq, Psyrri and Gazi. Bus nos. A16, B16, Γ16, E16, E63, 801, 836, 845, 865, 866 to bus-stop: Diomidios or Dafni, just before Dafni Monastery.
Driving: From Piraeos Ave turn west onto Iera Odos and follow it all the way up to Dafni, parallel to Athinon Ave (Kavalas). On the left (south) side, just before the streets merge.
Geotag: @38.010568,23.643351

KOLONOS, LARISSA (ATHENS) RAILWAY STATION, REGIONAL BUS TERMINAL AREAS, WESTERN ATHENS

Plato's Academy site & playground, Kolonos

This free archaeological site and park has a playground

Rate: 3 (out of the way, little shade)
Location: About 5km/3mi west of central Athens, between Larissa (Athens) railway station and Regional Bus Terminal A.
Better for summer or winter (shade/shelter): Playground has very little shade.
Toilets/facilities: No.
Stroller accessible: Yes.
Age appropriate: Babies to 8 yrs.
Details: If you're going to the long-distance **KTEL Bus Terminal A** at 100 Kifissou St, chances are you'll be leaving early, but in the event you have time to kill before your bus leaves, you can stop along the way at Plato's Academy—a little visited but important and very large archaeological park and site that also has a nice children's **playground**, with slides, swings and rocking horses. Good for **picnics**. The origin of the word "academy" comes from this site, sacred to the gods, notably Athena. In 387 BC Plato founded his Academy of higher-learning using the site's ancient name, known since the Bronze Age.

Hours: Open during the day.
Entrance: Free.
Where: Drakondos or Kratylou St (changes names), **Kolonos**, western Athens.
Get there: Bus no. 051 from Menandrou St, near Omonia Sq, to bus-stop: Kratylou.
Geotag: @37.992645,23.707501

Little ones enjoy the spacious children's pool at Copa Copana Park, Haidari

Chapter 13: Drop-in Hotel & Destination Pools

If you're coming to Athens from May to October, consider staying, or spending an afternoon, at a hotel with a pool, where some **accept external guests—** especially welcome after hot and sticky sightseeing, and when patience is thin and children are cranky. All the hotels with pools, to my knowledge, that are located in central Athens plus in the northern suburbs are listed, plus a couple of "destination" pools that children will love. Note that there are also about a dozen hotels with pools located along the beach-lined coastal road (Poseidonos Ave), so if you are staying outside of central Athens along the coast, check the hotel's facilities. *Note: Rates are 2012 and 2013; some not yet known at time of writing.*

Heads Up

At hotel pools there are usually no lifeguards, and often you're left on your own, so you must watch your own children, or be in the pool with them. Some pools don't have shade on the deck, so take care when the sun is beating down. It only takes a few minutes to get "touched" by the sun, but it takes a good three days of feeling ill to get over it. You also cannot wear sunscreen in the pool.

Disposable swim diapers and diaper swimming pants for older babies may be hard to find in Athens, especially out of season. **UV swimsuits** for babies and children are also not normally found here, so *bring your own*. They can also be ordered from sites such as ebay. Between two and three years old, my child would only go in the water in an inflated ring "boat", and thereafter only with water-wings/arm-bands, so consider bringing these items as well, otherwise they can be found at various shops and kiosks near beaches and at toy shops (*see Chapter 5*).

Swimming with Babies

Check websites and with your doctor for advice on acquainting babies with the water. A summary from *www.about.com* suggests doing simple, gentle passes with your baby in the pool, supporting with your arms under their armpits, passing the child to another person. At no time is the child unsupported. Then when the baby is comfortable, progress to brief passes with the baby's face just through the surface of the water (not completely submerged), by saying something like "ready, set, go". When this is comfortable, you can progress to submerging the face for two seconds, with the cue, "1, 2, 3, breath" and submerse and glide the baby to the other person.

Caution however, that *the baby does not ingest water* (drinking or otherwise) too much and too fast, as young children are in danger of water intoxication. Have fun but be aware.

Hotel Pools (by area)

EVANGELISMOS, KOLONAKI, EMBASSY, ILISSIA

Art Suites Athens (A)
Small outdoor pool for **guests only.**
• *88A Michalakopoulou and 3 Sevastias sts, Ilissia, 210-747-3180, www.artsuitesathens.gr*
Get there: From Megaron Mousikis Metro station on Line 3, Ilissia exit, then 5 minutes' walk. Turn right on Lampsakou St, opposite the Concert Hall (Megaron Mousikis).

Crowne Plaza (A)
Rooftop pool for **guests only.** Pool has a shallow end, large deck area with sunbeds and umbrellas, snack bar.
• *50 Michalakopoulou St, Ilissia, 210-727-8000, www.cpathens.com*
Get there: Megaron Mousikis Metro station on Line 3, Ilissia exit, then 5 minutes' walk.

Divani Caravel (deluxe)
Outdoor pool is heated and covered during the winter.
• *Year-round daily 10am–7pm.* • *Mon-Fri adults €30 Sat–Sun €40, under 3 yrs free, 3–12 yrs €15, Sat–Sun €20.* • *2 **Vas. Alexandrou Ave, Ilissia**, 210-720-7000, www.divanis.com*
Get there: From Evangelismos Metro station on Line 3, Rigillis exit, then 10 minutes' walk.

Girl on top of a rainbow, spring 2013 ☺ 5.5 yrs

Hilton Athens (deluxe)
The ground-level outdoor pool (*pictured*) is the biggest in the centre of Athens at 25m, plus a separate shaded wading pool. Pleasant but somewhat noisy from traffic. Locker, change-room, showers, bath towel and sunbed included. Pool **snack bar** (pricey) and grill restaurant.
• *Jun–Aug 8am–9pm; May, Sept, Oct 9am–8pm.* • *Mon–Fri adults €25, Sat–Sun €40, up to 6 yrs free, multiple-visit discounts (3x and 5x or membership) available.* • **46 Vas. Sofias Ave, Ilissia**, *210-728-1000, pool: 210-728-1801, www.hiltonathens.gr*
Get there: *From Evangelismos Metro station on Line 3, Rigillis exit, then 5 minutes' walk.*

Saint George Lycabettus (deluxe)
Rooftop pool (small) with **pool bar** serving snacks, light meals, coffee, fresh juices, cocktails, ice creams.
• *May–Oct 9am–9pm (or to 6pm later in the season) weather permitting.* • *Adults €34 incl refreshment, 0–12 yrs €17 (half-price).* • **2 Kleomenous, Kolonaki**, *210-741-6000, www.sglycabettus.gr*
Get there: *Walk (uphill) from Syntagma or Kolonaki (Evangelismos Metro station is closest) or take bus nos. 022, 060 to bus-stop: Loukianou.*

LARISSA (ATHENS) RAILWAY STATION, OMONIA SQUARE, METAXOURGIO SQUARE

Candia (B)
Rooftop pool for **guests only**.
• *40 Deligianni St, **Larissa Station**, 210-524-6112 to 7, www.candia-hotel.gr*
Get there: *Larissa Station Metro station on Line 2, Deligianni St exit.*

Dorian Inn (B)
Good-sized, deep, rooftop pool with shallow pool attached, small deck area has a few loungers and chairs but no shade. Panoramic view. Washrooms near the elevator, **snack bar**, rinsing shower on the deck. Towels available after 4.30pm.
• *Summer months daily 11am–7.30pm.* • *€20 per person, under 3 yrs free).* • **15-19 Piraeos St, Omonia**, *210-523-9782, www.dorianinnhotel.com*
Get there: *Omonia Metro station on Lines 1 and 2, then 5 minutes' walk up Piraeos St.*

Fresh (A)
Rooftop pool (*pictured*) has a bar that serves snacks. Nice deck area with shaded deck chairs, quite a small, deep (for kids) pool at ~1.5m–1.6m throughout, some shade, change in the bathroom of

the **snack bar** on the same floor (few steps lower), rinsing shower on the deck.
• *May–Oct 10am–7pm.* • *Adults €20, 3–12 yrs €15, under 3 yrs free, includes towels and a*
refreshment. • ***26 Sofokleous and Kleisthenous sts, Agora/Omonia**, 210-524-8511,*
www.freshhotel.gr
Get there: *From Omonia (Lines 1, 2) or Monastiraki (Lines 1, 3) Metro stations, then 5–10 min walk.*

Melia Hotel (A)
Lengthy (22m) rooftop pool, sunbeds, **snack bar**, small Jacuzzi that kids use.
• *May–Oct daily weather permitting, 10am–6pm.* • *Adults €20, up to 12 yrs free.* • ***4 Halkokondyli and***
***28th Octovriou sts, Omonia**, 210-332-0100, www.melia-athens.com*
Get there: *From Omonia Metro station on Lines 1 and 2, then 5 minutes' walk up 28th Octovriou St.*

Novotel Athenes (A)
Rooftop pool is good, but no shade, ~10m long, 50cm shallow end and 2.50m at
the deep end. Shower and change area, **snack bar**.
• *In season daily 9am–6pm.* • *Adults €20, under 12 yrs €10 includes towel and a refreshment or*
coffee. • ***4-6 Michael Voda St, Vathis Square**, 210-820-0700, www.novotel.com*
Get there: *From Larissa Station Metro station on Line 2, Filadelfia St exit, then 5 minutes' walk.*

Novus Athens (A)

Small plunge pool (uniform
1.20m/4ft) on the rooftop
with a panoramic view
(***pictured***), including of the
Acropolis and Lycabettus
hills. No shade on the small
deck, few deck chairs,
shaded tables and chairs at
the **snack bar** a few steps to
the lower level. Change in
the bathroom, no shower.
Short walk from the Metro
but have to cross busy streets with no crosswalks (roundabout).
• *Open end-April–Oct daily 11am–sunset.*
• *Adults €20, includes parking, towels and refreshment, under 5 yrs free, 6–12 yrs €10.*
• ***23 Karolou St, Karaiskakis Square, Metaxourgio**, 211-105-3000, www.novushotel.gr*
Get there: *5 min walk from Metaxourgio Metro station on Line 2, Deligianni St exit.*

Oscar (B)
Rooftop pool for **guests only**.
• *25 Filadelfias & Samou sts, **Larissa Station**, 210-883-4215 to 9, www.oscar.gr*
Get there: *Larissa Station Metro station on Line 2, Filadelfia St exit.*

Stanley (A)
Good-sized rooftop pool
(***pictured***) from ~1 to 2.5
metres deep—higher if the
pool is filled all the way.
Children of 120cm (4ft) can
stand with their head out (no
shallow end), and there's not

really a place to grab on to on the ledge, apart from the deck. Pool has shade. Deck area shower, change in the washroom. Large deck has a **snack bar**. Low-key, friendly service. Located right outside Metro station exit so no need to walk anywhere in this busy, down-at-heel area.

• *May–Oct daily 10am–7pm.* • *Adults €10, up to 12 yrs €5.* • ***1 Odysseos St, Karaiskaki Square, Metaxourgio***, *210-524-1611*, *www.hotelstanley.gr*
Get there*: At Metaxourgio Metro station on Line 2, Karaiskaki Sq exit.*

ACROPOLIS, MAKRIYANNI, SYNTAGMA

Divani Palace Acropolis (deluxe)
Outdoor pool (small) for **guests only**.

• *19–25 Parthenonos St, **Makriyanni**, 210-928-0100, www.divanis.com*
Get there*: From Akropolis Metro Station on Line 2, then 10 minutes' walk.*

Electra Palace (A)
Outdoor pool for **guests only**. **Indoor spa pool** is open to external guests of all ages, ask at reception if children are eligible for discounts.

• *Year-round daily 8am–9pm.* • *€15 per person.* • ***18 Nikodimou St, Plaka/Syntagma***, *210-337-0000*, *www.electrahotels.gr*
Get there*: From Syntagma Metro station on Lines 2, 3, then 10–15 minutes' walk.*

Grand Bretagne (deluxe)
Rooftop pool (***pictured***) for **guests only**. The GB Spa is the best in central Athens, and located on the floor below the lobby of this landmark hotel. The **indoor spa pool** (*see Chapter 15, At a Day Spa section*), sauna, and steam rooms are free to use for hotel guests and their children. Children aged 16 years and older can use the indoor pool on their own. **Snack bar** at both pools.

• *Indoor pool open year-round daily 6am–10pm; sauna/steam rooms daily 9am–10pm.* • *€45 per person, plus a treatment (massage, facial, etc) worth at least €50.* • ***Syntagma Square, Syntagma***, *210-333-0000, www.grandebretagne.gr*
Get there*: Syntagma Metro station on Lines 2 and 3.*

Royal Olympic (deluxe)
Rooftop pool (smallish) for **guests only**.

• *28–34 Athanasiou Diakou St, **Makriyanni**, 210-928-8400, www.royalolympic.com*
Get there*: From Akropoli Metro station on Line 2, then 5 minutes' walk.*

NEOS KOSMOS

Athenaeum Intercontinental (deluxe)
Seasonal rooftop pool for **guests only**.

• *89–93 Syngrou Ave, **Neos Kosmos**, 210-920-6000, www.intercontinental.com*
***Get there**: Neos Kosmos Metro station on Line 2; or trolley no. 10; bus nos. A2, B2, E22, E90, 040, 550 to bus-stop: Panteios; or tram-stop: Kasomouli, then 5 minutes' walk. ~10 minutes' journey from the centre.*

JK Hotel (A)
Small but nice rooftop plunge pool on the 5th floor with two steps (rarely found) at the shallow end (***pictured***) and steep gradient to about 1.8m at the deep end. Children must be accompanied in the pool. Deck chairs around the small deck. Washroom and private shower, no towels. Gazebo lounge

area around the pool. **Refreshments** but no food available. Early evening is a good time to go (not busy), and suitable for young kids (3–7 yrs), especially if they know how to swim; weekends are busy. Parking along or behind Ilia Iliou St.

• *May–Oct daily 8am–8pm or till sunset.* • *Adults €5, up to 6 yrs free.* • ***71 Ilia Iliou St, Neos Kosmos**, 210-901-0933, www.jkhotel.gr*
***Get there**: Just opposite Neos Kosmos Metro station on Line 2; or tram-stop: Neos Kosmos (same exit point).*

Ledra Marriott (deluxe)
Rooftop pool has a poolside **bar/restaurant** serving snacks, light meals, coffee, fresh juices, cocktails.

• *May–Oct daily 10am–6pm.* • *Free for guests, external guests of up to four people are charged a flat rate of €69, and get a room with towels and private facilities.* • ***115 Syngrou Avenue, Neos Kosmos**, 210-930-0000, www.marriott.com*
***Get there**: Trolley no. 10; bus nos. A2, B2, E22, E90, 040, 550 to bus-stop: Panteios; or tram-stop: Kasomouli, and then 5–10 minutes' walk. ~10 minutes' journey from the centre.*

KIFISSIAS AVE (AMBELOKIPI) & ALEXANDRAS AVE (PEDION AREOS)

President (A)
Pleasantly large outdoor pool (***pictured***) that's about 1.15m on either end and 2.10m in the middle. Some shade from poolside umbrellas. Deck area has sunbeds and umbrellas, shower, change rooms, WC. Atmosphere is a little bit strict.

• *Summer months daily 10.30am–7pm.* • *Adults €20, up to 6 yrs free, then full price. Mandatory €10 deposit per towel.* • *43 Kifissias Ave, Ambelokipi, 210-698-9000, www.president.gr*
Get there: *From Ambelokipi or Panormou Metro stations on Line 3, then 10 minutes' walk.*

Radisson Blu Park (deluxe)
Rooftop pool with chaises-longues, pool bar serving light snacks, coffee, fresh juices, cocktails.
• *May–Oct weather permitting, Sun–Fri 10.30am–6.30pm, Sat 10.30am–6pm.* • *Adults €25 includes coffee or juice, up to 12 yrs €12.50.* • *10 Alexandras Ave, Pedion Areos, 210-889-4500, 210-883-2711 to 19, www.athensparkhotel.gr*
Get there: *From Victoria Metro station on Line 1, then 10 minutes' walk. Located near Aigyptou Square and 28th Octovriou St (Patission), a junction with Alexandras Ave, there are many buses going past here, including trolley nos. 2, 3, 4, 5, 6, 7, 8, 9, 11, 13, 14, 15, 18 and 19, bus-stops in the centre on Amalias Ave or Panepistimiou St.*

Zafolia (A)
Rooftop pool 9.5x5m, 90cm to 2.5m, shaded, sunbeds, showers, **snack bar**.
• *May–Oct daily noon-7pm.* • *Entrance €15 incl refreshment, up to 2 yrs free.* • *87–89 Alexandras Ave, Pedion Areos, 210-644-9002, www.zafoliahotel.gr*
Get there: *From Ambelokipi Metro station on Line 3, Panormou exit, then 5-10 minutes' walk.*

KIFISSIA, METAMORFOSI, EKALI

Anessis (C)
Outdoor pool (20x10m) varies in depth from 1.3m to 2.7m. Shade on deck with umbrellas and sunbeds, snack bar.
• *May to Oct, daily 10am–6pm.* • *Adults €8 includes coffee or refreshment, 4 yrs and under free, 5–12 yrs half-price.* • *227 Tatoiou Ave, Metamorfosi, 210-281-4840.*
Get there: *Metamorfosi Suburban railway station then 5 min walk; or bus no. 541 from Maroussi*

Metro station on Line 1 to bus-stop: Polykandrioti; or bus nos. 604, 724 from Tachydromio bus-stop on Irakliou Ave near Nea Ionia Metro station on Line 1 to bus-stop: Polykandrioti (604), 2nd Tatoiou (724); or bus no. B9 from Halkokondyli St at Tritis Septemvriou St, Omonia Sq to bus-stop: Evis (Hbhs).

Life Gallery Athens (deluxe)

There are two pools at this deluxe hotel surrounded by grass and pines, so the pools also get shade from trees and buildings. One side of the plunge pool (15x5m) is glass so you can see swimmers underwater. There are gradual steps in the larger pool (20x10m), with a depth of 1.5m to 1.8m; the smaller pool's depth is ~1.4m to 1.7m. Lifeguard. Towels included, plus refreshments, other inclusions unknown at time of writing.

• *May–Oct, daily 10am–8pm.* • *Admission ~€15-20 for adults, free 2 yrs and under, half-price 3–12 yrs.*
• ***103 Thisseos Ave, Ekali****, 211-106-7400, www.bluegr.com.*
Get there*: Kifissia Metro station on Line 1, walk through park to Kifissias Ave to bus-stop: Pl Kifissias, then take bus nos. 507, 508, 509 or 536 to bus-stop: Narkissos. ~an hour's journey from the centre.*

Semiramis (deluxe)

This Yes (brand) hotel has a luxurious kidney-shaped pool that's about 20m long with depths of 1.5 or 1.6m, and steps on the side to 1.1m. There's no shade in the pool but there are umbrellas and sunbeds on the deck, it is lifeguarded, and towels are available. Snack bar. Apart from drop-ins, club members can use the pool and gym for an annual €750 fee.

• *May 15–Oct 15, daily 11am–7pm.* • *Admission expected to be ~€25 adults weekdays, more on weekends, under 2 yrs free, 3–12 yrs half-price, coffee, refreshment included.* • ***48 Harilaou Trikoupi St, Kifissia****, 210-628-4400, www.yeshotels.gr.*
Get there*: Kifissia Metro station on Line 1, then ~15 minutes' walk, through the park across Kifissias Ave to Kassabeti St, left/north on Georganta St, right on Kolokotroni St to the square (Kefalariou) and veer right/east on Filadelfeos along the side of the park a block to Har. Trikoupi St.*

'Destination' Pools

Sometimes children prefer to swim in pools than go to the beach, in which case they will love both of these options. One is located near the south coastal road not far from central Athens; the other is out west past Dafni, but kids of all ages will definitely remember the experience.

Acqua e Sole, Alimos

This conveniently street level, outdoor facility near the coast and beach Akti Alimou, Loutra Alimou, the Alimos Yacht Club, and on the way to Glyfada, about 10km/6mi from Athens, has two pools, and one is shallower and heated, thus suitable for babies. The other is unheated (except by the sun) and has a small slide

(*pictured*) and fountain, and is very popular with children. Both pools are **lifeguarded.**
   It's surrounded by sunbeds as well as tables with umbrellas. Licensed bar, **snacks** and light **lunches** are served, washrooms, change-rooms with warm showers for both pools. There's also an **outdoor play area** with swings, slides, bouncy castle and trampolines, as well as mini-soccer.
• *Stroller accessible.* • *Open year-round but not heated, so essentially May–Oct. Pool daily 9.30am until sunset; venue daily 9.30am–1am.* • *Adults €7 includes refreshment/coffee, 0–3 yrs free, 3–16 yrs €5 includes refreshment or granita (slushy).* • *Near Poseidonos and Alimou aves,* **Eptanissou and Cavafy sts, Alimos,** *210-984-1527,* www.acquaesole.gr, www.mini-soccer.gr
Get there: *Tram-stop: Zefyros; or bus nos. 109, 247 from Ag. Dimitrios Metro stn to bus-stop: Cavafy or 2nd Alimou; bus no. 141 from Dafni Metro stn to bus-stop: 2nd Alimou; or bus nos. A2, B2, E22 along Poseidonos Ave to bus-stop: 5th Kalamakiou.*

Copa Copana (water) Park, Haidari

This is a large waterslide and swimming pool complex with pools for all ages that children will adore. There are palm trees and "islands" for evening drinks, and all kinds of **waterslides**

(*pictured*). The **large circular pool** around the islands is about 1.5m throughout, and the **children's pool** (*paidòtopos*) is knee-deep at 0.4m (*pictured, beginning of the chapter*). There's a pirate boat with slides, fountains, and smaller waterslides for younger children. The big slides, including being able to go down in tandem on inner tubes, as from 2013, a jacuzzi, are up the steps (Aqua), under which are lockers, showers and washrooms, as well as a shop selling clothes, swimsuits, pool toys and accessories.
   There are **lifeguards** stationed throughout the site, including in front of each set of slides. It gets packed in summer; best to go in the morning or between 3pm and 5pm in the afternoon.
Snack bars, *souvlàki,* ice cream, and an air-conditioned **café/restaurant** including self-serve (*daily noon–2am*) with pastas, pizza, salads and more. You aren't supposed to bring your own food. Also **events in winter.**

• *Stroller accessible.* • *Pools open summer months 10am–7.30pm; slides 10am–6pm.* • *Adults €18, up to 3 yrs free, 3–5 yrs €7, 6–12 yrs, students & university students w/card €14. Family discounts: 1 adult +1 child 6–12 yrs €28. 1+2 ch €40. 2+1 ch €45. 2+2 ch €50. 2+3 ch €55. 2+4 ch €60. Also group discounts. With every ticket you can return Mon to Fri using the same ticket free of charge, within a*

month. • *Gefyra Schistou, Afaia Skaramanga, Haidari, on Athinon Ave (13.5km/8mi from Athens, heading towards Corinth), 210-557-6006, www.copacopanapark.com*
Get there: *Bus nos. A16, B16, Γ16 from Koumoundourou (Eleftherias) Sq on Piraeos St; or bus no. 866 from Egaleo Metro station on Line 3 from Iera Odos St; or bus no. 845 from Karaiskaki Sq at Metaxourgio Metro station on Line 2 to bus-stop: 2nd Afaia Haidariou. ~30-40 minutes' journey from the centre. Pool complex is in front of the bus-stop.*
Driving: *Take Athinon Ave (Kavalas, National Road) out of the city limits (built-up areas) and past the overhead bridge. You'll see a huge Copa Copana sign, and turn right immediately and right again into the parking lot. Leaving, follow the directions for the road over the highway heading towards Piraeus to the first traffic light and turn left to get back on to the National Road heading towards Athens.*

Kidom Fun Park, Rendi

And as a bonus, at Kidom amusement park *(see Chapter 12)*, 7.5km/4.5mi west of Athens, the shallow **swan boat pool** *(pictured)* and **snack bar** is open for little kids (only) during the heat of the day in summer, **supervised** and canopy-protected.

• *June–Aug daily 10am–11pm, Sept–May Mon–Thurs 5pm–11pm, Fri 5pm–midnight, Sat 10am–midnight, Sun 10am–11pm.* • *Children only (~3-5 yrs)* €4. • **Kifissou & Petrou Ralli aves, Agios Ioannis-Rendi**, *210-425-2600, www.allou.gr.*
Get there: *From Piraeos St, trolley no. 21; bus nos. B18, Γ18 to bus-stop: Kan Kan or Fix.*

Waterslide, Feb 2013 ☺ 5.5 yrs

Easy-to-reach Akti tou Iliou (Sunshine Coast) beach, Alimos

Chapter 14: Athens Area Beaches

Heads Up

Weather, season

The beaches along the Attica coastline, sometimes written in tourist literature as the Athenian or Athens Riviera, are among the best in Greece—sandy, shallow, clear and warm water. The south-facing beaches are less exposed to seasonal winds (if blowing from the north, the beaches should still be okay) than those along the east coast, but it's a good idea to check the wind forecast before heading out (try *www.meteo.gr*).

The water is chilly earlier in the season, but by August the salty, buoyant Aegean feels like you're walking into a bathtub.

You can reach a beach within half an hour to an hour from town, since from June to August, temperatures can exceed 40C/104F, and still reach the 30sC (86–94F) in mid-October.

The downside is that the beaches' proximity to Athens, population 4m, means they get very busy, especially at weekends, and those nearest the city, especially the free ones, get grubby. Early or later in the season the sea is clear.

Terrain

All the nearby beaches are sandy, but ones nearer to Athens have a bigger "drop" or a trough in the sea from the shoreline; those further out have a shallower gradient more suited for young children. Most young children wear water-wings/armbands. A beach that is shallow and near is at **Agios Kosmas** (*see below*).

Safety and facilities
There is a mix of free and pay (organized) beaches along the south coast. The free beaches are busier and scruffier, don't have sunbeds and may not have umbrellas, washrooms or showers, while the organized beaches have umbrellas and sunbeds, washrooms, facilities to change and shower, security at the entrance, and snack bars. Many people bring picnic lunches to both organized and free beaches. Alcohol is permitted; topless sunbathing is left for the more secluded beaches further down the coast.

In general there is not a theft problem at the beaches, but take precautions with belongings just the same. At the free beaches, many itinerant sellers come through selling things from sunglasses and cigarettes to jewellery, clothes, beach toys and doughnuts. It can get tiring. Canteens may set up nearby and sell hotdogs, skewers and refreshments.

Getting there
Getting to the beaches by trams that go all along the south coast to the suburb resort of Voula is the easiest way to locate a beach, and is a *stroller-friendly* means of public transport, but it is the slowest option. The quickest is by taxi, which costs about €10–20 one way, depending on the beach and traffic, but it easily racks up the cost of a day at the beach.

Attica Beaches (by proximity to Athens)

Nearest beaches
These beaches (selected) are *listed in order of proximity to Athens*. The nearest free beaches are at **Batis** and **Edem**, which also has a pay (organized) beach, both located where the **tram** reaches the coast and turns towards either **Piraeus (SEF)** or **Voula**, where there is also a large, organized beach with an **inflated water park**. *Note: Rates are 2012 and 2013; some not yet known at press time.*

Akti tou Iliou
Akti tou Iliou in Alimos is a long and wide stretch of coarse sand beach that's very near the centre, its entrance marked by flagpoles with a sun logo (Akti tou Iliou or "Sunshine Coast"). Plenty of umbrellas and sunbeds, which are included in the entrance price except on weekends, there are **canteens**, outdoor showers, washrooms and change huts. The entrance fee and security ensures there are no itinerant sellers along the beach.

The drawback here, as for any of

the beaches nearest town, is that there's a trough (*pictured*) when you just get into the water at the shoreline, so not too friendly for very young children, most have water-wings (armbands).

Since it's near Athens it gets busy and the water can get dirty, especially at weekends, when it's better to give these beaches a miss (too busy), apart from later or earlier in the season, when the sea is clear. In summer 2012, each time I visited, the beach had one or two women "exercising" provocatively. Hmmm.

• *Mon–Fri adults €5, 5–12 and seniors €3. Free sunbeds/umbrellas. Weekends and holidays adults €7, 5–12 yrs and seniors €4, sunbeds/umbrellas €2.* • *Akti Alimos-Plaz, 62 Posidonos Ave, Alimos, 210-985-5169.*

Get there: *Tram in the direction of Voula to tram-stop: Kalamaki (stroller accessible ramp) or the next one, Zephyros (steps); or bus nos. E22, A2, B2 from Akadimias St or Amalias or Syngrou aves to bus-stop: 4th Kalamaki. ~20–30 minutes' journey from the centre.*

FREE Agios Kosmas

This is a free, two-cove beach near Athens in Elliniko, on the tram line. Akrotiri nightclub, visible from Poseidonos Ave, is at the end of the access road. There are a few umbrellas and a snack bar with washroom facilities in front of the burnt-out club that has yet to be cleared. The first cove is sandy and shallow, hence many bathers and young children. The second small cove (*pictured*) in front of the burnt club is rockier but still shallow, and is sandy near the little spit dividing the beach, but no umbrellas.

You can get refreshments, meat skewers and hotdogs from a **canteen** here, and other supplies from itinerant sellers walking through the beach.

• *Agios Kosmas beach, **Alimos**.*

Get there: *Tram in the direction of Voula to tram-stop: 2nd Ag. Kosmas; or bus nos. A1, A2 from Akadimias St, Amalias or Syngrou aves to bus-stop: 2nd Ag. Kosmas. ~30 min journey from the centre.*

Asteria Glyfada and Balux

Across from the tony suburb and beach resort of Glyfada, this beach is 17km/11mi from Athens. Glyfada has many hotels, restaurants and bars that catered to Europeans flying in to the old airport on beach breaks. The beach is part of a complex of bars, play areas, lounges and a pool, with a wide swathe of sand, umbrellas and over-stuffed sunbeds, as well as grass.

The year-round **Balux House Project bar-café-restaurant** (*210-898-3577*, *www.baluxcafe.com*) (*pictured*) has a **play area for young kids** (games €2, inflatable play area €6, day pass €10), and entrees from ~€10. Balux serves drinks directly to your sunbed, with more canteens and bars, including the **Summer Balux Café** (*210-894-0566*) beside a **pool** (14 yrs and up) that has daybeds with privacy drapes.

• *Daily 8.30am–8pm, beach bars 9am–2/3am.* • *Adults €4 Mon–Fri, free up to 4 yrs, 4–12 yrs €2, Sat–Sun adults €6, 4–12 yrs €3.* • *58 **Poseidonos Ave**, **Glyfada**, 210-894-1620, www.asterascomplex.com*
Get there*: From Syntagma to tram-stop: Metaxa Agg; or bus nos. A2, E22 from Akadimias St, Amalias or Syngrou aves to bus-stop: Asteria (Glyfada). Free parking. ~40 minutes' journey.*

Voula A

This beach is 19km/12mi south of Athens at the end of the tram line in Voula, a suburb resort next to Glyfada. It's a long, wide stretch of sand that's been revamped and upgraded in the last year (2012), with additions like a swimming pool, inflatable water park (€10 for a parent and child), water-sports, **snack bars** and bars (Oxyzen), free wifi. Lots of padded wooden sunbeds and wide umbrellas. Very popular with teens and 20-somethings, suitable for young children as well.

• *Daily 8am–sunset (beach closes); beachfront cafe & other facilities stay open at night.* • *Weekdays adults €4.50, weekends €5.50, 6–12 yrs and seniors ~€3.50, free under 6 yrs.* • *4 K. Karamanlis St (Poseidonos Ave), Voula, 210-895-8800, www.south-coast.gr*
Get there*: From Syntagma to tram-stop: Asklipiou Voula; bus nos. A2, E22 to stop: A Plaz Voulas. ~50 minutes' journey.*

Asteri Vouliagmeni

Arguably the best beach this close to town, Asteri (*pictured*) is just across the street from a yacht club, 25km/15.5mi from Athens. It's also the priciest, but the payoff is more comfort, with cushioned teak sunbeds, nice facilities and warm showers. The sea has a shallow gradient in this large bay, and you can try water-sports such as waterskiing. Shops sell drinks and **snacks** (also a **restaurant**) books, toys, sunglasses and swimwear. Also on a swampy site are the ancient remains of a 6th century BC temple, Apollo Zoster. Kids can squish their feet and look for tiny frogs.

• *May 16–Sept 15 8am–9pm.* • *Mon–Fri adults €13, 5–12 yrs €7; Sat–Sun adults €23, 5–12 yrs €12.* • *Apr–May 15/Sept 16–Oct 31 9am–7pm, Mon–Fri adults €10, under 12 yrs free; Sat–Sun adults €18, under 12 yrs free.*
• *Astir Beach, 40 Apollonos St, Vouliagmeni, 210-890-1774, 210-890-1621, www.astir-beach.com*
Get there*: From Syntagma to tram-stop: Glyfada (Voula-bound); or bus nos. A2, B3, E22 to Glyfada from Akadimias St, Amalias or Syngrou aves. At Glyfada, transfer to bus no. 114 to bus-stop: Astir Vouliagmenis. ~60 minutes' journey, or 40 minutes by taxi.*

Akti Vouliagmenis

A very nice but very busy, child-friendly beach 26km/16mi from the centre with an easy gradient into the water that's shallow for quite a few metres. There are **canteens**/bars, outdoor showers, change huts and washrooms, and grassy areas with trees.

• *Daily 8am–9pm in summer, 8am–7pm shoulder seasons and 9am–6pm in winter.* • *Adults €4, under 5 yrs free, 6–18 yrs and seniors €3.* • ***Poseidonos Ave, Vouliagmeni**, 210-896-0697, www.etasa.gr* **Get there**: *From Akadimias St, Amalias or Syngrou aves bus no. E22; or from Glyfada bus nos. 114, 116, 149 to bus-stop: A Plaz Vouliagmenis. Free parking. ~60 minutes' journey from the centre.*

Vouliagmeni Lake

Just past Akti Vouliagmenis, the hot-spring lake is unique in that it's fed by mineral-rich underground thermal springs (21–27C/70–80F) which have many health benefits for all kinds of ailments. The water covers the top of an enormous cave, surrounded by cliffs. **Café**, sunbeds, tables and umbrellas on a deck forming a semi-circle, lifeguard, doctor on duty, plus aids to help those with difficulties enter the water.

• *Year-round 8am–7.30pm, last entrance 7pm.* • *Adults €8, 5–12 yrs €5, under 4 yrs free.* • ***Lake Vouliagmenis, Vouliagmeni**, 210-896-2237/9, www.limnivouliagmenis.gr* **Get there**: *Bus no. E22; or from Glyfada bus nos. 114, 116, 149 to bus-stop: Limni. Free parking.*

Yabanaki Varkiza

This is the furthest organized beach within easy striking distance from Athens (30km/19mi), about half-way to Sounion (67km/41mi). Varkiza is a seaside resort with a wonderful sandy beach (shallow gradient) that's very popular with young people, with rows of sunbeds and blaring **cafe-bars**. Also **restaurants**, waterslides, beach volleyball, windsurfing and water-skiing.

• *June–Oct daily 8am–7pm.* • *Mon–Fri adults €5.50, 6 yrs and under free, 7–12 yrs and seniors €3.50. Sat–Sun, holidays adults €6.50, 7–12 yrs and seniors €3.50, 6 yrs and under free. Sat–Sun and holidays sunbeds/umbrellas are €5.* • ***Sounion Ave, Vari**, 210-897-2414, www.yabanaki.com* **Get there**: *From Akadimias St, Amalias or Syngrou aves bus no. E22 to bus-stop: Varkiza (Akti), or by taxi. Free parking. ~70-90 minutes' journey from the centre.*

Eat

Across from Yabanaki in Varkiza, is a taverna called **Zachos**, which has many tables set out front. Very busy, the service is prompt. Typical meal for four under €20 is chips (fries) x 2, 2 *kalamaki* (skewers of pork), a pork *merida* (dish with pork and chips), *souvlaki* in a pita, which kids can open and eat from, and they do have ketchup.

• *Daily 12.30pm–1am.* • *94 Vas. Konstantinou St, Varkiza, 210-897-5652.*
*Also branches in **Saronida** (58 Saronidos Ave, 22910-60687), and in **Glyfada** (7 Kondyli St, Glyfada Square, 210-894-2343).*

Monster, unfinished, March 2013 ☺ 5.5 yrs

**FREE Artemis
(Artemida, Loutsa)**
Loutsa beach (*pictured*) is
a long shallow stretch (but
watch for currents) on the
east coast, about
30km/18mi from Athens.
It can get windy but in late
summer the water is like a
bath. A Greek fast-food
restaurant across the
street beside the
amusement park (Ferris
wheel, bumper cars, mini-
train, etc) serves the
umbrellas and sunbeds

with cheap food and drinks (so don't bring your own beer for example, if you're
using the umbrellas). Washrooms and foot rinse at the restaurant, no public
showers.

• *Loutsa Beach,* **Artemida (Loutsa)**.
Get there: *From Nomismatokopeio Metro station on Line 2, bus nos. 305, 316 to bus-stop: Palaio Terma. Bus no. 304 to the Metro station turns further down (south) on the Paiania–Loutsa Road (Konstantine Karamanlis St) at the corner of Artemidos Ave, past the marina. There is also beach front near here (a long beach). ~90 minutes' journey.*

Beach & Island Day Trip: Aegina & Angistri

A good way to hit a beach without the hassle of traffic along the Poseidonos Ave
(south) coast is to go to the nearby island of Aegina (28km/17mi from Athens), or
its satellite, Angistri (or Agistri) on a day trip.
   Ferries and flying dolphins (hydrofoils) for the Saronic islands leave from
Gate E8 at the port of **Piraeus**, across the busy street (overpass) from Piraeus
Metro station on Line 1, which takes about 20 minutes to reach from Monastiraki
station in town. Allow about 20–30 minutes at the other end to get your tickets

(from booths inside the
port opposite the boat
departure point) and get
on the ferry. Many daily
departures, and the
journey takes about an
hour on a hydrofoil (add
10 minutes for Angistri) or
two hours by ferry, which
is much more pleasant.
   Snack bars are on the
boats but they're usually
pricey.
   Boat schedules are on
www.gtp.gr and
www.openseas.gr.

Tickets are about €14 per person (discounts for children) by hydrofoil, and €9 by ferry.

Aegina
Aegina is big (85km2/33mi2) and ferries may go directly to **Agia Marina** (*pictured, previous page*) a busy beach resort (free) on the east side of the island. **Aegina town** is on the island's west coast, with its neoclassical 19th century buildings, plethora of tavernas and narrow streets. The beach, **Avra** (*pictured*) is a few minutes' walk along the shoreline, past the seafood tavernas towards the Kolona, or ancient column, visible from the **archaeological site** (*Aegina Archaeological Museum and site, Tues–Sun 8.30am–3pm, adults €3, 22970-22248, www.culture.gr*) located beside the free beach.

Or take a taxi to **Marathonas** in the other direction, a small, shallow and quiet beach with a couple of **tavernas** and villas to rent, or go to the fishing village of **Perdika** 9km/5.5mi from Aegina town on the southwest tip of the island.

Angistri (Agistri)
At next-door Angistri (13km2/5mi2), if the hydrofoil goes to **Skala port**, the shallow, protected beach (*pictured*), is a few steps from the ferry dock, and has umbrellas and sunbeds (free with drink or food purchase), as **tavernas and cafes** line the shore. There are many hotels if you decide to stay overnight. If the hydrofoil goes to **Mylos** (aka

Megalohori), there's a waiting bus (small fee) that brings you the five-minute trip to Skala.

Waterpainting, June 2011 ☺ *3.5 yrs*

Traditional Greek dances under the stars, Dora Stratou Theatre, Filopappou Hill (see Chapter 10, Venues section)

Chapter 15: Parent Time Out

On the Town

If you can manage some "me" time, here are suggestions for a night out nearby, having a spa treatment, or just getting a hair cut (children too). (*See chapters 10 & 11 for concerts, special events, theatre, cinema and activities*).

Dinner & drinks

If you're able to get a babysitter, here is a selection of places for dinner and drinks within walking distance of the hotels located in the areas around the Acropolis and central Athens. For an excellent guide to nightlife in English, pick up the free *Athens City Guide* which also has maps.

In Plaka, colourful Vrettos ouzo, raki and brandy bar is one of Europe's oldest. 41 Kydathinaion St, Plaka, 210-323-2110, www.brettosplaka.com

SYNTAGMA SQUARE, PLAKA

7 Jokers
Right in the central shopping district, this bar/cafe serves drinks till late in the night.
• *Mon–Sat 8.30am–late, Sun from 3.30pm.* • **7 Voulis St, Syntagma**, *210-321-9225.*

Boheme
Or from Syntagma, go up the hill to this small, friendly bar in the business district.
• *36 Omirou St,* **Panepistimio**, *210-360-8018.*

GB Roof Garden
For a special night out at a restaurant, the best setting is the GB Roof Garden in the **Grande Bretagne Hotel**. The décor is teak, with an open, Asian feel, the food is Mediterranean grill. Also an attractive, translucent marble, backlit **bar**.
• *Entrees €19–€46.* • *Daily 6–11am/1pm–2am.* • **Syntagma Sq**, *210-333-0766, www.gbroofgarden.gr*

Filomousou Etairia Square (Kydathinaion St), Plaka
On the main street of Plaka for food and drinks, Kydathinaion St, is a small public square completely surrounded by seating and umbrellas for café-bars, restaurants and ouzeries. Come here to enjoy the evening atmosphere and people-watching.

Karytzi Square, Agia Irini Square
The nearest **nightlife areas** are at **Christou Lada St** and Karytzi Square, or head further down towards **Monastiraki** at Agia Irini Square on Aiolou St.

THISSIO

Filistron
The roof garden at this meze restaurant has an incomparable view of the Acropolis and Lycabettus Hill.
• *Meze €4–€12.* • *April–Oct daily noon–midnight, Fri–Sat to 1am.* • **24 Apostolou Pavlou St, Thissio**, *210-346-7554, www.filistron.com*

Thissio Square, Irakleidon St
Then go around the corner to Irakleidon St or across **Apostolou Pavlou St** to Thissio Square (*pictured*) for a nightcap at one of countless **sidewalk café/bars**.

GAZI

Kerameikos Metro station area

Or make for nearby Gazi, where **Mamacas** (*41 Persefonis St, Gazi, 210-347-0280, www.mamacasbar.gr*) beside Kerameikos Metro station (Technopolis/Gazi exit) has passed the test of time for hearty Greek food and has sidewalk dining in mild weather. **Mamacas bar** (*daily 10pm till late, 37–39 Persefonis St, Gazi, 210-347-0280, www.mamacasbar.gr*) is handily across the street, but there's a **plethora of bars and cafes**, especially on the other side of the station (*pictured*). You can't miss them.

MAKRIYANNI, KOUKAKI

Drakou St

Go down to Drakou St (*pictured*) for a nightcap at one of the **sidewalk cafes**. It's the pedestrian street where the Syngrou-Fix Metro station exits. Have a beer at **Vini's** (*10 Drakou St, Koukaki, 210-922-6225*) or at another **outdoor café/bar** along here (all within two or three blocks).

Edodi

Just down the street from Makriyanni in Koukaki, Edodi is arguably the best restaurant this side of Filopappou Hill, where you choose from fresh ingredients brought to your table, and sommelier wine by the glass.
• *Entrees €28–€32, fixed menu €34.* • *Sept–June Mon–Sat 5.30pm–12.30am.* • **80 Veikou St, Koukaki**, *210-921-3013, www.edodi.gr*

Mani Mani

This nouvelle cuisine restaurant puts a modern twist on Greek dishes.
• *Entrees €8.50–€14.50.* • *Tues–Sun 2pm–11pm.* • **10 Falirou St, Makriyanni**, *210-921-8180, www.manimani.com.gr*

Olympou St

After dinner at Edodi, have a drink at one of the many **café/bars** on pedestrian Olympou St that has a local neighbourhood feel, or go back to Drakou St.

Strofi
Dine on traditional taverna fare in the roof garden with a beautiful view of the Acropolis, just off pedestrian Dion. Areopagitou St near that monument's entrance.
• *Entrees ~€11–€25* • *Daily noon–1am.* • *25 Rovertou Galli St, Makriyanni/Koukaki, 210-921-4130, www.strofi.gr*

KOLONAKI

Altamira
If your tastes run to the exotic, this airy restaurant/bar has crocodile, reindeer and ostrich on the menu.
• *Entrees €10–€15.* • *Mon–Sat 1pm–1.30am, closed mid-July to Aug.* • *36A Tsakalof St, Kolonaki, 210-361-4695, www.altamira.com.gr*

Filippos
Or eat a traditional taverna meal at the well-loved Filippos in the middle of a residential, upmarket neighbourhood.
• *Entrees €6–€14.* • *Mon–Fri 1–5pm/8.30pm–midnight, Sat 1–5pm.* • *19 Xenokratous St, Kolonaki, 210-721-6390.*

Milioni St, Kolonaki Square, Haritos St
For a nightcap go to pedestrian Milioni St— where you can also eat at **Jackson Hall** (*4 Milioni St, Kolonaki, 210-361-6098, www.jacksonhall.gr*) that runs off Athens' poster-child of café society, Kolonaki Square (*pictured*), or head to one of the tiny, more intimate **bars** near the end of pedestrian Haritos St.

Ouzadiko
This *meze* restaurant is in the most unlikely setting—inside a rather empty mall complex (one building among the residential apartment blocks), increasingly occupied by **bars and clubs**. The food is great.
• *Entrees from €8.* • *Sept–July Mon–Sat noon–12.30am, closed Dec 25, Jan 1, Orthodox Easter Sun.*
• *25-29 Karneadou St, Lemos Intl Centre, Kolonaki, 210-729-5484.*

MONASTIRAKI

Café Avyssinia
Have a memorable, unique local food dinner on the top floor of this restaurant with a view of the Acropolis, located inside the antique and flea market at **Avyssinia Square**, between Ermou and Ifestou sts.
• *Entrees €7.50–€15.* • *Tues–Sat 11am–1am, Sun 11am–7pm.* • **7 Kynetou St, Avyssinia Sq, Monastiraki**, 210-322-4501, www.avissinia.gr

James Joyce Irish Pub
This Irish pub has a more foreign clientele, live evenings, and three large screens for sports events.
• *Daily noon till around 2am.* • **12 Astiggos St, Monastiraki**, 210-323-5055, www.jjoyceirishpubathens.com

Six Dogs
This arty place (***pictured***) is out of the way in a narrow street in the shopping district which has a large, treed space at the back (downstairs) in a courtyard/garden full of tables and quiet corners.
• **6-8 Avramiotou St, Monastiraki**, 210-321-0510, www.sixdogs.gr

TAF/The Art Foundation
The popular TAF hangout is a 19th century building turned art space with a courtyard for drinks.
• **5 Normanou St, Monastiraki**, 210-323-8757, www.theartfoundation.gr

PSYRRI

Nearby, across Ermou St (north) and Athinas St (west) is Psyrri, which has a number of bars and restaurants. **Silfio** (*24 Taki and Lepeniotou sts, Psyrri, 210-324-7028*), with the distinctive black cat in a yellow background sign, is a good bet for dining. Some also have **live bouzouki music**. Take care not to venture too far north, towards the **Central Market (Agorà)** and **Evripidou St** at night, as it becomes rather unsavoury.

KALIMARMARA (STADIO), PANGRATI

Half Note Jazz Club
A place for **blues and jazz** is this club, opposite the First Cemetery, which also has a lot of foreign acts.
• *17 Trivonianou, **Mets**, 210-921-3310, after 8pm: 210-921-3360, www.halfnote.gr*

Spondi

With two Michelin stars to its credit, this restaurant in Pangrati, the area behind the Panathenian (Kalimarmara) Stadium, serves French cuisine and also has a formidable (1,300-bottle) wine list.

• *Entrees €38–€55.* • *Daily 8pm-midnight.* • **5 Pyrronos St, Pl. Varnavas, Pangrati, 210-756-4021, www.spondi.gr**
Get there: *Taxi or walk from Syntagma, where you can also get bus no. 209 to bus-stop: Pl. Varnavas; or trolley no. 4 to bus-stop: ELTA, rtn bus-stop: Nearhou on Filellinon St.*

Special Events & Concerts

If you've timed your visit for an international gig (or are just lucky), take the opportunity and hire a sitter, if necessary. For an excellent guide to nightlife in English, pick up the free *Athens City Guide*. (*See chapters 10 & 11*).

Spectator Sports

Soccer/football fans can check if there's a match taking place while here. Soccer (football) games are not known to be particularly family-friendly, but if older children are ardent fans...

Tickets (other than season tickets) are usually made available when the games are announced, about a week or so before each match.

The three main clubs are **AEK** and **Panathinaikòs** of Athens, and **Olympiacòs** of Piraeus.

The **football clubs** (FC) are listed below; the websites for the **basketball clubs** are *www.aek.gr*, *www.paobc.gr* and *www.olympiacosbc.gr* respectively.

AEK FC
Athletic Union of Constantinople, 210-612-1371, www.aekfc.gr
Get **tickets** by calling 801-100-2121, or 210-805-6740 for credit card purchase; buy online; at the **OAKA Stadium** grounds; or at the AEK official shop in Nea Filadelphia.

• **AEK official shop**: *Mon, Wed, Sat 9am–4pm, Tues, Thurs, Fri 9am–9pm.* • **146 Dekeleias St, Nea Filadelphia**, *210-252-5784.* • **Get there**: *On Proastiakos suburban rail from Larissa (Athens) Station railway station on Metro Line 2 to Pindou station.*

Olympiakos FC
210-414-3000, www.olympiacos.org
Tickets can be bought at their home ground, **Karaiskaki Stadium** in Neo Faliro, but check announcements on the website about a week before games for online and other points of purchase.

• **Karaiskaki Stadium**: *Opposite Neo Faliro Metro station on Line 1, ~10 minutes' journey.*

Olympic Stadium (OAKA)
Panathinaikos and AEK currently share the home ground at OAKA Stadium in Maroussi (11km/7mi), also known as the **Olympic Stadium**.

• **Olympic Centre of Athens, Maroussi**, *210-683-4060, www.oaka.com.gr*
Get there: *Irini Metro station on Line 1. ~30 minutes' journey.*

Panathinaikos FC

210-870-9000, www.pao.gr
Tickets through their website, at the grounds, telephone orders 210-647-0970, and from official stores.
• *Panathinaikos Official Store: daily 10am–8.30pm.* • **47 Pandrossou St, Monastiraki,** *210-321-6230, www.greenteam.gr*
• **The Mall Athens, Maroussi:** *Neratziotissa suburban rail and Metro station on Line 1. ~30 minutes' journey from the centre.*

Sports Cafes

Most café bars, such as in the **Thissio area,** have wide screen TVs indoors and/or outdoors for patrons to watch spectator sports, usually football/soccer. Foreigners gather at a couple of places in town.

Athens Sports Bar

This small bar draws an international backpacker's crowd. Their site and Facebook page has upcoming games. Eat fish n' chips and burgers from the **Fish Café** (*www.fishcafe.gr*) next door in the same building (same owners), as it's also part of the **Athens Studios** (*www.athensstudios.gr*) complex.
• *Daily 7.30am till late.* • **3A Veikou St, Makriyanni,** *210-923-5811, www.athenssportsbar.com*
Get there: *Akropoli Metro station on Line 2, then 5 minutes' walk.*

James Joyce Irish Pub

This pub screens sports events on three large screens, and has an expat crowd.
• *Daily noon–~2am.* • **12 Astiggos St, Monastiraki,** *210-323-5055, www.jjoyceirishpubathens.com*
Get there: *Thissio or Monastiraki Metro stations on Lines 1 or 3, then 5 minutes' walk.*

At a Day Spa

Doctor Fish

A day spa with a twist is Doctor Fish, where, apart from the list of waxes, tints, manicures and express massages, you can get your feet nibble-cleaned by fish (€10 for a 10-minute trial or €20 for 30 minutes). Located near Monastiraki Metro station.
• *59 Adrianou St and Areos,* **Plaka,** *210-325-1515, www.doctor-fish.gr*

Open-air theatre

See a film under the stars in summer on the rooftop at **Cine Paris**, 22 Kydathenaion St, Plaka, 210-322-2071. Or in a garden at **Thission**, 7 Apostolou Pavlou St, Thissio, 210-347-0980 (**pictured**), or at **Aegli**, inside the Zappeion Gardens, Syntagma/Zappeio, 210-336-9369, www.aeglizappiou.gr (See also Chapter 10, Cinema section).

Fish Spa

Fish Spa, across the street from Quick Spa, has a €5 massage and incorporates the latest in pedicure fads: the use of fish (€10).

• *45 Aiolou St, **Monastiraki**, 211-800-3700, www.fishspa.gr*

GB Spa

The Grande Bretagne hotel's spa on Syntagma Square in central Athens is a luxury, full-service spa complete with indoor pool with hydrojets (*pictured*), sauna and steam rooms ("Thermal Suite") as well as offers facials, massages and body-care treatments. For non-guests (free for guests) you must buy a treatment

worth at least €50 and pay an additional €45 to use the facilities.

• *Treatments, consultations, Thermal Suite daily 9am–9.30pm, indoor pool daily 6am–10pm.* • *Spa cuisine 11am–4pm.* • ***Grande Bretagne Hotel, Syntagma Sq**, 210-333-0799; www.gbspa.gr*

Hammam

For a traditional hamam experience, at Hammam (*pictured*) you can enjoy the steam room for €25 or have a masseuse exfoliate your body like they did in the Turkish baths of old for €45. Also other treatments, including for couples. Suitable for children 8 or 9 yrs and up.

• *Tues–Fri 1pm–10pm, Sat/Sun 10am–10pm.* • ***17 Agion Asomaton and 1 Melidoni sts, Thissio** Metro station, 210-323-1073, www.hammam.gr*

Quick Spa

Countless nail bars in the city offer **manicures and pedicures**, but Quick Spa, in a blink-or-miss lane off Aiolou St in Monastiraki, has good prices and does massages and facials as well.

• *50–52 Aiolou and 31 Miltiadou sts, **Monastiraki**, 210-325-5545, www.quickspa.gr*

At a Salon

If a new haircut for grown-ups (or children) is in order, a colour, highlights, special hairdo, or even just to redo your roots, here are some hairdressers located around the centre. Most speak English, especially around Syntagma. Cuts start ~€15, children's cuts are usually €8–€12, colours/highlights ~€30. Blow-drying is usually charged extra.

D. Frank
There are a few salons in upmarket **Kolonaki**; one is D. Frank.
• *50 Sina and Anagnostopoulou sts, Kolonaki, 210-360-3297.*

Eau
Around **Syntagma**, Eau does women, men and children.
• *17 Nikis St, Syntagma, 210-331-8072-3.*

Giorgos Hatzigiorgiou
Giorgos Hatzigiorgiou does hair for men, women and children as well as manicures, pedicures, waxing and make-up.
• *45–47 Voulis St, Syntagma/Plaka, 210-331-1891.*

Yianni Hair Spa
The salon inside the Grande Bretagne Hotel, Yanni, is a local chain started by a well-known and internationally-trained stylist (by appointment). He uses natural products, and is conveniently open on Sundays.
• *Daily 11am–7pm.* • ***Syntagma Square**, 210-333-0799, www.gbspa.gr*

Take your pick of places to get your hair cut if you walk along arterial **Veikou** or **Dimitrakopoulou** sts in **Makriyanni** and **Koukaki**. Choose one that appeals— they are reasonably priced and often have weekday deals.

George and Georgia
This hairdresser's on the pedestrian road has English-speaking staff, which also does a nice scalp massage while washing your hair.
• *17–19 Olympiou St, Koukaki, 210-921-6119.*

Panos Evageliou
You can get good colour/highlighting and quick cuts done at this salon (***pictured***), also catering to men and children.
• *3 Orlof St, Koukaki, 210-923-6777.*

In **Thissio** try **Kaiti** (*7 Akamandos St*), **Nikolaou Team** (*16 Nileos St, 210-342-5221*), **Hair Trick** (*24 Nileos St, 210-345-1352*), one on Poulopoulou at Apostolou Pavlou St, or the one at 3–5 Erysixthonos St at Thessalonikis St.

Valentine, Feb 2013 ☺ 5.5 yrs

One of the city's most beautiful churches is the 12th century Agii Theodori church near Klafthmonos Square on Evripidou St, central Athens

Chapter 16: Biblical Athens & Worship

Athens has early roots in Christianity. Apostle Paul preached to ancient Greeks worshipping the pantheon of Mount Olympus gods at **Areopagus Hill**, near the Acropolis. There are still a few **Eastern Orthodox churches** built in the mediaeval Attica style that remain from the time when the city was a small, provincial town in the Byzantine (Eastern Roman) Empire, the centre of which was at Constantinople, renamed Istanbul. The churches are typically domed and cruciform, and the earliest date from the 9th century. Some may be open to view the colourful interiors and light a candle (say a prayer).

The **Byzantine and Christian Museum** has many relics and rare sculptures, while Christian artefacts are also found in the **Benaki Museum** and the **National History Museum**. (*See Chapter 6 for descriptions of the above-mentioned sites*).

Attend a Greek Orthodox Church Service

To experience a worshipping ritual that hasn't changed in hundreds of years (hence "orthodox"), attend a **service**, part of one, or visit a church while services are being held, at one of the numerous churches around town and in every neighbourhood. There are no Greek Orthodox services held in English under the auspices of the **Archdiocese of Athens**. Services are long and held early Sunday

mornings from 7am, but people arrive until about 8.30am. The main Orthodox church is aesthetically-maligned **Metropolitan cathedral**, on Mitropoleos St.
• *Archdiocese, 21 Agias Filotheis St, Mitropoleos/Plaka, 210-335-2300, www.iaath.gr*
You'll be able to hear the unique chants (typical example:
http://www.youtube.com/watch?v=ITojhvuyJg0), and smell the frankincense—used since antiquity with its purportedly purifying and calming effects—when the censer is shaken down the aisle to disperse the wafting incense among the faithful.

Women usually sit or stand on the left side of the church, men on the right.

The interior is plastered with colourful, usually two-dimensional wall paintings and silver icons of Christ, Mary, apostles, saints and biblical scenes. Congregants are always facing east.

Light a candle

Typical ornate Greek Orthodox church, Agia Marina, Thissio

If you don't want to stay for the service, near the entrance are candles you can buy (donation) and light—the flame is from Jerusalem, brought each year at Easter—and say prayers, leaving your candle(s) in a sandpit or special candelabra (***pictured, at left***). You can also do this or drop in for prayer whenever a church has its doors open during the day.

Wendy A Kollias

Agia Sofia church produced leaflets in English on the subject: *Lighting a Candle*. "The early Christians used candles (for) the purpose of (lighting) the dark catacombs where they were congregated for their sacred masses. Today, Christians are lighting candles in churches in order to honour this event. They are also lighting candles as a symbol of their flaming faith, as well as in memory of their beloved deceased. The amount of money gathered is used for the maintenance of this church and (for) the purpose of helping (the) Meropion Foundation, a Nursing Home for elderly destitute ladies."
• *Agia Sofia church, 45 Dion. Areopagitou St, opposite the Herodes Atticus Theatre on the Acropolis walkway, 210-921-9398.*

English-language Church Services

1st Greek Evangelical Church
Sun 11am in Greek with English translation, winter Sun 7pm, summer 8pm with translation by appt, winter Wed 7pm, summer 8pm with translation by appt.
• *50 Amalias Ave, **Plaka/Makriyanni/Zappeion**, 210-323-1079, www.aeee.gr, www.gec.gr*

2nd Evangelical Church is unadorned, inside and out

2nd Greek Evangelical Church

June–Oct Sun 10.30am, Nov–May 11am, Sun 7pm; prayer service Wed 7.30pm. English translation Sun mornings, Wed eve prayers may be led by visiting theology students. Many resident UK and US congregants and visitors.
• *24 Androutsou and 35 Anast. Zinni sts, **Koukaki**, 210-923-4071, www.beee.gec.gr*

Athens Baptist Church
Sun at 11am–12.30pm in English and Greek (Greek with English translation, hymns alternating languages, then English-language liturgy).
• *14 V. Dipla St, **Neos Kosmos**, 6944-058-1001.*

Church of Christ
Sun 6pm–7.30pm in English.
• *10 Evrou St, **Ambelokipi**, 210-779-4840.*

Church of Christ
Sun 6pm–7pm in English.
• *1st floor, 28 Piraeos (Pan Tsaldari) St, **Omonia**, 210-523-7030, 210-524-5527, www.athenschurchofchrist.net.*

International Christian Fellowship of Athens
Sun 9.45am in English.
• *7th fl, 68-70 Aiolou St, Kotzia Square, **Omonia**, 211-710-9235, www.icfofathens.com*

Saint Denis/Agios Dionysus Roman Catholic Cathedral
Oct–March Sun 6pm, Apr–Sept Sun 7pm mass in English. **Office**: Mon–Fri 9am–1pm.
• *22 Panepistimiou (Elef Venizelou) and 9 Omirou sts, **Panepistimio**, 210-362-3603.*

Saint Paul's Anglican Church
Sun 10.15am, Tues 10am (communion) in English.
• *27 Filellinon St, **Syntagma**, 210-721-4906, www.anglicanchurch.gr*

Trinity International Baptist Church
Sun 9am in English. Held at the 3rd Greek Evangelical Church.
• *37 Heldraich St, **Neos Kosmos**, 210-932-6761, www.actsseventeen.com*

Non-Christian, Buddhist & Meditation Services

Art of Living
(Founder: Sri Sri Ravi Shankar, *210-752-3087*, *www.theartofliving.gr*) holds guided meditation upstairs at:
* **Avocado Restaurant** Tues 6.30pm. May also have special events such as children's yoga and free seminars for parents downstairs.
• *30 Nikis St, **Syntagma**, 210-323-7878, www.avocadoathens.com*
* Also satsangs on the first and third Wednesday of the month; check in summer, held different locations, often at **Fish Spa**.
• *1st floor, 45 Aiolou St, **Monastiraki**, 311-800-3700.*

Bhavana Yoga Center
Drop-in yoga with meditation classes for €17 or €8 (contact the centre). Kundalini Yoga for English-speakers, Mon 6.30pm, and Pranayama/Yoga Nidra for Greek-speakers Wed 6.30pm.
• *43 Aiolou and Kolokotroni sts, **Monastiraki**, 210-323-8133, www.bhavanayoga.com*

Pathgate Dharma Centre Buddhist Association
Guru Yoga and Mahakala practice. Classical Buddhist Qigong & Meditation Mon, Wed 7–8pm, Sun 10am; Tara Puja Wed 8–9pm, Sun 9–10am, Meditation and teachings Sun 11am–noon. Meditation classes €6 per hour, Puja and audiotape meditation free. In English. Children can take part or keep busy by watching children's DVDs, etc.
• *7 Menandrou St, Theatrou Square, **Agora (Central Market)**, 210-330-3471, www.palyulnyingma-gr.org*

Inside Goraba mosque, Kato Patissia, Athens

Derek Gatopoulos

Mosques
There are a number of unofficial mosques operating around Athens that cater to the immigrant community, and services are not likely to be in English. You can find local **prayer times** on *www.islamicfinder.org*, and a **list of mosques** at *www.islam.gr* in Arabic and Greek only under "Useful: Masjiids in Greece." Use an auto-translator.

Synagogue
Beth Shalom Synagogue
Services Mon, Thurs 8.30am, Sat 8.30am, and Fri–Sat at sunset. In Greek and

Hebrew. For security reasons call ahead before visiting; they may request ID.
• *5 Melidoni St, **Thissio/Psyrri**, 210-325-2875/23. More info on www.chabad.gr*

Excursions to Monasteries

There are a few monasteries around Athens, both deserted and functioning. They must be popular with visitors, as taxi operators include a selection for visits and full-day tours (try "monasteries Attiki" in a search). Listed here are the two best-known deserted ones, plus two functioning monasteries. Conservative dress for visiting is expected; male-only ones may not allow women to enter.

FREE Dafni Monastery, Haidari

An important monastery near Athens is Dafni (Daphni, Daphne) Monastery. Now in ruins, the main draw here are the remarkable 11th century mosaics, with charming biblical depictions that include the baptism of Christ and a Pantocrator said to be the best Byzantine example, but you need to climb ladder steps to see them, so parents will have to take it in turns if caring for little ones. There is also a small **museum** here.

Founded in the 6th century on the site of an ancient temple of Apollo, Ionic columns had been used in its construction, removed by **Lord Elgin** in the 19th century. Originally a three-aisled basilica which is rare in these parts, it was dedicated to the Dormition of the Virgin in the 11th century (depicted in mosaic) and used as a monastery for Frankish Cistercian monks. By 1458, the then Turkish rulers had returned it to the Orthodox Church. During the 19th century Greek War of Independence, it was used as a garrison, and Bavarian troops accompanying the first king of Greece stayed here. It housed psychiatric patients from 1883 to 1885. It was first excavated in 1892 following earthquake damage.

There are also two **playgrounds**, one beside the monastery and another in the nearby **Diomidis Botanical Gardens** (*see Chapter 12*), which has a **canteen**. There are **no shops or restaurants** in the vicinity.
• *Tues and Fri 9am–2pm. • Free entrance. • **Moni Dafniou, Haidari**, ~10km/6mi west of Athens at the end of Iera Odos road, 210-581-1558, www.culture.gr*
Get there: *From Koumoundourou (aka Eleftherias) Sq, near Omonia on Piraeos (Panagi Tsaldari) St, bus nos: B16, Γ16, 801, 836, 845, 865, 866 to bus-stop: Moni Dafniou. ~45 minutes' journey.*

Attica plain from Mt Hymettus

Kaisariani Monastery, Kaisariani, Mt Hymettus

It's an effort to get here if you don't have a car as the public transport stops some way down the hill, but if you can make the journey 5km/3mi east of Athens you'll find an abandoned 11th century monastery (now belonging to the culture ministry) on the slopes of Mt Hymettus, and there are blink-or-miss views if you're able to drive along the mountain rood. Mythical Aphrodite's sacred spring is also the source of the Ilissos River, which begins here. Best time to go is in the wild-flower-resplendent spring, when you can have a **picnic** on the mountainside.

• *No food or drink available, apart from spring water.* • *Stroller accessible only to the church.*
• *Tues–Sun 8am–3pm (2.45pm last entrance.* • *Entrance €2, free under 18 yrs, EU students free, other students half-price.* • *Moni Kaisarianis, Kaisariani, Ymittos. Continuation of Ethnikis Antistaseos Ave, Kaisariani, 210-723-6619.*
Get there: From Evangelismos Metro station on Line 3, bus no. 250 (bus-stops on Vas. Sofias Ave or Rigillis St) takes you closest, to bus-stop: Grammateia, then a long walk (15-30 minutes) uphill to the monastery and grounds. ~an hour's journey.

Kleiston Monastery, Fyli

Thought to be the oldest monastery in Attica, the actual founding date of Moni Kleiston is unknown. Dedicated to the Dormition of the Virgin (*feast day: Aug 15*) in the pretty foothills of Mt Parnitha, this monastery is located ~3km/2mi past the village of Fyli, a Sunday grill destination, which is ~25km/15mi from Syntagma Square. Believed to have been established following the appearance of an icon of the Virgin in the crevice across the gorge, it attracts many visitors. Relics include the head of St Polyeuctos, a part of the head of St Peter the Patriarch of Alexandria, and relics of Sts George and Haralambos. The monastery was rededicated as a convent in 1930, with eight resident nuns who also create **handicrafts, some for sale**.

• *Visiting hours: Mon–Sat 8am–noon/3.30pm–5.30pm, all day Sunday.* • *Moni Kleiston, near Fyli, Parnitha, 210-241-1314.*
Get there: No direct public transport. From Ano Liosia suburban railway station, bus no. 723 to the terminus, then try and get a taxi, which would likely wait for the return journey/fare.
Driving:Ttake Athinon Ave (Kavalas) to the National Road (No. 1), head westbound on Attiki Odos (toll) (exit 8) and get off at exit 6 Fylis Ave towards Ano Liosia, go past Fyli towards the mountain and turn right instead of left at the junction (sign-posted). ~45 minutes' journey.

Easter 2012 ☺ 4.5 yrs

Holocaust memorial near the synagogue, opposite Thissio Metro station

Chapter 17: Special Interest—Jewish Athens

Jews are thought to have been present in Greece at least from the 3rd century BC, with a reference to Moschos, son of Moschos from Viotia (north of Athens), found in Oropos, eastern Attica. The *Book of I Maccabees* (2nd century BC) refers to communities throughout what is now modern Greece, while Apostle Paul proselytized to Jews at Athens' **Areopagus Hill** in 51 AD (*see Chapter 6 for description*) and Nero apparently sent 6,000 to help dig the Corinth canal in the 1st century AD. By the 12th century, the small town of Thiva (Thebes) 97km/60mi north of Athens, had the largest community of 2,000, mainly involved in the silk trade. Following the Spanish Inquisition and by the 16th century, the northern port city of Thessaloniki had the largest Jewish population in the world, at some 90,000 in 1917. Following the atrocities of WWII, the decimated community numbered around 10,000 in Greece, with many leaving for the US or Israel. The western Greek city of Arta has the country's oldest Jewish population.

Jewish Museum of Greece
At the Jewish Museum of Greece, some 8,000 remnants from 4,000 years of history have been collected, including 600-year-old textiles, displayed on various small levels that are *stroller accessible* in this neoclassical building near **Syntagma Square**.

• *Mon–Fri 9am–2.30pm, Sun 10am–2pm.* • *Entrance €6, students 6–15 yrs €3, under 6 yrs free.*
• **39 Nikis St, Syntagma**, *210-322-5582, www.jewishmuseum.gr*

Athens has **two synagogues** across the street from each other on Melidoni St, near Thissio Metro station in Psyrri, catering to some 3,000 Athenian Jews. The white Pentelic marble **Beth Shalom** synagogue at no. 5 was built in 1975 and is used for services.

Etz Hayyim is the older one at no. 8, dedicated in 1906. The name is believed to be associated with Romaniote Jews of Greek origin dating to the 3rd century BC.

• **Services** *Mon, Thurs 8.30am, Sat 8.30am, and Fri–Sat at sunset. In Greek and Hebrew.*
• **5 and 8 Melidoni St, Thissio/Psyrri**, *210-325-2875/23, www.chabad.gr*

Inside Beth Shalom synagogue

A **Holocaust memorial** dedicated in 2008 resembles a Star of David symbolizing the locations of Jewish communities, just west of the Byzantine Ag. Asomaton church.
• *Across from* **Thissio** *Metro station on Ermou St.*

The **Ancient Agora** contains foundations of what may have been a **synagogue** dating to the 2nd century BC. Found following excavations by the Germans in the early 1930s, it includes part of the mosaic floor and a fragment of Pentelic marble on which a menorah and lulav were carved, where the "Metroon" registry building was located.

• *Daily 8am–3pm.* • *Adults €4 or part of the Acropolis coupon, under 18 yrs free.* • *Entrance to the site from* **Adrianou and Agiou Filippou sts, Monastiraki**, *alongside the train tracks between Thissio and Monastiraki Metro stations; the west end of* **Polygnotou St, Plaka**; *or at* **Thissio Square**, *beside the playground. 210-321-0185, www.culture.gr*
Get there: *Monastiraki or Thissio Metro stations on Lines 1 and 3, then 5 min walk.*

Avyssinia Square in **Monastiraki**, where the antique and flea market opens to Ermou St, was once known as Yusurum Square, after a Jewish merchant.

Many of the **textile shops** in **Monastiraki**, from *Mitropoleos to Athinaidos sts around Aiolou St*, were Jewish-owned, at least until the 1950s.

The **First Cemetery** of Athens has a closed-off Jewish section. Ask the grounds-keeper to open the entrance if you want to go inside.
• *Apr–Oct 8am–8pm, Nov–Mar 8am–5.30pm.* • **Anapafseos and Trivonianou sts, Mets**, *210-923-6720.*

Get there: Bus A3, A4, 103, 108, 111, 155, 206, 208, 237, 856, 057, or 227 to bus-stop: A' (Proto) Nekrotafio.

WWII memorials are located at the Jewish section of the city's largest **Third Cemetery**, about 7.5km/4.5mi west of Athens, at the far northwest end of the cemetery. Donations for the memorial and upkeep can be made at the **office** *(Mon–Fri 8am–2pm).*
• *Daily summer 7.30am–5pm; winter 7.30am–7pm.* • *Kotyoron St at Antigonis St, Nikaia, 210-561-2206, 210-545-2921.*
Get there: From Piraeos St, trolley no. 21; or Omonia Sq (Menandrou St) and Piraeos St, bus nos. B18, Γ18 (closer) to bus-stop: Γ' (Trito) Nekrotafios. ~20 minutes' journey plus 10–20 minutes' walk.

At the **playground** opposite Agia Trianda church is a memorial to the 13,000 children who perished during the Holocaust in WWII.
• *Pafou and Acharnon sts, Agios Nikolaos/Kato Patissia.*
Get there: Trolley no. 6 from Ippokratous and Panepistimiou sts to bus-stop: Paradeisos; or from Panepistimio Metro station on Line 2 to Agios Nikolaos Metro station on Line 1.

The **Jewish Community Centre** binds the community and also runs a **private school** (pre-k to grade 6) in the suburb of Psychiko.
• *9 Vissarionos St at Sina St, Akadimias, 210-360-8896 after 5pm, www.athjcom.gr*

Resteion Elderly Care Centre is a rest-home some 30km/18mi from Athens.
• *180 Labton St, Doussi-Koropi, 210-965-6736, www.resteion.gr*

Gostijo in Chabad House specializes in **kosher** meat (*besari*) and Sephardic dishes under the supervision of a rabbi, also a mini-shop of kosher products. May deliver to visitors at their hotels.
• *Daily from 5pm, Fri Shabbat dinner and Sat Shabbat lunch by reservation, Sat night (Motzari shabbat) opens one hour after sundown.* • *10 Aisopou St, Psyrri, 210-323-3825, www.chabad.gr*

A list of **kosher foods** and where they can be bought is on *www.chabad.gr*.

Buy the ***Cookbook of the Jews of Greece*** by Nicholas Stavroulakis, Jason Aronson Inc, 1996, in English, or the ***Tastes of Sephardic Thessaloniki:*** *Recipes of the Jews of Thessaloniki (Γεύση από Σεφαραδίτικη Θεσσαλονίκη: Συνταγές των Εβραίων της Θεσσαλονίκης)* by Nina Benpoubi and Epikouros, Fytraki Press, 2002, in Greek.

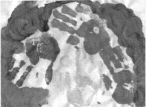

Fingerpaint, April 2013 ☺ 5.5 yrs

The Greek tourism org (see Tourist Info section) has a useful free map

Chapter 18: Planning & Reference

Babysitting

Ask if your hotel arranges babysitting, how much notice they need, how much it will cost and if a tip is included. The going rate in Athens outside hotels is €6–9 per hour.If there's an event you really want to attend, arrange babysitting before you arrive.

You'll find many places to go that are nearby, whether out for dinner, for a stroll, drinks, or a combination thereof, all in close proximity.

Bathing

Many smaller hotels may only have a shower stall. This is actually easy for bathing small children because the shower head is attached to a flexible hose, but if you must have a bathtub, check beforehand. Also note that washcloths may not be provided.

Beggars

There are many beggars around Athens, more since the economic crisis began. They are not aggressive, but some may have exposed medical conditions which may be upsetting to young children.

While it's impossible to shelter children completely from the harsher side of life, be aware, as such images can leave lasting imprints.

Crime

Greece has the reputation for being among the safest countries, and Athens still has a safe feel, although some areas are a little seedy and approaching dangerous. It's quite safe to walk around the Acropolis vicinity (north, south, east, west slopes) and connecting neighbourhoods as well as nightlife areas at night, but use common sense, such as avoiding dark and deserted lanes. Be wary of anyone approaching you for parties or to go to hostess bars, don't accept food and water at archaeological sites, keep your valuables safe from pick-pockets (especially on the Monastiraki to Omonia portion of the Metro), and from possible motorcycle thieves who come up alongside to pull off bags or necklaces, pulling over the victim in the process. Shield the keypad while entering your PIN number at an ATM (bank machine).

Demonstrations

Athens has many public demonstrations. A few are short and usually take place in the daytime along Stadiou St to Syntagma Square, in front of Parliament. The streets are closed to traffic, so buses that go along this route will be suspended for the duration—an hour or so. It's safe to be out and about but inconvenient if you were planning on taking a bus.

In the event of a wider demonstration or protest march, such as the annual march to the US Embassy on November 17th each year, it's strongly advised to stay away from the area. If it gets out of hand, tear gas may be fired which lasts a long time and is obviously irritating to the eyes, and shops along the route may be targeted. Bystanders are not attacked, but you don't want to be caught anywhere where it's volatile or where violence may flare at any moment. Check with your hotel, or buy the daily *International Herald Tribune* (€2.50) which has the English-language *Kathimerini* at the back and which posts the latest goings-on, good and bad. You can also check their site, *www.ekathimerini.com*. The site *www.apergia.gr* has a handy monthly calendar format showing who is striking when, including transport, but it is in Greek. Ask your hotel to keep you posted as well.

Discount cards

There are a lot of deals following the economic crisis, but visitors can pick up the free **Athens Spotlighted discount card** (*www.athenspotlighted.gr*), valid for ten days up to eight people, seven days a week, at the **airport only**, at one of two booths in the Baggage Claim area or in the Arrivals hall level Business Centre between 6am and 10pm, and outside these hours from

info booths 5 & 6 in the Arrivals hall (10pm–6am). Special prices and discounts are given at museums, restaurants, tours, theatres, shops, bookstores and deli mini-markets, even private hospitals (IASO).

Earthquakes

While the chances of a big one during your stay are rare, Greece is in an earthquake zone, and most people keep a robe or easily pulled-on clothes handy in the event of a quake at night. Stay calm. If you are inside, crawl under a sturdy table or brace yourself in a door frame. Keep away from windows. Do not use elevators. There is a greater danger from falling objects outside, but extra caution must be taken in and around older buildings. If you are outside, get to an open area. Avoid driving or using the phones to leave both the roads and phone lines open for emergency use.

Electricity

Greece runs on 220 volts and has a round, two-pronged plug. Check if your appliance (phone, laptop, etc) has dual (110/220) voltage, if not, a transformer is needed. Simple plug adapters can be purchased at numerous electrical appliance and light shops for a few euros. Bring a multi-plug for your gadgets.

Embassies in Athens (selected)

UK Embassy (waffle), Vas. Sofias Ave

• **American**: 91 Vas. Sofias Ave, Embassy (Megaron Mousikis area), 210-721-2951, *athens.usembassy.gov*

• **Australian**: *Thon Building, 6th fl, Kifissias and Alexandras aves, Ambelokipi, 210-870-4000, www.greece.embassy.gov.au*
• **British**: *1 Ploutarchou St, Kolonaki, 210-727-2600, www.ukingreece.fco.gov.uk*
• **Bulgarian**: *33A Stratigou Kallari St, Paleo Psychiko, 210-674-8105, embassbg@otenet.gr*

• **Canadian**: *4 Ioannou Gennadiou St, Kolonaki, 210-727-3400, www.athens.gc.ca*
• **Chinese**: *2A Krinon St, Paleo Psychiko, 210-672-3282, gr.china-embassy.org/eng*
• **Cypriot**: *2A Xenofondos St, Syntagma, 210-373-4800, www.mfa.gov.cy/mfa/Embassies/Embassy_Athens.nsf*
• **Dutch**: *5-7 Vas. Konstantinou Ave, Stadio, 210-725-4900, greece.nlembassy.org*
• **Egyptian**: *3 Vas. Sofias Ave, Syntagma, 210-361-8612, (www.touregypt.net)*
• **French**: *7 Vas. Sofias Ave, Syntagma, 210-339-1000, www.ambafrance-gr.org*
• **German**: *3 Karaoli and Dimitriou St (continuation of Loukianou St), Kolonaki, 210-728-5111, www.athen.diplo.de*
• **Irish**: *7 Vas. Konstantinou St, opposite Panathenian Stadium (Stadio), 210-723-2771, www.embassyofireland.gr*
• **Israeli**: *1 Marathonodromon St, Paleo Psychiko, 210-670-5500, embassies.gov.il/athens*
• **Italian**: *2 Sekeri St, Syntagma, 210-361-7260, www.embatene.esteri.it*
• **Japanese**: *46 Ethnikis Antistasseos St, Halandri, 210-670-9900, www.gr.emb-japan.go.jp*
• **New Zealand Consulate**: *76 Kifissias Ave, Ambelokipi, 210-692-4136*
• **Russian**: *28 Nikiforou Litra St, Paleo Psychiko, 210-672-5235, athens.rusembassy.org*
• **South African**: *60 Kifissias Ave, Maroussi, 210-617-8020, www.dfa.gov.za*
• **Spanish**: *21 Dion. Areopagitou St, Makriyanni, 210-921-3123, www.emb-esp.gr*
• **Turkish**: *8 Vas. Georgiou B' St, Rigillis, 210-726-3000, atina.be.mfa.gov.tr*
• **UAE**: *290 Kifissias Ave and 2 Paritsi St, Neo Psychiko, 210-677-0220.*

Environment

The light blue bins/dumpsters (**pictured**) are for recycling paper and cardboard, plastic and metal, if you want to do your bit in helping to reduce waste.

Health hazards

Accommodation: With toddlers especially, be vigilant and take extra precautions, checking rooms for potential accidents. Hazards include a slippery floor, so take care in bathrooms and put down towels or dry the floor if it gets wet from the shower. Bring masking or packing tape to cover exposed electrical outlets, and consider bringing a kitchen sponge to cut up and tape over sharp furniture corners at eye level. Inspect the balcony and take precautions if unsafe, or stay on the ground floor, checking that patios are safe. In self-catering, move hazardous objects and cleaning supplies out of reach, or keep cupboard handles together with a child-safe device or tamper-proof elastic band. Make sure the children are not in reach of hot elements or dials. When not in use, locate the fuse box and flip off the fuse for the stove.

Cold: Temperatures can hover near freezing, so if you are coming in winter or early spring, bring a sweater and jacket, scarf and hat, and even gloves/mittens for babies/children and consider bringing for yourself.

Driving: Car accidents are a major problem in Greece. The silver lining is that the hospitals have a wealth of experience catering to accident victims with grazes, broken bones and disfigurements. Keep your eyes open for dangerous drivers, traffic lights located at the side of the road (and further obscured from view by leaves) rather than overhead, and direction signs that are usually located right at the turn-off. One way streets are another annoyance that make driving in the centre of Athens difficult. Drivers are quite aggressive and will often tailgate, until you move out of their way.

As a pedestrian, watch for cars at pedestrian crossings, as drivers usually take the right of way, including turning when the "green man" is also lit, and look both ways, even when crossing one-way streets.

Food: Take care with what you eat when it's hot, such as a ready-made or made-to-order sandwich, as it's easy to get food poisoning, which can obviously cut into your holiday time.

Heat: It gets very hot in spring, summer and fall, and the ozone layer can be thin, so wear sunscreen at all times during daylight (as I've been advised by a dermatologist— skin cancer is high risk here, especially for the light-skinned), a hat to avoid sunstroke (at least three days to recover from even a mild case), sunglasses, including for your children, and always bring a bottle of water with you. Water is price-controlled, and small bottles are widely available at kiosks and cost 50 cents. Clothing should be loose-fitting. Bring salve or nappy cream in case your child develops a rash from tight-fitting trousers in the heat. You can buy non-irritating, non-bleached toilet paper at health food (and supply) shops.

Mosquitoes: Bring mosquito repellent and bite cream especially in summer. You can get electric plugs with liquid or tablet mosquito repellent for use overnight from supermarkets and minimarkets, but most hotels supply them.

Pavements: Pavements and sidewalks are often broken, or have trees, parked bikes or cars obstructing the way. Often steps also infringe on pavement space (*pictured*). Smooth marble paving stone is also common, and these get very slippery when wet. Watch your step.

Swimming: Being nearly surrounded by sea, the drowning rate is also high. Keep a close eye on your children around water, especially as not all areas are lifeguarded, or they have to scan a wide area. If children get in trouble it just takes a few seconds and they may be impossible to find or see under a wide expanse of water, where reflection also obscures visibility. Very young children playing at the shoreline also need to be watched like a hawk. Armbands or water wings give added security for locating quickly in/near the water.

Insurance

European Union members should apply for the European Health Insurance Card which entitles **free medical treatment throughout the EU**. Non-EU members should check with their insurance providers, or buy additional travel insurance. It may be offered or covered by your home or auto insurance, or get extra coverage with an insurer you trust, or you can buy online through sites such as *www.comparethemarket.com*. Do a search on the provider offered to make sure it's reputable or not about to close, such as running the name through a search engine's "news" filter. As an example of cost, treatment at Ag. Kyriakou chldren's hospital (*see Medical Care section*) may start at €300.

Internet

Hotels usually have computers and internet access or **wifi** that's also free in many cafes and areas around town, including at the airport, at Syntagma Square, Kotzia Square on Athinas St, Thissio Metro station, and at Thissio Square. **Everest sandwich shop** at **Syntagma Square** has a free wifi zone upstairs. There are also **internet cafes** around town that cost one or two euros for 30 minutes to an hour.

Athens Internet
Starting at €3 per hour.
• *3A Veikou St, 210-923-5811*, **Makriyanni**, *www.athensinternet.gr*

Bits and Bytes
• *19 Kapnikareas*, **Monastiraki/Plaka**, *210-325-3142, www.bnb.gr*

Fivos Hotel
Walk-in internet access.
• *23 Athinas St*, **Monastiraki**, *210-322-6657, www.hotelfivos.gr*

Volcano.Net
Near Syngrou-Fix Metro station around the corner from the pedestrian street (Drakou St).
• *61 Veikou St*, **Koukaki**, *211-119-7216.*

Language

The language spoken is Greek but fortunately, since most Greeks learn

English at afterschool cramming schools (*frontistìria*) and/or may have much contact with foreigners in the tourism industry or as sailors, most people speak English. Signs are usually in both Greek and Latin script, with the Latinized rendering varying widely, as there is not an exact "fit", so for example the "ch" as in "chris" may be rendered as "ch" or "h" (pronounced as in "loch"), "f" or "ph", "i" or "e", etc.

Vas. Sofias Ave street sign

Knowing a few words is appreciated—these are the basics: *efharistò* (**thank you**), *parakalò* (**please/you're welcome**), *Yiàssas* (polite first and last greeting, such as "**hello**" and "**goodbye**"), *signòmi* (excuse me or sorry, although "**sorry**" is also widely used), *nai* (**yes**), *òchi* (**no**), *Ti kànete?* ("**How are you**", polite form), *Kalà* (**fine**). The **washroom** (toilet, signed as WC) is *toualèta*. **Tickets** are *eisitìria*. **How much** (money): *Pòso kànee?*

Laundry

Bring a handful of clothes pegs, and get a travel laundry line of twisted, elasticated string with hooks or suction cups on either end. You insert the clothes in the "twists."

A flat rubber plug (not plastic) that fits all sinks is another item to bring, plus laundry powder in a tightly-fitting small-sized container.

Often you can do your own smalls in the hotel sink, but if it's prohibited, you don't want to use their own service or there isn't one, there are a few centrally-located laundrettes/laundromats:

**American Laundry
& Dry Cleaners**
Further down, near Syngrou-Fix Metro station.
• *43 Dimitrakopoulou St and Drakou St, Koukaki, 210-922-4504.*

Athens Launderette
Near the Acropolis Museum, in the same building as Athens Studios, with entrances on both Veikou and Dimitrakopoulou sts.
• *Daily 8am–midnight • 3A Veikou St, Makriyanni, www.athenslaunderette.gr*

National Dry Cleaners
Beside the Hermes and other hotels around that very convenient location.
• *17 Apollonos St, Plaka/Syntagma, 210-323-2226, www.nationaldrycleaners.gr*

Medical Attention

For all treatments, have your insurance info with you, and bring your children's immunization and/or medical book with you.

Bring a small first-aid kit that includes plasters and perhaps a small bottle of Betadine; diarrhoea and nausea (motion sickness) antidotes will save time if you need them, and maybe also an antihistamine. These are all available at pharmacies; the plasters are commonly found at kiosks as well. If your child needs antibiotics such as for an **infection** that does not clear up with antibiotic cream (topical), you can get it at pharmacies over the counter. The usual prescription (obviously check with a doctor if your child has any allergies, including to penicillin, or has medical conditions) is **Ceclor** (cefaclor) (*pictured*) manufactured by Pharmaserv Lilly

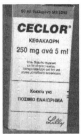

(*www.lilly.gr*), a pink powder which you mix with water and you get three bottles of it (250mg in 5ml doses, measuring cap included or ask pharmacist for a syringe, €5.50 per bottle), which is what my paediatrician recommends for a seven- to ten-day course and not less. The usual dosage is 5ml every eight hours, but I'm supposing it also depends on the weight of the child, so ask the pedi or pharmacist.

For **fevers** that are high (bring a thermometer), doctors here recommend giving **Ponstan** and **Depon** (liquid) alternating every four hours. Dosage depends on the weight of the child.

There are many **cough syrups**, prescriptions differ depending on whether it's a dry or productive cough, but tests in Canada have shown they are ineffective and are no longer given for coughs, and instead advise letting them run their course.

To stop a coughing fit, try sucking on a hard-boiled, sweet candy with sugar, as sugar-free and "cool" ones are ineffective (I find).

Medical Care
The level of medical care is good in Greece, even though the buildings may not be in the best condition at public hospitals, while during these times of economic crisis, supplies and services are becoming increasingly limited.

There are separate hospitals for children and women, hence more specialized in their care. If WHO World Health Statistics 2011 are to be believed (given the country's reputation for falsifying data), the child mortality rate before age five in Greece is 4 per 1,000 live births (8 in the US; 5/1,000 in the UK and 6/1,000 in Canada), while the maternal mortality rate is the lowest in the world, at 2 per 100,000 live births (24 in the US and 12 in Canada and the UK).

While "tipping" some doctors is still unfortunately common practice (and obviously illegal), visitors are not expected or asked to pay extra. Do however, double check your bill for mistakes/over-charging, at both public and private hospitals.

Doctors of every specialty, including pathologists (GPs), paediatricians and dentists, have offices in almost every neighbourhood and most speak English. They charge around €50–€70 per visit, and can include a check-up and fillings at the **dentist**, many with US or UK training. Ask at your hotel if you want to visit one near you.

If you lose or need **contact lenses**, you don't need to visit a doctor, just take your prescription to an **optical shop**, where they may also do vision tests if you need glasses.

Embassies have lists of doctors, while hotels usually have doctors they call for emergencies.

For a list of paediatricians recommended by expats, contact Theme Attica (see title page).

EMERGENCIES

• **Ambulance 166**
• **EU Emergency hotline** (English-speaking) **112** for **police, fire, ambulance.**
• **Fire 199**
• **Poison Centre** (Athens) **210-779-3777**
• **Police 100**
• **SOS crisis helpline 197**
• **Children's helpline 1056**
• **Tourist police** (English-speaking) dial **171.**
*Tourist police office: 43 Veikou St, **Koukaki**, 210-920-0724, daily 7:30am–10pm.*
***Get there**: Syngrou-Fix Metro station on Line 2; or trolley nos. 1, 5, 15, bus-stop: Gargaretta.*

HOSPITALS

Public hospitals operate on a rotation basis for emergencies. Find someone to call **14944** for a *recorded message in Greek* of the nearest **hospital on duty**;
* Or call the **ambulance** (**166**);
* Or call **112**, the **EU Emergency hotline**, for all kinds of emergencies with English-speaking assistance (they will make the arrangements);
* Or call **171**, the English-speaking **tourist police** for assistance.

Polykliniki
There's a **public clinic** in the downtown area near Omonia Square, which has doctors of every specialization.
*• Daily 8am–8pm. • **3 Piraeos (P. Tsaldari) and Socratous sts, Omonia**, 210-389-9000, appt 210-389-9100, www.polykliniki.gr*

Alexandras
The main Athens **public women's hospital** is Alexandras.
*• 80 Vas. Sofias Ave, **Embassy**,*

213-216-2000, 210-338-1100, www.hospital-alexandra.gr
***Get there**: 5-minute walk from Megaron Mousikis Metro Station on Line 3, on the south side of Vas. Sofias Ave.*

Euroclinic
Athens has many **private hospitals**; a central one is Euroclinic. Check before going to make sure they can treat your ailment.
*• 9 Athanasiadou St, **Ambelokipi**, 210-641-6600, www.euroclinic.gr*
***Get there**: Ambelokipi Metro Station on Line 3, Soutzou St exit.*

IASO
The biggest **private women's** (and **maternity**) **hospital** in Athens is IASO.
*• 37–39 Kifissias Ave, **Maroussi**, 210-618-4000, www.iaso.gr*
***Get there**: About 30 minutes from central Athens by taxi.*

HOSPITALS, CHILDREN'S

There are separate public hospitals just for children, known as *"Pàidon."* The two main ones, **Agia Sofia** and **Aglaia Kyriakou**, are located next to each other, one or the other will be open for **emergencies**. They are in the area of (bordering) Goudi, which is east of Ambelokipi, at the top of Michalakopoulou St which runs northeast from beside the Hilton Hotel, if coming from central Athens.

Agia Sofia
*• Thivon and Papadiamantopoulou Sts, **Ambelokipi**, 210-746-7000, www.paidon-agiasofia.gr*
***Get there**: All taxis know "Paìthon, Goutheè" (Paidon, Goudi - soft "th" sound). Bus no. 815 from Piraeos St, Akadimias St, or Vas. Sofias Ave near Evangelismos Metro station on Line 3, bus-stop: Nos. Paidon.*

Aglaia Kyriakou

• *Thivon and Livadeias sts,* **Ambelokipi***,
213-200-9000,* www.aglaiakyriakou.gr
Get there*: All taxis know "Paíthon, Goutheè"
(Paidon, Goudi - soft "th" sound). Bus no.
815 from Piraeos St, Akadimias St, or Vas.
Sofias Ave near Evangelismos Metro station
on Line 3, bus-stop: Nos. Paidon.*

Aglaia Kyriakou, Syngrou Ave branch

A branch of Aglaia Kyriakou
public children's hospital is
nearer central Athens, but call
before going, as it may not be on
emergency duty.
• *290 Syngrou Ave,* **Kallithea***,
213-200-9900.*
Get there*: Trolley no. 10, bus no. 550 to
bus-stop: Skra.*

Paidon Penteli

Up on the mountainside (less busy),
call switchboard (Mon–Fri 8am–
2pm) for recorded message (in
Greek) of emergency hours, or wait
for someone to pick up. Admission
with ID, health book, AMKA no.
and tax no.
• *Paidon Pentelis, Ippokratous St,* **Paleo
Pendeli***, 213-205-2200,*
www.paidon-pentelis.gr
Get there*: Halandri Metro station on Line 3,
bus no. 460, 461 to bus-stop: 1ˢᵗ
Nosokomeio Paidon; or Maroussi Metro
station on Line 1, bus no. 446 to bus-stop:
1ˢᵗ Nosokomeio Paidon.*

IASO Paidon

A **private children's hospital** is
IASO Paidon.
• *37-39 Kifissias Ave,* **Maroussi***,
210-638-3000,* www.iaso.gr
Get there*: About 30 min from central Athens
by taxi.*

HOUSE CALLS

Two **medical services** in Athens
make **24-hour house calls**. They
can advise hospitalization if
needed.

• **SOS Doctors:** *1016,* www.sosiatroi.gr
• **Homed:** *1144,* www.hospitalathome.gr

NON-EMERGENCY MEDICAL & DENTAL

It's worth noting that if you need or
want to take any **medical tests** that
take a long time or are expensive in
your home country, to consider
getting them done in Greece. The
labs and diagnostic centres are
state-of-the-art and include things
like MRIs that cost around €250
(and cost $thousands in the US),
while blood tests are quite
inexpensive. Often no appointment
is necessary, and all hand over the
results, including x-rays, on the
spot or within a day or so.

Biocheck

Can do blood tests among other
tests.
• *1 Venteri and Vas. Sofias Ave, beside the
Hilton*, 210 -724-1416.*
Get there*: Megaron Mousikis Metro station
on Line 3, Ilissia exit.*

Iatropolis

Can do MRIs, bone density testing
and digital mammograms among
others.
• *64 Vas. Sofias Ave,* **Ilissia***, 210-996-9000,*
www.iatropoli.gr
Get there*: Megaron Mousikis Metro station
on Line 3, Ilissia exit.*

Money

Currency is the euro, and it's a cash
society. The usual denominations
are €50, €20, €10 and €5 bills, and
€2, €1, 50, 20, 10, 5, 2 and 1 cent
coins. Change money at exchange
bureaus or use local bank ATMs
connected to your bank's global
banking system. **HSBC** and
Citibank have branches here. If an
ATM isn't working, try denominations of €50 or another machine.

Greek news in English: the daily 'Kathimerini' is inside the IHT ('Athens News' is not publishing at present), or www.enetenglish.gr

News & current info

There is one local English language newspaper, the daily *Kathimerini* (*www.ekathimerini.com*) which is part of the *International Herald Tribune*. (The weekly *Athens News* was confirmed closed in March 2013 after 50 years of publication.) The *IHT* is available where the foreign press is sold, including all the kiosks at Syntagma Square, just in front of McDonald's and the main post office. For online daily news, visit *www.enetenglish.gr*. For tons of free information about Athens and where to go, pick up a copy of the *Athens City Guide*, same publishers as the free weekly Greek-language paper, *Athens Voice*.

Pharmacies/Chemists

There are **pharmacies** in every neighbourhood, look for signs of green or red crosses, where you can also buy baby formula powder (Stage 1), which is available at supermarkets from six months and up (Stage 2) only. Check if your brand is available here or a substitute. For example, Cow and Gate in the UK is Almiron in Greece. And make sure you slap on sunscreen, summer and winter.

You can get many drugs over the counter, including antibiotics. Hours are usually 8am–2pm, reopening 5pm–8pm on Tuesdays, Thursdays and Fridays.

After-hours pharmacies are listed in the windows of pharmacies, or find out by dialling **14944** (phone charges apply). Ask a Greek-speaker for assistance, also to look them up *www.fsa.gr/duties.asp*.

Post office

The **main post office** (ELTA) branch is at Syntagma.
• *Mon–Fri 7.30am–8pm, Sat 7.30am–2pm, Sun 9am–1.30pm.* • **Syntagma Sq** and *Mitropoleos St, 210-331-9500, www.elta.gr*

There's another **post office** further down the street that's also used for **parcels** over two kilos, that you need to have open for inspection.
• *Mon–Fri 7.30am–8pm.*
• **60 Mitropoleos St, Monastiraki,** *210-321-8156 or 210-321-8143.*

Smoking

Bans are ignored and people smoke where-ever they like.

Strollers/Buggies

Strollers take a beating on uneven Athens streets and up and down steps. Narrow, compact ones are best for getting through tight spaces and inside elevators. Metro station elevators may not always be at the most convenient exit. At Syngrou-Fix Metro station, for example, the elevator brings you out across busy Syngrou Ave, where you then cross at the nearest traffic light.

Telephony

The country code is 30. Ten digits are needed to complete calls. Making and receiving calls on a cell/mobile that's tri-band-enabled can be pricey while in Greece, which uses the Europe-wide Global System for Mobiles (GSM). You can buy a pay-as-you-go phone to use here for around €35 that includes a phone number and SIM (memory) card, and a phone card of units from €10. (*See Chapter 5*).

Phone booths require phone cards that you can buy at kiosks and newsstands, or buy pre-paid calling cards for a few euros and make your call on any phone. Some kiosks and corner stores have metered phones you can use. Otherwise use an internet connection.

* **International operator: 139**
* **Directory enquiries: 11888**

Time

Greece is GMT+2, Eastern European Time. Daylight savings is observed, and occurs a week or so later than the US and Canada in spring, and a week or so earlier in autumn.

Tipping

A service charge is often included in restaurant bills, but it's customary to leave change on the table, or 10–20% at restaurants and bars. In a taxi, round up to the nearest euro. Chambermaids and bellhops should also receive gratuities of €1 or €2 a day.

Toilets

There are public washrooms, denoted by "WC" or coin-operated, and some playgrounds also have toilets, but most people go to restaurants and cafes, and if you have kids, they readily oblige. As a courtesy, you could buy a soft drink, juice or take-out snack. Most bathrooms are very small, but some child-friendly places do provide change tables.

There are clean, free **public toilets** (*steps*) in **Makriyanni**, near Akropoli Metro station, opposite the Greek National Tourism Organization information building, near the entrance to the Theatre of Dionysus.

Tourist Info

The **Greek National Tourism Organization** information office (*pictured*) is opposite the Acropolis Museum, beside the ancient Theatre of Dionysus entrance, behind the statue of Makriyianni greenery. They have excellent **free maps** and other info, including all the museums and bus **schedules**.

• *May–Sept Mon–Fri 8am–8pm, Sat–Sun 10–4pm; Oct–April shorter hours (usually 9am or 10am to 7pm).* • **18-20 Dion. Areopagitou St, Makriyanni**, 210-331-0392, www.gnto.gr **Get there**: *Akropoli Metro station, then 2 minutes' walk.*

Tours & excursions

You can walk around Athens quite easily, or take a popular **tour** that hits the main places around town (s*ee Chapter 7*).

PACKAGE TOURS

Package holidays are good value and may be just what's needed for young families, including all-inclusive options. Check the hotel's location carefully however with traveller's reviews, and plug in your parameters (such as "family holiday") in online menu selections.

Whether you DIY or not, you can often **join the excursions of package tour operators**, which is useful if there is no travel agency/booking office offering excursions in the vicinity of your accommodation. Just contact the organizer on the posted excursion.

* Online packages and deals can be found on **Expedia**, **Travelocity**, **Last-minute**, **Booking**, and in Greece, try *www.touristorama.com (210-325-2263 to 5)*, but you'll need language assistance for the website.

* One UK operator with well-located properties on the islands of Rhodes and Symi for instance, is **Olympic Holidays** (*0800-093-3322 in the UK, www.olympicholidays.com*).

SAILING HOLIDAYS

A sailing yacht vacation or day-trip adventure can be affordable, given you stay on the boat, can make your own meals, you don't bother anybody else and can be part of a flotilla that may include other families. There's an **Athens Sailing meetup group** (*www.meetup.com*), or try **Nautilus Yachting** (*www.nautilusyachting.com*), or **Sunsail** (*www.sunsail.eu*). Don't forget motion-sickness pills.

Water
Tap water varies around the country whether it is potable or not. Most city water is, including Athens water, which is hard. Most people prefer to drink bottled water, which is price-controlled and therefore relatively cheap, at 50 cents for a half-litre (small) bottle at a kiosk.

Weather

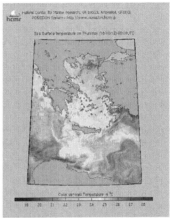

Poseidon System (www.hcmr.gr) sea surface temperature map

It usually gets hot (high 20s–30s C/70s–90s F), from May to October, and cold (0–15 C/40–65 F) from November to March, where snow can occur at higher elevations and even in Athens, and roads may close. In summer the afternoon sun is oppressive, so most people are not outdoors except at the beach, hence the siesta from 3pm till 5.30pm. Sea water is warmer in August and September. The autumn and spring seasons are short, where the temperatures are pleasant for sightseeing, but can also get quite hot or quite cold, and shorts and a jacket and sweater are advised, as well as a rain cover for strollers. Short torrential rains occur in spring and fall, while it can get very windy too, with the seasonal north (Etesian, *Meltèmi*) wind occurring from mid-July to Mid-August, which can stop ferries from operating.

* Check **weather conditions**, including **wind**, at _www.meteo.gr_. Very high temperatures are marked in red, while wind (Beaufort) is noted with a swaying palm tree and a reading.

* Check **weather conditions**, including **sea temperature and ozone** (UV) readings at _www.hnms.gr_.

* Check **daily pollution levels** through the Environment Ministry: _http://www.ypeka.gr/Default.aspx?t abid=708&locale=en-US&language=el-GR_.

Warnings to stay indoors are posted on this site and occur especially on very hot days with no wind since Athens is in a basin.

What's on the calendar

There are many festivals, religious festivities and special events throughout the year.

Athens usually empties during the **August 15** holiday of the **Assumption of the Virgin**, when most Greeks take their holidays, and many shops are closed around this time.

Most hotels in resort areas close from October to April. (_See also_ Chapter 11).

MUSEUMS AND SITES FREE, CLOSED DAYS

State-run (public) museums have many **free entrance days** in the year: Mar 6, Apr 18, May 18, June 5, Sept 27, last weekend of September, Sundays between Nov 1 and Mar 31, first Sunday every month, except in July, Aug, Sept.

Museums may not be open during public holidays, or have reduced hours.

The hours of operation usually change in April/May and October, staying open longer during the summer months. Check _www.culture.gr_ or call ahead.

State-run sites and museums are **closed**: Jan 1, March 25, Orthodox Good Friday morning (_see below for dates_), Orthodox Easter Sunday, May 1, Dec 25-26, and occasionally when there is a strike.

State-run sites and museums observe their **Sunday schedule**: Jan 6, Orthodox Ash (Clean) Monday, Orthodox Easter Saturday, Orthodox Easter Monday, Orthodox Whit Sunday, Aug 15, Oct 28.

NATIONAL HOLIDAYS

Jan 1: New Year's Day.
Jan 6: Epiphany.
Feb/Mar: Clean (Ash) Monday (_Katharà Deftèra_) (_March 3, 2014; February 23, 2015_).
Mar 25: Independence Day and the Feast of the Annunciation.
April/May: Orthodox Easter (_Pàscha_) Sunday, Monday (_April 20&21, 2014; April 12&13, 2015_).
May 1: Labour Day, May Day (_Protomaià_).
May/June: Whit Monday (_June 24, 2013; June 9, 2014; June 1, 2015_).
Aug 15: Assumption of the Virgin.
Oct 28: _Ochi_ (No) Day.
Nov 17: Unofficial student protest day.
Dec 25 and 26: Christmas.

Evzone, Oct 2011 ☺ 4 yrs

202

Index

1st Greek Evangelical
  Church, 181
2nd Greek Evangelical
  Church, 182
7 Jokers, 172

Academy of Athens, 92
  library, 92
Accommodation, 19–30
  hotels & hostels, 21–30
  Kolonaki, Evangelismos,
    29–30
  location, 20
  Makriyanni (Acropolis),
    Koukaki, 25–27
  Monastiraki, Psyrri (east), 29
  Neos Kosmos, 27–28
  Plaka, Syntagma, 21–25
  self-catering, 20–21
  Thissio, Psyrri (west), 28
Achilleas hotel, 21
Acqua e Sole pool, 161–162
Acropolis area, 2, 6, 7, 20,
  21, 25, 28, 44, 47, 67–68,
  80, 128, 132, 134, 147,
  158, 171, 190
Acropolis Bikes, 95
Acropolis Hill, 6, 66, 67–68
Acropolis House hotel, 21–22
Acropolis Museum, 7, 80
Acropolis walkway, 5–6, 7,
  44, 125
Admiral shoes, 58
Adonis hotel, 22
Adrian hotel, 22
Adrianou St, Monastiraki,
  7, 42
Adrianou St, Plaka, 48, 51,
  54, 57, 59
Adventure Park, 112
Aegaleo (Egaleo), 6
Aegean Air, 8
Aegina, 91, 169–170
Aegli café, 133
Aegli open-air cinema,
  118, 177
AEK club, 60, 176
Agia Irini Square, 172
Agia Marina church,
  82, 122, 125, 181
Agia Sofia church, 181
Agia Sofia Paidon, 196
Agii Apostoli Solaki (Holy
  Apostles of Solakis)
  church, 73
Agii Asomati church, 74
Agii Theodori church, 91
Agios Dimitrios Loumbar-
  diaris (St James Bomb-
  bardier) church, 81–82

Agios Dimitrios playground,
  145
Agios Dionysus/St Denis
  Roman Catholic
  Cathedral, 182
Agios Eleftherios/Panagia
  Gorgoepikoos church, 72
Agios Georgios (St George)
  church, 86
Agios Kosmas, 166
Aglaia Kyriakou Paidon, 197
  Syngrou Ave branch, 197
Agorà (*see Central Market*)
Airport (*see Athens Intl
  Airport*)
Akti tou Iliou, 165–166
Akti Vouliagmenis, 168
Alexandras hospital, 196
Alimos, 10, 120, 148–151,
  161–162, 165–166
  photo, 164
Allou Fun Park and Kidom,
  151–152, pool, 163
Alpeis café, 91
Altamira, 174
Amalias Ave, 6, 44
American Laundry & Dry
  Cleaners, 194
Ambelokipi, 160
Amphitrion, 10
Amusement parks, indoor &
  supervised play areas,
  145–152
Anafiotika, 69
Anavasi book shop, 52
Ancient Agora, 7, 73
  museum, 73, photo, 65
  synagogue, 187
Ancient Assembly, 7, 82
Ancient Epidavros
  (Epidaurus) Theatre,
  79, 124
Ancient Greek food
  (Archaion Gefseis), 44–45
Ancient Theatre of Dionysus,
  7, 68, 78–79
Anessis hotel, 160
Angistri (Agistri), 170
Antonis Tritsis Park,
  106–107
Apollonos St, 57
Apostle Paul, 69, 73, 98
Apostolou Pavlou St,
  7, 73, 125, 172
Archaeological site
  unification, 5, 7
Archaion Gefseis, 44–45
Archdiocese of Athens,
  180–181
Ardittou Hill, 6, 66, 85
Areopagus (Mars, Ares) Hill,

  6, 66, 68–69, 180, 186
Art & Hobby, 62
Art Gallery hotel, 25
Art of Living, 183
Art Suites Athens hotel, 155
Art-Athina intl art fair, 124
Artemis (Loutsa) beach, 169
Artemisia health food, 36
Arts and entertainment,
  114–126, 171–179
Asklepion, 79
Assumption of the Virgin
  (Aug 15), 123, 201
Asteri Vouliagmeni (Astir
  Beach), 167
Asteria Glyfada and Balux,
  166–167
Astor hotel, 24
Athena (goddess), 67
Athena Apollo Museum, 80
Athenaeum Intercontinental
  hotel, 27, pool, 159
Athens Backpackers, 25
Athens Baptist Church, 182
Athens Best Yogurt (ABY), 48
Athens by Bike, 95
Athens City Guide, 171, 176,
  198
Athens Classic Marathon, 126
Athens Cypria hotel, 22
Athens Epidaurus Festival,
  124-125
Athens Heart mall, 55
  skating, 119
  supervised play area, 146
Athens International Airport
  (AIA, Eleftherios
  Venizelos), 6, 8, 9–10
Athens Internet, 193
Athens Launderette, 194
Athens map, indicative, 212
Athens Metro Mall, 55
  skating, 119
  supervised play area,
    146–147
Athens Olympics 2004
  Marathon race/Pana-
    thenian Stadium, 85
  Olympic (OAKA) Stadium,
    108, souvenirs, 60
Athens Open Tour, 96
Athens Piraeus Electric
  Railways Museum
  (Metro), 103
Athens railway station (*see
  Larissa railway station*)
Athens Sports Bar, 177
Athens Studios, 25, 177
Athens Walking Tour, 97
Athens (geog, pop), 6
Athenstyle hostel/hotel, 29

Athinas St, 7, 59
Athinon (Kavalas) Ave, 6
Athos hotel, 24
Attica Department Store, 55
Attica (Messogeia) Plain, 6
Attica Zoological Park, 110–111
Attika radio taxi, 14
Attiki Odos, 6
Automobile Assoc (ELPA), 12
Ava hotel, 22–23
Averof, Velos museums, 102-103
Avocado Restaurant, 46, 183
Avyssinias Square, 51, 187

Babies & toddlers (flying, luggage), 9
Baby food, 32–33, 36–38
Babysitting, 19, 171, 189
Badminton Theatre, 115
Bags and purses, 59
Balux Café (House Project) (*see also Asteria Glyfada and Balux*), 109, 167
Bank of Greece, 57
Baptism & christening, 51, 54
Bathhouse of the Winds (*Loutro ton Aeridon*), 71
Bathing, 189
Bathing suits, 53, 61
Battle of Crete, 125
Bazaar supermarket, 36
Beaches, Attica, 164–170
    getting there, 165
    nearest to Athens, 165
    safety & facilities, 165
    terrain, 164–5
    weather, season, 164
Beggars, 189
Benaki Museum, 87, 180
    toys & souvenirs, 61
Benaki Museum Piraeos St Annex, 77–78
Beule Gate, 67
Bhavana Yoga Center, 183
Biocheck, 197
Bits and Bytes, 193
Blanos Sports Park
    bowling, 117
    ice skating, 120
Bo café, 47
    photo, 173
Boat schedules, 15, 169
Boheme, 172
Books & magazines (newspapers), 52, 198
Botanical Gardens, 107, 152–153
    playground, 153
Botanical Museum, 100
Bouzouki music, 175
Bowling, 117–118

Bus travel, 10
    KTEL terminals, 16
    long-distance, 16
Byzantine and Christian Museum, 87–88, 180
Byzantine architecture, 72, 73, 74, 91, 105, 107
Byzantino, Hilton, 45

Café Avyssinia, 175
Café Lycabettus, 86
Calendar (what's on), 201
Callicrates, 67
Candia hotel, 156
Car rental, car seats, 11
Carnival (*Apokriès*), 124
Carrefour Marinopoulos, 36
Caryatids, 80
Casio mobile/cell phone shop, 57
Ceclor, 195
Central hotel, 23
Central Market/Agorà, 7, 34, 56, 59, 175
Ceramic Folk Art Museum (Tzisdarakis Tzami), 72
Chamber of Hotels, Greek, 19
Changing of the Guard, 88, 89
Chat Tours, 96
Children's hospitals (*see Paidon children's hospitals*)
Children's Museum, 70
    toys & souvenirs, Greek-made, 61
Christmas, 123
Church of Christ, 182
Church services, 180–183
Cine Paris open-air cinema, 119, 177
Cinema, and open-air, 118–119, 177
City of Athens Museum, 91–92
City Sightseeing Bus, 97
Clean Monday (*Kathara Deftèra*), 122, 201
Clothes, children's, 52–53
Clothes, general, 53–54
Clothes, Greek-made, 54
Clothes, men's, women's, 53–54
Concert Hall (Megaron Mousikis), 116
Contact lenses, 195
Copa Copana Park pool, 162–163
Coronet Theatre, 115
Cosmos radio taxi, 14
Cosmote network, 58
Costumes, Greek, 53

Cough syrups, 195
Crime, 190
Crowne Plaza hotel, 155
Cruise ship arrival, 12
Cycladic Art Museum, 87

D. Frank, 179
Dafni (Daphne, Daphni) Monastery, 107, 184
Damigos toys, 63
Dee.es children's shoes, 58
Delinolanis, 44
Demonstrations, 190
Dentists, 195
Department & chain stores, 55–56
Depon, 195
Dexameni playground, 136
Diakopto (Diakofto), 18
Diamond Homtel hotel, 25
Dining (*see also Food & Restaurants*), 31–49
Dinner & drinks
    Gazi, 173
    Kalimarmara (Stadio), Pangrati, 175–176
    Kolonaki, 174
    Makriyanni, Koukaki, 173–174
    Monastiraki, 175
    Psyrri, 175
    Syntagma Sq, Plaka, 172
    Thissio, 172, 171–176
Dinner hour, 5
Diomidis Botanical Gardens (*see Botanical Gardens*)
Dion. Areopagitou St, 7, 44
Dionysus Theatre (*see Ancient Theatre of Dionysus*)
Discount cards (Athens Spotlighted), 10, 190
Divani Caravel hotel, 155
Divani Palace Acropolis, 26
    pool, 158
Diving Excursion, Lessons, 112–113
    Aqua Divers Club, 113
    Athina Diving, 112
    Divers Club, 113
    Paralos Diving Academy, 113
    Sotiriou Diving Centre, 113
Doctor Fish, 177
Doctors, 195
Domestic airlines, 8
Dora Stratou Theatre, 82, 115
Dorian Inn hotel,
Doric architecture, 67
Drakou St, 44, 173
Drug stores (*see Pharmacies*)

Early Learning Centre, 61
Earthquakes, 190–191
Easter (Orthodox), 122–123
Eau, 179
Edodi, 173
Efi's (Greek-made clothes), 54
Ekavi, 62
Electra Palace hotel, 23
    pool, 158
Electricity, 191
Eleftheroudakis books, 52
Embassies, 191
Emergencies, 196
Emotions Museum of
    Childhood, 81
En Athinais, 47
English (language), 5
Entertainment and events,
    114–126, 171–179
Environment, 63, 66, 102,
    103, 106, 107, 109–110,
    191, 201
Epiphany, 122
Epitropakis baptism, 51
Erechtheion, 67, 68
Ermou St, 7, 77
    shoes, 58
    shopping, 51, 53
Euro shop, 52
Euroclinic hospital, 196
Evangelismos, 20, 29–30,
    86–88, 136–138, 155–156
Events and holidays (see
    also Special events &
    concerts), 121–126
Everest sandwich chain,
    40, 47, 51, 193
Evrika sports, souvenirs, 60
Evripidou St, shopping, 50
Exarchia, 7, 52, 93–94, 136, 140
Experience in Visual Arts
    museum, 75–76

Ferry travel, 15–16, 169
Fetiye Mosque (Roman
    Agora), 72
Fil. Etairia Sq (Kydathinaion
    St), Plaka, 172
Filippos, 174
Filistron, 172
Filopappou Hill, 7, 81, 122
Filopappou Hill playground, 131
Filopappou Monument,
    7, 82–83
First Cemetery, 85–86
    Jewish section, 187
Fish Café, 177
Fish Spa, 178, 183
Fivos Hotel, 193
Flea market, 51
Fleiyo, 48
Flisvos Marina, 101, 148

Flisvos Park playground, 149
    Parko Flisvou café, 149
Flying Dolphins (hydrofoils),
    15, 169–170
Fokas clothing dept store, 54
Folk Art Museum, 70
Food & restaurants
    babies & toddlers, 32
    bread & cheese, 34–35
    central supermarkets &
        health food shops, 36–38
    dining out, 38–49
    farmer's markets (Laiki), 34
    fast food, souvlaki, 40
    feed & change spots,
        33, 71
    groceries & supermarkets,
        36–38
    kosher/halal, 36
    Middle Eastern pastries,
        35–36
    restaurant chains, 40–41
    street food, 33–34
    tavernas & local cuisine,
        38–44
    tipping, 39–40
    Tavernas and Greek
        restaurants, 41–44
    ancient Greek, 44–45
    brunch, 45
    ethnic, 45–46
    Makriyanni (Acropolis),
        Koukaki, 44
    Monastiraki, 42
    Plaka, 43
    vegetarian, 46
    Syntagma, 42
    Thissio, 43
    Ice cream & frozen yogurt,
        46–49
    Kolonaki, 49
    Koukaki, Makriyanni
        (Acropolis), 47
    Monastiraki, 48–49
    Syntagma, Plaka,
        47–48
    Thissio, 47, 31–49
Food, herbs and Greek
    specialties, 56
Formula, 32, 36
Fresh hotel, 156–157
Fro-yo, 48
Fruit shop, 37
Full moon festival, 125
Fun runs, 124–125
Funbike, 96
Funky Ride, 96
Furin Kazan (Japanese), 45
Fyli, 185

Gazi, 7, 28, 29, 73–78, 120,
    129, 131–132, 173
GB Roof Garden, 172

GB Spa, 178
Gefsi Peripatou, 47
Gelato, 47
Germanos phone and
    electronics, 55, 58
Getting around on foot, 6
Giorgos Hatzigiorgiou, 179
George and Georgia, 179
Glyfada, 10, 109, 118, 119,
    161, 166–167
Golf (Glyfada Golf Course), 119
Goody's, 41
Gostijo (Jewish), 45, 188
Goudi, 115, 144, 196–197
Goulandris Natural History
    Museum, 104
Grande Bretagne hotel, 23
    own-brand products, 56
    pool, 158
    Roof Garden, 172
    GB Spa, 178
    Yianni Hair Spa, 179
Greek language, 98
Greek National Tourism
    Organization, 199
    map download, 20
Greek Reptile Centre, Tritsis
    Park, 107
Green Store health food, 37
Gyristroula souvlaki, 40, 51

H&M, 53, 55
Hadrian's Arch, 84, 44
Hadrian's Library (Roman
    Agora), 73
Hairdressers (salon), 179
Halal food, 36
Half Note Jazz Club, 175
Hammam, 178
Happy Train, 97
Hard Rock Café, 41
Haritos St, 174
Hats, men's & women's, 54
Hatzi bakery, 35
Health Ecology health food &
    vegetarian dining, 37, 46
Health food shops and
    supermarkets, 36–38
Health hazards
    (accommodation, cold,
    driving, pedestrian, food,
    heat, mosquitoes,
    pavements, swimming),
    192–193
Heldraix (Heldreich) Square
    playground, 140–141
Hellenic Cosmos, 101
Hellenic Motor Museum, 93
Hellenic Ornithological
    Society, 106
Hellenic Railways Org
    (OSE), 17

Hephaisteion temple (see
    Thisseion temple)
Herb shop, 56
Hercules (Irakles), 5
Hermes hotel, 23
Herodes Atticus, 83, 84, 85
Herodes Atticus Odeon
    Theatre, 7, 68, 78, 79, 83
Herodion hotel, 26
Hill of the Muses (Mouseion),
    6, 66, 82–83
Hill of the Nymphs
    (Nymphon), 6, 66, 82
Hilton Athens hotel, 30
    pool, 156
Holocaust and WWII
    memorials, 187, 188
Homed, 197
Hondos Center, 53, 61
    Plan Toys, 63
Hospitals, 196–197
Hotel Tony,
Hotels & hostels (see
    Accommodation), 21–30
House calls, 197
Hydrofoils, 15, 169–170

Ianos books (Plan Toys), 63
IASO hospital, 196
IASO Paidon (children's), 197
Iatropolis, 197
Ice Scream! Lazaridis, 48
Ice skating, 119–120
Icons, 57
Ictinus, 67
Ifestou St, 51
Igglesi costumes, 53
Ikea & River West Mall, 102
    freezer gel packs, 49
Ilissia park playground,
    137–138
Improv Vegetarian
    Restaurant/bar, 46
In Between, 40, 47, 51
Independence Day, 122
Indian Kitchen, 45-46
Institute of Agricultural
    Sciences, 109
Insurance, 193
Intercontinental hotel
    (see Athenaeum
    Intercontinental)
International Christian
    Fellowship of Athens, 182
International Film Festival, 126
International Herald Tribune,
    114, 190, 198
International Trade Fair, 126
Internet, 193
Irakleidon St, 74, 172
Islamic Art Museum, 74

Jackson Hall, 174
James Joyce Irish Pub,
    175, 177
Japanese dining (Furin
    Kazan), 45
Jason Inn hotel, 28
Jazz club (see Half Note)
Jewellery, 57
Jewish Athens, 186–188
Jewish Community Centre,
    188
Jewish food (Gostijo), 45
Jewish Museum of Greece,
    89, 186–187
JK Apartments hotel, 27
    pool, 159
Jumbo toys, 63–64

Kaisariani Monastery,
    105–106, 184–185
Kaisariani Park playground,
    138–139
Kalavryta rail journey, 18
Kalimarmara, 175
Kallirois Ave, 7
Kallirois playground, 141–142
Kallisperi St playground, 134
Kalogirou shoes, 59
Kalyvioti toys, 62
Kapnikarea church, 71
Karagiozis (see Shadow
    puppets)
Karaiskaki Stadium, 176
Karaklou Gulluoglu bakery, 35
Karytsi Square, 172
Kastelorizo, 86
Kathara Defterà (see Clean
    Monday), 122
Kathimerini, 114, 190, 198
Kefitoys, 62
Kentrikon, 42
Kerameikos ancient
    cemetery, museum, 76
Kerameikos Metro station
    area (see Gazi)
Key Tours, 96
Kidom Amusement Park
    (see Allou Fun Park)
Kifissias Ave, 6
King George Palace, 23–24
King Midas, 91, 104
Kitsiki playground, 136–137
Kleiston Monastery, 185
Kolonaki, 20, 29–30, 34, 49,
    51, 52, 57–59, 86–88,
    132, 133, 136–137, 139,
    155–156, 174, 179
Kolonaki Square, 174
Konstantinidis bakery, 36
Kosher food, 36, 45, 188
Kostis bakery, 36
Koukaki, 20, 25–27, 34, 36, 37,

44, 47, 52, 59, 78–81, 131,
    133, 134–135, 140, 147,
    173–174, 179, 182, 196
KTEL long-distance bus, 16
Kydathinaion St, 48
Kymaion St playground, 129
Kyristes, Andronikos, 72

Labour Day (May Day,
    Protomaià), 123
Lambraki Hill playground,
    142–143
Language, 193–194
Lapin House, 53
Larissa (Athens) railway station,
    10, 12, 13, 17, 153, 156, 157
    photo, 17
Latinized spelling, variations, 7
Laundry, 194
Leap Frog, 9
Ledra Marriott hotel, 159
Lentzos, 53
Life Gallery Athens hotel, 161
Live shows, events,
    exhibitions, 114–117,
    121–126, 176–177
Loca Fun Park, 150, 151
Loutro ton Aeridon
    (Bathhouse of the Winds), 71
Luxurious Furnished
    Apartments, 28
Lycabettus (Lykavittos) Hill,
    6, 29, 66, 86, 136–137, 156
    funicular/teleferik, 86
    photos, 5, 86
    theatre, 86
Lysicrates monument, 79–80

Makriyanni, 20, 25–28, 33, 34,
    36, 37, 44, 47, 52, 59, 78–81,
    84, 98, 132–134, 141–142,
    147, 158–159, 173–174, 177,
    179, 181, 199
Makriyanni St, 44, 47
Mama Psomi, 47
Mamacas, 173
Mani Mani, 173
Maps, download
    city/prefecture, 199
    public transport 13
    port of Piraeus, 12
Maps,
    indicative (Attica/Attiki,
    central Athens,
    public transport,
    port of Piraeus), 209–212
    sea surface temperature,
    200–201
    weather, pollution, ozone,
    200–201
Marble House hotel, 26
Marina Alimou playground,

150–151
Marinopoulos supermarket, 37
Market In supermarket, 37
Marks & Spencer, 53, 55
Mars Hill (see Areopagus Hill)
Mastiha Shop, 50
Mattonella Gelateria, 48
May Day, Protomaià, 123
McDonald's, 41
Medical attention, 194–195
Medical care, 195–197
Meditation services (see
    Non-Christian, Buddhist &
    meditation services)
Megaron Mousikis (Concert
    Hall), 116
Melia hotel,
Melina Cultural Centre
    (shadow puppet
    museum), 76
Messogeia (Attica) Plain, 6
Messogeion Ave, 6
Metaxourgio, 13, 20, 44–45,
    156–158
Metro, 12–13
    map, indicative, 210
Metropolitan Cathedral, 181
    icons, 57
Mets, 84–86, 141, 142, 175, 187
Michael Cacoyannis
    Foundation, 116
Mikres Istories supervised
    play area, 147
Milioni St, 174
Milk Bar, 48
Mitropoleos St, 42, 51
Mompso, 59–60
Monasteries, 184–185
Monastiraki, 7, 20, 29, 33,
    51, 175
Money, 57, 197
Mosque/s, 67, 72, 183
Mothercare, 61
Moustakas toys, 64
Mouyer, 55, 58
Mt Hymettus (Ymettos,
    Ymittos), 6, 105–106
Mt Parnitha (Parnes),
    6, 109–110
    gondola/teleferik, 110
    Little Museum, 110
    National Forest, 110
Mt Penteli (Pendeli), 6, 68
Museo, 7, 16, 93–94
Museum of Greek Children's
    Art, 69–70
Museum of Greek Popular
    Musical Instruments, 70
Museum of Mineralogy and
    Petrology, 100
Museum of Traditional
    Pottery, 75
Museums and sites closed

days, 121, 201
Museums and sites free
    entrance days, 66, 201
Musical instruments, 62
Mycenaean palace, 67
Myrto hotel, 25
Mythology, 67

National Archaeological
    Museum, 7, 67, 93, 94
National Dry Cleaners, 194
National Gardens and
    playground, 132–133
    children's library, 132
    zoo, 132
National History Museum,
    90, 180
    toys & souvenirs, 62
National holidays,
    121–123, 201
National Library, 93
National Observatory (old),
    82
National Opera (Olympia), 116
National Road (Highway
    No. 1), 6
National Tourism
    Organization, 199
    map download, 20
Natural history museums,
    Panepistimioupoli,
    99–101
Nautilus Yachting, 200
Nea Smyrni Alsos
    playground, 143
Neapolis Sq playground, 140
Neos Kosmos, 27–28, 34, 36,
    116, 117, 118, 133, 140–
    143, 147, 159–160, 182
Network providers (Cosmote,
    Vodafone, Wind), 55
New hotel, 24
New Year's, 121
New York Sandwiches, 45
News & current info, 52, 198
Newspapers, 52, 198
Niki hotel, 24
Nikorellos, 54
NJV Athens Plaza hotel, 24
Non-Christian, Buddhist &
    meditation services, 183
Non-emergency medical &
    dental, 197
North slope, 7, 68–69
November 17, 123
Novotel Athenes hotel, 157
Novus Athens hotel, 157
Numismatic Museum, 90–91

Ochi Day, 123
Odeon Starcity cinema, 118

Odeon Starcity Planet
    Bowling, 118
Old Prints, Maps & Books, 60
Olympiakos (Olympiacos)
    club, 60, 176
Olympic Air, 8
Olympic Games (see Athens
    Olympics)
Olympic Holidays, 200
Olympic Stadium (OAKA),
    108, 176
Olympou St, 173–174
Omonia Sq, 7, 13, 20, 29, 34,
    36, 37, 38, 46, 52, 57, 61,
    63, 90, 93, 156–158, 196
    mobile/cell phones, 57
Onassis Cultural Centre, 116
O Petros souvlaki, 40
Open-air museums, 74
Operators (directory
    enquiries, intl), 199
Organic health food shop, 37
Organization Earth, 106–107
Orizontes, 86
Orthodox church service,
    180–181
Oscar hotel, 157
OSE (Hellenic Railways), 17
Ouzadiko, 174

Pacific (tour co), 10
Package tours, 200
Paidiki Hara playground, 135
Paidon children's hospitals,
    196–197
Paidon Penteli, 197
Paidon Sq playground, 144
Paidotopos (see Amusement
    parks, indoor &
    supervised play areas)
Paleontology and Geology
    Museum, 100
Panagia Chrysospiliotissa
    (Our Lady of the Golden
    Cave) shrine, 78–79
Panagia Gorgoepikoos/Agios
    Eleftherios church, 72
Panathenian (Panathinaic,
    Marble, Kalimarmara)
    Stadium, 66, 83, 84–85
Panathinaikos club, 60, 61,
    176–177
Pandrossou St, 51, 53, 63
Panepistimiou St, 7, 92–93
Pangrati, 84–86, 115, 133,
    138, 175–176
Panos Evageliou, 179
Papasotiriou bookstore, 125
Parliament, 6, 7, 88, 89
Parnassos Concert Hall, 116
Parthenon, 67
Pathgate Dharma Centre

Buddhist Association, 183
Patission Ave, 6
Patras, bus to/from, 16
train station, 17
Pausanias, 73
Pegasus music, 62
Pelion peninsula rack-and-pinion touristic rail journey, 18
Percy Jackson, 5
Pericles, 67, 82
Pericles Odeon, 79
Periscope hotel, 30
Pharmacies (drug stores, chemists), 32, 61, 198
Phidias, 67, 80, 84
Phidias hotel, 28
Philippos hotel, 27
Philopappos (see Filopappou)
Phones, mobile/cell, 61
Piraeos Ave, 6
Piraeus, Port, 6, 16, 107–108, 122
map download, 12
map, indicative, 211
Mikrolimani, 107
Pita Pan souvlaki, 40
Pizza, Pizza Hut, 41
Plaisio electronics, 55
Plaka, 7, 20, 21–25, 29, 43, 47–48, 54, 61, 63, 68, 69–73, 79–80, 84, 96, 117, 119, 124, 132, 133, 141, 158, 171, 172, 179, 181
Plaka restaurants (see Food & restaurants),
Plan Toys, 63
Planetarium, 101
Planning & reference, 189–201
Platanos Taverna, 43
Plato's Academy site & playground, 153
Playgrounds, 20, 127–153
children's hospital, Goudi, 144
Ilissia, Embassy, 137–140
Kolonaki, 136–137
Makriyanni, Koukaki, 134–135
Monastiraki, Thissio, Ano Petralona, 128–132
Nea Smyrni, 143
Neos Kosmos, 140–143
Syntagma, Zappeion, 132–133
Vouliagmenis Ave, Agios Dimitrios (Athens Metro Mall station), 145
Playgrounds & supervised play areas, Greater Athens, 148–153
Kolonos, Larissa (Athens) railway station, regional bus terminal areas,

Western Athens, 153
Rendi & Dafni, Haidari, Western Athens, 151–153
South Coast, near Athens/Piraeus (Paleo Faliro, Flisvos, Kalamaki, Alimos), 148–150
Playmobil Funpark, 104
Pnyx (Pnika) Hill, 6, 66, 68, 81–82
Polykliniki, 196
Ponstan, 195
Pools, 154–163
Acropolis, Makriyanni, Syntagma, 158–159
destination pools, 161–163
Evangelismos, Kolonaki, Embassy, Ilissia, 155–156
Kifissia, Metamorfosi, Ekali, 160–161
Kifissias Ave (Ambelokipi) & Alexandras Ave (Pedion Areos), 160
Larissa (Athens) railway station, Omonia Sq, Metaxourgio Sq, 156–158
Neos Kosmos, 159
Port Authority, 15–16
Agios Konstantinos, 15
Corfu (Kerkyra), 15
Igoumenitsa, 15
Lavrion, 15
Patras, 15
Piraeus, 16
Rafina, 16
Poseidon (god), 67
Poseidonos Ave, 6
Post office, 198
Postal and Philatelic Museum, 85
Praktiker, 56
Praxitelous St, 51, 62
Prenatal, 53
President hotel, 160
Proodos radio taxi, 14
Propylaia, 67, 68
Protoporia books, 63
Psyrri, 28, 29, 33, 36, 45, 48, 62, 73–78, 128-130, 175, 183–184, 187, 188
Public store, 52, 55, 56, 62, 63, 124
Public transport, 12–15
map download, 13
map, indicative, 210

Quick Spa, 178

Rack-and-pinion touristic railways: Kalavryta, Pelion, Volos, 17–18
Radisson Blu Park hotel, 160
Railway, intercity, 16–17
touristic rail journeys, 17–18
Railway (Train) Museum, 99
Railway station, 10, 12, 13, 17, 153, 156, 157
Raxevsky (Greek clothing chain), 54
Reed slippers, 59
Reference, 189–201
Regency Casino Mont Parnes, 110
Restaurants (see Food & restaurants)
Resteion Elderly Care Centre, 188
Ring-road (Alsos Petralona) playground, 130
River West Mall & Ikea, 102
Rockwave Festival, 125
Roller skating, 118
Roman Agora, 72–73
Roman Catholic church, 182
Romvis St, 51
Roussos Art and Jewelry, 60
Royal Olympic hotel, 158
Ruby's, 48, 57
Russian church (Sotira Likodimou), 90

Sacred Way (Iera Odos), Sacred Gate, 76
Sailing holidays, 200
Saint Denis/Agios Dionysus Roman Catholic Cathedral, 182
Saint George Lycabettus hotel, 156
Saint Paul's Anglican Church, 182
Savvas (see Mitropoleos St)
Scholarhio (Kouklis), 43
Sea surface temperature maps, 200–201
Segway, 98
Self-catering (see also Accommodation), 20–21
Semiramis hotel, 161
Shadow puppets (Karagiozis), 117
Koukles kai Figoures, 117
Michael Cacoyannis Foundation, 117
museum, 76
Shoes, Children's, 58
Shoes, Women's, 58–59
Shopping, 50–64
Shopping Center Plaka, 60
Sidewalks/pavements, 6

Silfio, 175
SIM card, 58
Six Dogs, 175
Sklavenitis supermarket, 55
Smoking, 198
Sofitel Athens hotel, 11
Sofos supermarket, 37
SOS Doctors, 197
Sotira Likodimou church
   (Russian church), 90
Sounion, Temple of
   Poseidon, 16, 112
South slope, 7, 67, 78
Souvenirs, 59–60
Spar supermarket, 37
Spas, 177–178
Spata, 10, 110–111, 120
Special events & concerts,
   176, 114–117, 121–126
Spectator sports, 176–177
Spelling, variations, 7
Spetses Armata, 125
Spiliopoulos shoes, 59
Spondi, 176
Sports cafes/bars, 177
Sports teams, 60, 176–177
Stadio, 175
Stadiou St, 7, 38, 42, 53, 88,
   90–92, 190
Stanley hotel, 157–158
Starbucks, 41
Steki tou Ilia, 43
Stoa of Attalos, 73
Stoa of Eumenes, 79
Strefi Hill, 1, 6, 66, 94
Strofi, 44, 174
Strollers/buggies, 6, 198
Sunsail, 200
Sunshine Express, 97
Supermarkets, 36–38
Supervised play areas,
   127–128, 145–148, 150
Swimming, babies, 155
Swimsuits, 53, 61
Synagogue, Beth Shalom,
   183–184, 187
Syngrou Ave, 6
Syngrou Estate park,
   108–109
Syntagma Metro station, 74
Syntagma Sq, 6, 7, 10, 13, 19,
   20, 21–25, 30, 33, 35, 42, 47–
   48, 51, 52, 57–59, 74, 88–93,
   132–133, 136, 156, 158–159,
   172, 178, 179, 182, 183, 186,
   187, 190, 198

Ta Souvlakis tou Hasapi, 40
Tae Kwon Do Centre, 114
TAF/The Art Foundation, 175
Tatoi royal estate, 111–112
Taverna tou Psara, 43
Tavernas (see Food &

restaurants)
Taxibeat app, 14
Taxis, 11, 13–15
   ordering, 14
   scams, 14–15
   surcharges, 14
Technopolis cultural centre &
   museum, 77
   Café tou Dimou Gaz a
      L'eau, 131
   ice skating, 120
   play area, 131
Telephony, mobile/cell
   phones, 57–58, 199
Tempi hotel, 29
Temple of Athena Nike,
   67–68
Temple of Olympian Zeus, 84
Temple of Poseidon,
   Sounion, 112
Temple of Tyche (Fortune), 85
Tesseris Epoches, 37–38, 46
TGIFriday's, 41
Thanasis (see Mitropoleos St)
The Mall Athens, 56
Theatre (see Cinema)
Theocharakis Foundation, 117
Thespis, 79
Thisseion (Hephaisteion)
   temple, 73, 74, photo, 65
Thissio, 7, 20, 28, 29, 33, 40, 42,
   43, 47, 51, 69, 73–78, 82, 97,
   118, 120, 122, 125, 128–132,
   172, 177, 179, 187 photos,
   65, 122, 127, 172, 181, 186
Thissio Metro station, 73–74
Thissio Square, 75, 125, 172
Thissio Sq playground, 128
Thission open-air cinema,
   119, 177
Thomas Cook European Rail
   Timetable, 17
Ticket House, 114
Time, 199
Tipping, 199
To Horiatiko, 48
Toiletries, 61
Toilets, 199
Tomb of the Unknown
   Soldier, 88, 89
Tourist information, 199
Tourist Police, 196
Tours, 95–98, 199–200
   bicycle tours, 95–96
   coach, excursions, day
      cruises, 96
   horse & buggy, 82,
      photo, 98
   mini-trains, 97
   open-top buses, 96–97
   package, 200
   sailing, 200
   walking, 97–98, 199

Tower of the Winds, 72
Toys of the World, 63
Toys, hobbies, music,
   Greek-made, 61–64
Train Museum, 99
Tram, 12–13
Travel Bookstore, 52
Trekking Hellas, 98
Trinity International Baptist
   Church, 182
Tritsis Park, 106–107
Trolley buses, 13
Tzisdarakis Tzami (Ceramic
   Folk Art Museum), 72

Ulysses (Odysseus), 5
Unification of arch. sites, 5–7
University of Athens, 92

Variety Cruises, 96
Vas. Sofias Ave, 6, 12
Vasilopoulou Delicatessen, 38
Vathis Square, 20, 156–158
Vegetarian dining, 44
Velos museum, 103
Village cinema, 118
Vini's, 44, 173
Vodafone network, 55, 58
Volcano.Net, 193
Volos railway station, 18
Volta Fun Park, 146–147, 148
Voula A beach, 167
Vouliagmeni beach, 168
Vouliagmeni Lake, 168
Vouliagmenis Ave, 6
Vrettos, 171
Vtech, 9

Waldorf Shop, 63
War Museum, 88
Water, 200
Weather, 5, 164, 200–201
White Fantasy ice skating, 120
Wind network, 55, 58
Worship services, 180–183

Yabanaki Varkiza, 168
Yanni Hair Spa, 179
Yiaourtaki, 48
Yum…me, 48–49

Zachos, 168
Zafolia hotel, 160
Zappeion, 25, 84–86, 119, 177
   Aegli café, 133
   Gardens, playground,
      132–134
Zara, 53, 55
Zografou playground,
   139–140
Zoological Museum, 101

Attica (Attiki)

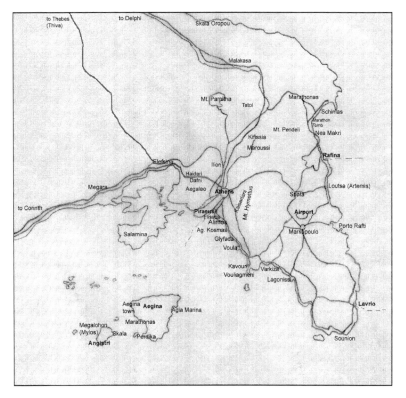

Indicative orientation map of Attica. Pick up free maps at the airport, from your hotel, at the Greek National Tourism Organization (*www.gnto.gr*) information office in Athens (*see Chapter 18*) or from numerous map images online.

Athens Public Transport (Metro, suburban rail, tram)

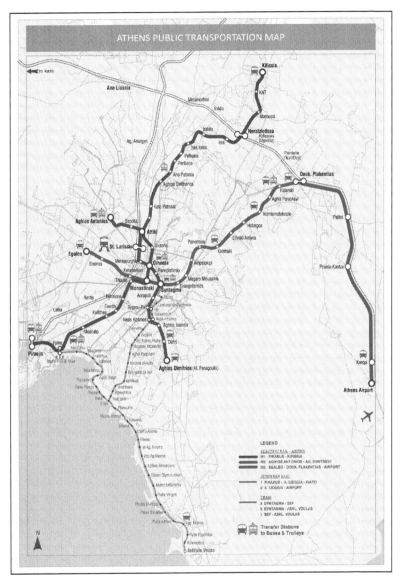

Indicative map. See original or download from the Greek National Tourism Organization at *www.visitgreece.gr* or from the Athens Urban Transport Organization at *www.oasa.gr*, which also has bus route maps.

Port of Piraeus

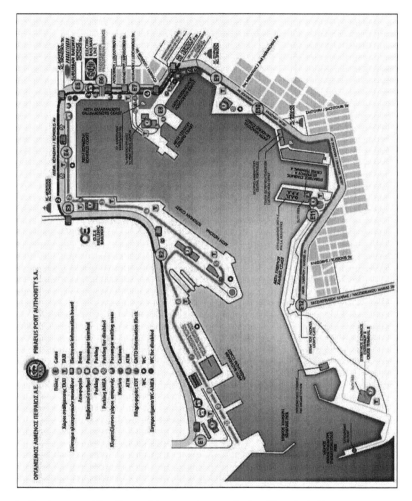

Indicative map. The Piraeus Metro station, marked as Electric Railway Line 1, is opp. Gate E6, and the cruise ship terminal is at Gates E11, E12. For more details on gates and the map itself, see the Piraeus Port Authority's site at *www.olp.gr* under Coastal Shipping, Gates and Destinations.

Central Athens

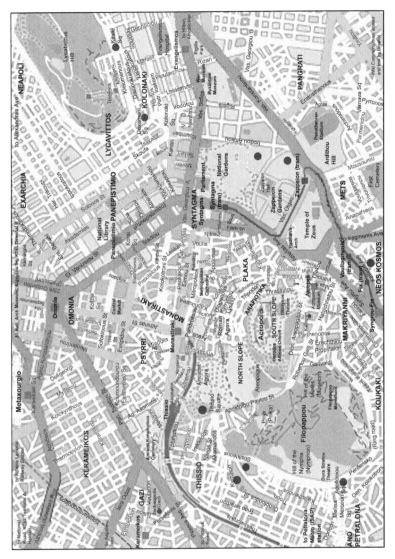

Indicative map of central Athens for basic orientation, including streets mentioned in this guide. Black dots are playground locations. For the marked playgrounds mentioned in the guide in the greater Athens area that are outside the map, plus complete street names and landmarks, see the accompanying Google map at *http://goo.gl/maps/IEnSh*

30643802R00121

Made in the USA
Lexington, KY
11 March 2014